EUROPEAN INTEGRATION

FROM COMMUNITY TO UNION

MARTIN HOLLAND

PINTER
PUBLISHERS
LONDON

Pinter Publishers
25 Floral Street, Covent Garden, London, WC2E 9DS, United Kingdom

First published in hardback as 'European Community Integration' in 1993

© Martin Holland, 1993, 1994

Reprinted 1995

British Library Cataloguing in Publication Data

A CIP catalogue record for this book is available from The British Library

ISBN 1 85567 241 3 (PBK)
    0 86187 108 1 (HBK)

Printed and bound in Great Britain by SRP, Exeter.

Contents

**To Ove
with thanks**

Preface

Today in Europe the pace of integration is accelerating.

The challenges which face the European Community (EC) come from both within and without. The development of the EC's 'internal market' – an economic area of 350 million people in twelve countries without internal frontiers – has brought in its train an irresistible movement towards economic and monetary union. Events in the rest of the European continent, resulting from the collapse of the Communist system and the disintegration of the Soviet Union, have shown how vital is the EC's role as a pole of stability and attraction for those countries seeking to nurture the growth of democracy and the market economy.

The successful outcome of the Maastricht Summit in December 1991 marked another milestone on the path towards the development of a federal system in Europe, capable of harnessing the energy of its people and the potential of its resources, while at the same time preserving the diversity of its nations and cultures. In this way, the ideas and methods of Jean Monnet, the pioneer of European integration, continue to bear a rich fruit.

Martin Holland's book, which describes and analyses the process of European integration, comes to its readers at a moment when the nature and causes of this process deserve to be more fully understood, both by the citizens of Europe and by the rest of the world. I commend it to a wide and attentive readership.

Frans Andriessen   Brussels
Vice-President   January 1992
Commission of the European Communities

Introduction: the idea of Europe

This book is about the idea of Europe. It is not primarily a factual text that details the precise workings of European Community policies and institutions: for such useful sources the reader should consult some of the popular texts, such as Lodge (1983, 1989), Nugent (1989), Nicoll and Salmon (1990), Pryce (1987) or Wallace (1990). Such necessary descriptive accounts suffer from two weaknesses: the limited period of time for which they are relevant or provide an accurate discussion of EC procedures; and secondly, often the political and social context of integration is under-emphasized, or at best only approached in a technical and theoretically sterile way. Exceptions to the rule are George (1985), Burgess (1989) and Pinder (1991).

This volume adopts a conscious political and polemical stance. The organizing principle that underpins all the chapters is the concept of Europe espoused by Jean Monnet and his contemporaries: in particular, the implicit federal institutional elements contained within the various communities that have come to structure post-1945 European politics and society. The idea of Europe is an exciting one; unfortunately this element has all too often been buried beneath volumes of technicalities obscuring the political essence of the EC. This edition provides an antidote to this myopia by recalling the vision of Monnet and Schuman and exploring the federal agenda of the EC for the last decade of the twentieth century.

Chapter 1 provides a necessary, but too often ignored, theoretical context for comprehending the development of European integration over the past half-century. The ideas and achievements of one of the founding fathers of the EC, Jean Monnet, are presented. In particular, his views on federalism and functional integration are discussed and a re-evaluation of neofunctionalist thought undertaken. While acknowledging the diversity within the Community experience and the need for a pluralistic conceptual approach, this chapter follows a neofunctionalist approach to integration and it is this theory that provides the general structure for the remaining chapters.

Chapter 2 describes the historical development of the Community using the intergovernmental and supranational (or *communautaire*) elements within the Community's experience to distinguish between six periods of integration. These are: the immediate post-war period and the search for new European structures; the creation of the Community's functional organizations from 1950–57; the return to intergovernmentalism during the 1960s; the 1970s and the relaunch of the Community; 1979–84 and the crisis perpetrated by the 'British problem'; and, from 1985 onwards, the communautarization of the EC towards Political, Economic and Monetary Union.

Building on this description and expression of the Community idea, Chapter 3 explores the reform process within the Community at the institutional, policy-making and conceptual level. Three specific reform proposals are examined: the 1975 Tindemans Report; the Single European Act of 1986; and the Intergovernmental Conferences (IGC) of 1991 that led to the most recent reform, the Maastricht Treaty on European Union. While each of these three attempted reforms were dissimilar in their outcomes and in their historical contexts, clear thematic similarities are evident and the consistent elements in the reform of the European Community highlighted. As Monnet often remarked, the original Community structures were not an end-point, but a transitional stage towards a full Union of the peoples of Europe. While the final destination still remains unknown, the Community's future seems increasingly set along a federal road, irrespective of continuing British reservations and more recently, Denmark's hesitation with respect to the Maastricht Treaty. This historical interpretation and search for thematic threads in the Community's reform process provides the background for surveying the development of institutional relations within the Community.

The theme of Chapter 4 is the decline of independent national sovereignty and the development of pooled Community sovereignty and the transformation of the institutional structure of authority within the Community.

The Community's international role is investigated in Chapter 5: the origins and history of European Political Cooperation are considered and the issues pertaining to the creation of a Common Foreign and Security Policy are analysed. This progressive move towards defining the EC's international capabilities is interpreted within competing theoretical contexts. A series of case studies are provided that illustrate both the strengths and the weaknesses of Europe's collective foreign policy in the 1990s. From this theoretical and empirical combination, the availability of EC foreign policy instruments, the effectiveness of EC action and the Community's claim to be an international actor are explored.

The Community is much more than an expression of Europe's economic or political strength: integration and European Union have to be compatible with the concept of a people's Europe. Chapter 6 returns to a theme first raised by the functional theorists of the early 1960s. To what extent is European integration dependent on the attitudinal loyalties of Europe's population? The evidence supplied by the *Eurobarometre* surveys of any change in mass attitudes is evaluated together with the arguments concerning the democratic deficit and lack of representation within the EC's institutions. The inconsistencies within the European Parliament's electoral provisions and the requirements for an equitable Community are outlined. The chapter also examines the Maastricht Treaty provisions concerning the concept of Community citizenship, and provides a critical commentary on the rejection of a Community Social Charter. The verdict after assessing these four factors is that a people's Europe remains to be adequately constructed.

In Chapter 7 the challenge and the opportunities posed by further enlargement of the EC are considered. The Community cannot remain at twelve: the pressures to include Austria, Finland and Sweden are already unstoppable and the other current applicant states of Cyprus, Malta and Turkey are rapidly harmonizing their policies and legislation with a view to accession this century. In addition, other former EFTA states such as Switzerland and Norway seem poised to apply (albeit through lack of alternatives rather than a new found enthusiasm for the Community ideal). Beyond these immediate pressures the newly democratic countries of Central and Eastern Europe pose a fundamental question for the Community. Just how large a Community can the current institutional structures maintain? What are the consequences in terms of policy- and decision-making structures of a community that stretches from the Atlantic to the Urals? In attempting to answer these questions Chapter 7 examines the problems encountered and the solutions implemented during the Community's early experience of enlargement from the Six to the Twelve. The contemporary issues of future enlargement are evaluated within this historical context.

Chapter 8 addresses the scope of the Community's policies and examines the principle of subsidarity. Although the Community's policy competences have grown significantly since 1957, the member state governments have maintained control over vast areas of domestic legislation. To date there is only one comprehensive supranational Community policy, the Common Agricultural Policy. Typically, EC policies are rudimentary fragmented and supplement rather than replace national policies. The Maastricht agreement has the potential to alter this status quo. The decision to implement Economic and Monetary Union and to adopt the ECU as the single Community currency no later than 1999, lays the ground for further expansion of common EC policies.

The first edition of this book was completed after the signing of the Maastricht Treaty, but before the final completion of ratification. As the events of 1992 and 1993 proved, ratification was not a simple formality. It involved a lengthy procedure that was precarious and albeit temporarily, undermined the integration process. The Maastricht reform process took a full twelve months to produce the new treaty (The intergovernmental conferences lasted from December 1990 to December 1991). On 7 February 1992 the member states signed the treaty: From that point onwards it was left to each individual member state to ratify the treaty in accordance with its own national tradition and law. This varied from domestic parliamentary approval to a binding national referendum to determine ratification. In addition, the European Parliament had to give its assent to the Treaty. Ratification was complicated and delayed by events in three member states: the 'no' vote in the 2 June 1992 Danish Referendum, British parliamentary procedure and an appeal to the German courts that the treaty was unconstitutional . A second Danish Referendum held on 18 May 1993 gave a majority for ratification; after months of party management the British House of Commons gave its approval; and in September 1993 the German constitutional court rejected the claim that the treaty was incompatible with federal law.

Consequently, twenty-one months after the signing at Maastricht, only on 1 November 1993 did the Treaty on European Union come into force.

With the implementation of the Maastricht reforms the European Union was established in part replacing, in part complementing the existing structure of the Community. Thus as of November 1993 , in general the term European Union, rather than the European Community, became the correct name for those activities governed by the Treaty on European Union. Although this text examines the potential consequences of the Treaty reform, throughout the term 'European Community' is used for reasons of clarity.

Maastricht signifies the the most ambitious and clearly the most difficult stage of European integration so far attempted. The economic and political competences being transferred from the national to the Union level resemble the federal and functional objectives of Monnet and the Community's founding partners. For more than two decades the success of the supranational ideal seemed in doubt and the longevity of the Community even questioned. For all its faults that are so readily exposed by the international media, the success of the Community has been remarkable, indeed unprecedented. The challenge for the twenty-first century is to maintain and extend this achievement. The following chapters try to place the past Community and present Union within an appropriate and stimulating context to encourage both students and practitioners of politics to escape the confines of national boundaries and to conceptulize European politics at the supranational level.

References

Burgess, M., 1989, *Federalism and European Union: political ideas, influences and strategies in the European Community, 1972–87*, Routledge, London.

George, S.,1985, *Politics and policy in the European Community*, Clarendon Press, Oxford.

Lodge, J. (ed.),1983, *Institutions and policies of the European Community*, Pinter, London.

Lodge, J. (ed.),1989, *The European Community and the challenge of the future*, Pinter, London.

Nicoll, W. and Salmon, T.C., 1990, *Understanding the European Communities*, Barnes and Noble, Savage, Maryland.

Nugent, N.,1989, *The government and politics of the European Community*, Macmillan, London.

Pryce, R. (ed.), 1987, *The dynamics of European Union*, Croom Helm, London.

Pinder, J., 1991, *European Community: building of a union*, Oxford University Press, Oxford.

Wallace, W. (ed.), 1990, *The dynamics of European integration*, Pinter/RIIA, London.

1 Integration and the ideas of Jean Monnet: federalism versus intergovernmentalism

How are we to comprehend 'Europe'? In a period of massive change in both the international and European system, it is difficult to gain the correct focus on events, to detect underlying trends amid a mass of events which often appear volatile and seemingly contradictory. Is the EC still relevant in the last decade of the twentieth century? The distractions of contemporary affairs can lead to conclusions that are both disarming and specious. In this book an interpretation of the Community experiment is attempted. It remains an 'experiment' because, as is self-evident, the end-product/outcome remains hypothetical and a matter for conjecture: clearly, being axiomatic or predictive about the shape or content of Europe in the 1990s would be foolhardy. As Duchêne has observed, 'the earthquake in eastern Europe is probably the moment of truth for the Community. Everything depends on how the transition to a new system is secured. At this point, the Community issue becomes subsumed, as in fact it always has been, in the fate of the international order around it.' (1990, p. 21)

While some theoretical caution is manifestly required, it would be equally undesirable to reject theory in our search for an understanding of contemporary European integration. In this chapter a basis for interpreting the Community and European integration over the past half-century is suggested. In such a period of international flux, it is instructive to return to first principles – the ideas of Jean Monnet and the earlier federalist and neofunctionalist theorists who for almost two decades were mistakenly seen as increasingly irrelevant to the European debate. A re-evaluation of Monnet's ideas in the light of the Community experience and European integration is both appropriate and long overdue.

The heritage of Jean Monnet

Commenting on the establishment of the Organisation of European Economic Co-operation (OEEC) in 1948, Jean Monnet made the following remarks in his *Memoirs*: 'I could not help seeing the intrinsic weakness of a system that went no further than mere co-operation between Governments . . . The countries of Western Europe must turn their national efforts into a truly European effort. This will be possible only through a *federation of the West.'* (1978, pp. 272–3) (emphasis added) This recollection serves as a useful guiding principle for an analysis of the integration of the European Community in the post-war period. Two successive European civil wars had illustrated the inherent dangers of unrestrained nationalism and an international movement towards federalism inspired many of the post-1945 generation of political leaders (Burgess, 1989, p. 24).

There has been much debate over Monnet's approach to the idea of European Union (was he a federalist, a practical functionalist, or some strange combination of both?). While his philosophy towards integration may require qualification, there is no dispute over the magnitude of his contribution, although some of his critics would argue that this was to the detriment rather than to the advantage of the European integration. Schuman, Spaak and Spinelli can lay justifiable claim to being key contributors to Community development, but the role of catalyst and initiator lays properly with Jean Monnet. As one commentator has remarked, 'Monnet's role was vital, and still is' as the font for ideas that generated such 'a revolution in international affairs' (Mayne, 1966, p. 350). As the Community approaches the twenty-first century, it is instructive to return to Monnet's ideas and achievements in order to provide a context within which to evaluate the development of the Community.

Monnet's influence over the Community is remarkable given that he was not directly involved in the formal committee meetings that eventually produced a constitutional formula for European integration. Indeed, his only public role within a European institution in the post-war period was as the first President of the High Authority of the European Coal and Steel Community (ECSC) (1952–56). However, the principles behind both the Messina conference of 1955 and in the text of the 1957 Treaty of Rome, 'were very clearly the offspring of Monnet and his friends' and embodied his 'essential ideas' (Mayne, 1966, p. 367). What then, were these 'essential ideas'?

It is often forgotten that one of the main inspirations behind post-war European integration was the desire to secure a lasting peace. National sovereignty and the competition over resources were seen by an increasing number of influential individuals to be counter to this objective. In his *Memoirs* Monnet records that in 1950 the prevalent atmosphere was of an 'increasing acceptance of a war that is thought to be inevitable' (1978, p. 289). Hindsight should not make us undervalue this preoccupation: East–West relations were confrontational; the status of Berlin remained precarious; Germany was formally divided; French economic recovery was stagnating; and the proliferation of atomic weapons had begun. Echoing Winston Churchill's famous call for 'a kind of United States of Europe' built around a Franco-German axis (Patijn, 1970, p. 33), Monnet believed that the key to European peace was an alliance between France and Germany. The precise nature of such an agreement was less important than the realization of this historical reconciliation, although even at this early stage Monnet had begun to experiment with federal principles for the new Europe. In many senses, the ECSC of 1952 can be regarded as modern Europe's first peace movement: former national control over these key products for the armaments industry were placed under joint or pooled authority thereby, according to Monnet, creating 'the first concrete foundations of the European Federation which is indispensable to the maintenance of peace' (1978, p. 298). The importance of this objective is evident in the preamble to the 1952 Paris Treaty which begins:

> Considering that world peace can be safeguarded only by creative efforts commensurate with the dangers that threaten it,
>   Convinced that the contribution which an organised and vital Europe can make to civilisation is indispensable to the maintenance of peaceful relations,
>   . . .
>   Resolved to substitute for age-old rivalries the merging of their [the Six] essential interests; to create, by establishing an economic community, the basis for a broader and deeper community among peoples long divided by bloody conflicts; . . .
> Have decided to create a European Coal and Steel Community.

It is myopic to regard the past four decades of European integration as a technocratic economic exercise principally devoted to capital expansion: the complete success of the ECSC and latterly the European Community can disguise this original purpose of creating a European organization that would prohibit the outbreak of Europe's third civil war of the twentieth century. While Europe was a political and economic concept, it was above all 'a moral idea' (Monnet, 1978, p. 392).

The organization of Europe in a way that sublimated national rivalries and achieved peace and prosperity was regarded by Monnet as a continuous process, drawing as much on incrementalism as grand design. Thus, in 1950, in the formative years of European integration, Monnet observed that 'Europe will not be built all at once, or as a single whole: it will be built by concrete achievements which first create *de facto* solidarity' (p. 300). This practical approach has opened Monnet up to attack from more ideologically committed academics and politicians. Burgess has argued that despite his periodic usage of federalist language, Monnet cannot be regarded as 'a champion of the federal cause in Europe'; despite having a European federation as his ultimate goal, Monnet is best viewed as primarily an economic functionalist and only secondly as an incremental federalist (1989, p. 44).

There is considerable evidence in Monnet's *Memoirs* to support this view, although uncharacteristically for Monnet this issue lacks clarity and the case against his federalist principles is far from conclusive. There is a strong emphasis on 'concrete achievements' and acknowledgement of caution in pushing Europe too quickly along an ill-defined road (here Monnet's reticence over establishing the European Defence Community is illustrative) (1978, p. 343). But above all Monnet remained a pragmatist, a political opportunist who valued incrementalism over the purity of federalist principles, regarding such an *ad hoc* approach as the more effective strategy for uniting Europe. His acceptance of outcomes that were formed by compromises reflected a realization of the limitations of what was politically possible. Commenting on the draft EEC treaty, Monnet writes 'Myself, I never bothered to speculate on whether the new Community treaties might have been improved. I think they embodied as much as possible at that time and that stage in men's (sic) thinking.' (p. 423)

Ends, rather than means, characterize Monnet's political style. If the route towards European integration involved a temporary detour into intergovernmental territory, if it meant forgoing logically the most direct path to federation in order to safeguard current gains, these were the costs that Monnet was prepared to pay in order to secure the deepening and solidifying of European union. Commenting on the emergence of political union from the early economic integration created by the European Community, Monnet argued:

> Little by little the work of the Community will be felt . . . Then the everyday realities themselves will make it possible to form the political union which is the goal of our Community and to establish the United States of Europe . . . the idea is clear: political Europe will be created by human effort, when the time comes, on the basis of reality . . .
>
> For me there has been only one path: only its length remains unknown. The unification of Europe, like all peaceful revolutions, takes time. (pp. 431–2)

Quite what the specifics of European union might look like were left intentionally vague; however, the broad plan was consistent and indicates that Monnet was, at least in a general sense, a European federalist, and held beliefs that were not necessarily inconsistent with his avowed practical functionalist integration strategy. Functionalism for Monnet meant the creation of a supranational regime or organization that was based on the principle of international authority. The piecemeal nature of this approach was accepted as was the logic of functional expansion from one sector to another.

Federal references are easily found in Monnet's statements. The Community itself is not regarded by Monnet as the institutional form necessary for a political federation of Europe; rather he uses the term 'a pre-federal model' to describe the Community of the 1970s. None the less, his idea of Europe was one 'organized on a federal basis' (p. 295) where 'no state can secede by its own unilateral decision' and the Community is composed of 'nations which commit themselves to it with no limit in time and no looking back' (p. 326). Monnet's contribution as a bureaucrat to the creation of Europe lacked the high profile impact of some of his political contemporaries: however, this should not disguise his pervasive influence in the Community debate for more than three decades. In 1946 he was appointed France's Planning Commissioner, arguably the most important bureaucratic post, responsible for the post-war modernization of France. He can rightfully take credit for the 'idea' of the 1950 Schuman Plan and served as the first President of the High Authority of the European Coal and Steel Community (1952–5). The success of this first attempt at a supranationalism laid the foundations for the wider Community as set out in the 1957 Treaty of Rome. His resignation from the High Authority and reluctance to be a candidate for the newly established Commission in 1957 did not indicate a loss of commitment to the European cause, but rather reflected his pragmatic approach as how best to influence the development of the Community. Consequently, he exchanged the direct responsibility of public office and the public profile of the High Authority, for a more familiar informal role as an independent counsellor and source of ideas. In 1955 he formed the Action Committee for the United States of Europe and served as its inspiration and President until his resignation on 9 May 1975, the 25th anniversary of the Schuman Declaration.

Monnet's role as the President of the Action Committee for the United States of Europe provided him and his organization with the advantage of being able to influence political élites directly without having to face the disadvantage of public scrutiny. Europe was being constructed by a cohesive and remarkably small élite; while public support was welcomed, it was never a prerequisite for Monnet's Europe. Free from any institutional constraints, Monnet, through the Action Committee, was able to shape the debate and the emerging form of the new European Economic Community structures. Of course, Monnet was not always successful in his lobbying for a progressively federal arrangement for Europe. As Chapter 2 describes, for almost all of the 1960s the supremacy of the nation-states of the Community stood in stark contrast to ambitions of both the Action Committee and the Spaak Committee, and to the expectations developed from the ECSC experience. The inability of the Community to agree upon a single European 'District' to house the institutions should have been regarded as a prescient omen underlining the resilience of national self-interest; the two failed attempts at expansion, the constraints imposed on extending Community-level competences and most notoriously the inappropriately named Luxembourg Compromise all conspired to stifle the development of Community political integration. As de Gaulle scathingly commented in 1962, 'at present there is and can be no Europe other than a Europe of the states – except, of course, for myths, fictions and pageants' (p. 441).

Perhaps the attractiveness of Monnet's Europe was the breadth of its conception: uncluttered with precise institutional relations, or even a clearly described destination, the 'idea' of European integration could be sufficiently flexible to appeal to a broad political spectrum, from cautious intergovernmentalists to unabashed federalists. This ubiquity, however, has been challenged as both a strength and a weakness. It has allowed successful if pragmatic integration to a substantial degree, while simultaneously facilitating the opportunity for intergovernmentalism due to the very absence of precise institutional and policy objectives.

There is general agreement between the majority of writers who have commented on Monnet that his contribution to the construction of Europe has been fundamental. Duroselle, for example, argues that Monnet's Europe contained four themes: it was an anti-nationalist Europe; a Europe of concrete institutions; an 'open' Europe; and a Europe which was linked in partnership with the United States of America (1970, p. 195). Monnet equated nationalism with a 'spirit of domination' based on the inequality between states that had been responsible for the previous centuries of European wars. Consequently, he was opposed to the substitution of nationalism at the state-level by a new nationalism at the European level.

The Treaty of Rome reflected this desire to ameliorate the fervour of nationalism by establishing the principle of the 'protection of the minorities' within the Community's institutional balance. What had to be realized was a Community in which domination by one power (Germany) or an alliance (Franco-German) was impossible. Thus, for example, the origin of the ECSC was an attempt 'to sublimate national rivalry over these coal and steel resources by uniting Germany and France' (Monnet, 1978, p. 286).

The importance Monnet gave to institutions has already been noted in this chapter: for Monnet, institutions were the key to successful integration as 'only institutions grow wiser; they accumulate collective experience' (p. 393). Once established, institutions have a tangible impact that far outweighs the metaphysical influence of ideas or theories. Duroselle maintains that this emphasis on concrete institutions is Monnet's most enduring legacy for the Community: competing ideas concerning integration or Political Union have come and gone during the Community's turbulent history, and yet what has remained largely untouched since the Schuman Declaration of 1950 has been the institutional structure and relationships of the European Community. Only after four decades of supranational experience has the need arisen to reform the institutional balance and decision-making process. The 1991 IGC reform process should not, however, be regarded as invalidating Monnet's approach; rather the success of the Community has resulted in its enlargement to the point where the structures developed to accommodate the integration of six economically similar Western European states of the 1950s, are now in need of adaptation to the new political geometry of contemporary Europe.

Doubling the number of Community member states in the three decades that spanned 1957–86, and the probability of further enlargement before the year 2000, is evidence that Monnet's belief in an 'open' Europe has become ingrained within the Community idea. The conditions of membership set down in the Treaty of Rome were intentionally expansive: the preamble encourages 'other peoples of Europe who share their (the Community) ideal to join in their efforts', whereas Article 237 simply states that '[A]ny European State may apply to become a member of the Community' with accession determined by the unanimous approval of the Council of Ministers and since the Single European Act, majority support in the European Parliament. In practice, informal criteria (such as democratic legitimacy, compatibility of economic structures and, increasingly, a common approach to foreign and security issues) have been used to evaluate potential applicants (see Chapter 7). This general principle of 'openness' has not gone unchallenged: the aborted enlargements of the 1960s and the transitional problems experienced by applicant states have all periodically marred 'openness'. During the ECSC negotiations Monnet sought to express this principle by courting British participation; although unsuccessful and later thwarted on two separate occasions by de Gaulle, Monnet never deserted his assessment of the importance of a Franco-British union within the context of the Community. What is more remarkable, however, is Monnet's insistence that the division of Germany and East–West reconciliation could only be addressed within the Community context and with the backing of the United States. Despite periodic trade disputes, the United States has fully supported the development of the Community and the European-American partnership advocated by Monnet has been influential in the Community's history. The complexity of the linkages as well as the necessity for an Atlantic consensus, have become increasingly clear in the 1990s. The Community's extended competence in the sphere of security and defence has placed the question of NATO and American involvement in Europe back on the Community agenda of integration and Political Union.

Other writers have commented on Monnet's influence in more general, if equally complimentary, terms. Drawing on his personal experience as a member of Monnet's Action Committee staff, Mayne challenges the all too common assumption that Monnet was principally a 'technocrat' or economic expert and emphasizes his importance as an original thinker. Mayne documents that Monnet's contemporaries and colleagues stress the crucial role that he performed, not as 'a mere reflex of loyalty, but rather a sober recognition that this was how it happened, and that without Monnet's mercurial personality they doubt whether it would have happened at all' (1966, p. 351). It was not just that Monnet's ideas were remarkable, it was that he displayed an almost unique dedication to collective action at the expense of individual power: it was this personal philosophy that was translated, albeit imperfectly, to the principles of the European Community. Throughout his career in public office (which spanned some 40 years), a commitment to problem-solving by collective action rather than by single and independent national policies is evident. Perhaps his most direct influence was in drafting the Schuman Declaration and acting as the president of the French delegation that, together with the other five national delegations, produced the basic articles that shaped the ECSC. Although the full significance of this one event may not have been apparent to many of Europe's political élite at the time, as Monnet commented in an address to the ECSC Common Assembly,

The Schuman proposals are revolutionary or they are nothing . . .
    We can never sufficiently emphasize that the six Community countries are the fore-runners of a broader united Europe, whose bounds are set only by those who have not yet joined. Our Community is not a coal and steel producers' association: it is the beginning of Europe. (1978, pp. 316, 392)

Monnet's principle of collective action was recognized by the creation of the ECSC High Authority, and it is this 'method' that has shaped the development of the European Community into the 1990s. Monnet's absence from public office after May 1955 should not be taken as a sign of declining influence. The intergovernmental Spaak Committee, charged with the responsibility of drafting the terms of the new Community, included a number of Monnet's closest former aids and associates from the High Authority: as Mayne concludes, the 'resultant Rome Treaties establishing the European Economic Community and Euratom, were thus very clearly the offspring of Monnet and his friends' (1966, p. 367). Through his Action

Committee for the United States of Europe (which was launched on 13 October 1955), Monnet continued to exert influence and succeeded in embodying his essential ideas both formally within the constitutional provisions, and informally within the practices of the new European Community. The Action Committee became 'the world's most illustrious and influential action group, and has been described as "something like the collective democratic conscience of the European Community" ' (p. 369). A substantial number of its members subsequently served in both Community and national political office, thereby extending the influence of the Action Committee directly. Arguably, the events of the 1960s provide a necessary realistic antidote to unqualified euphoria concerning the influence of the Action Committee. For almost a decade de Gaulle's conception of 'L'Europe des patries' seemed to be ascendant. And yet paradoxically, the role of Monnet and the Action Committee was perhaps at no other time more important: they remained loyal to the principle of collective action and continued to argue for integration within the European debate. It is not simply coincidental that the relaunch of the Community in 1969 draws heavily from Monnet's approach to European Union: his influence has been pervasive and remarkably enduring.

Monnet's economic approach to integration through rational planning and collective action has been examined by George, who argues that had his belief in *dirigisme* (indicative planning) 'worked, economic co-ordination would also have slipped out of national hands. But Monnet's scheme did not work.' (1985, p. 5) To the contrary, rather than centralized market control that planned production and output, George suggests that the ECSC became an agent of the free market system due to national opposition from West German and Benelux industries. This interpretation suggests that Monnet's practical influence on the shape of the new communities was somewhat ineffectual and that supranationalism was ephemeral. George contends that in the Treaty of Rome there 'was no trace of *dirigisme* . . . The document enshrines the principles of *laissez-faire* throughout most of its articles.' (p. 7) However, such concessions to national authority over supranationalism were in keeping with Monnet's belief in incrementalism: while a *dirigist* Community with a dominant supranational institution such as the Commission may have been his objective, he realized that the idea of the Community would be jeopardized by an overly ambitious attack on national prerogatives. George's economic alternatives of the market and *dirigisme* may not be mutually exclusive. Given Monnet's sense of what was politically possible, it is hardly surprising to find market forces and *dirigisme* combined within the EEC Treaty. As a former member of the first Commission has recorded,

> If, however, we consider the objectives set out in the Treaty and the means made available for their achievement in the form of rules and institutions, it becomes clear that all the essential characteristics of a free market system are present. Moreover, these considerably restrict the latitude for national economic planning, since national subsidies or protectionist measures are either forbidden or subject to the control of Community institutions . . . (although)

they have no powers for any kind of *dirigiste* economic planning. (Groeben, 1987, p. 24)

Both these elements, however, are evident in the Community of the 1990s: while the single internal market of 1992 may be premised on the notion of free trade between member states, this freedom can only be possible through the imposition of positive supranational *dirigisme* that works to remove existing tariff and non-tariff barriers, rather than impose an economic plan. The perceived tension may not, necessarily, be antagonistic.

For Monnet, popular support for an integrated Europe was of secondary importance and would develop only after, and as a consequence of, the creation of institutions. As Pryce and Wessels have commented, Monnet's strategy was essentially élitist in origin (1987, p. 24), as well as being practical and the more successful strategy in the early 1950s (Cardozo, 1987, p. 73). The support of national élites across the political spectrum was required in order to establish a supranational authority. Possibly Monnet's greatest achievement was in engineering this élite consensus. Once a consensus in principle though not in detail was apparent, he encouraged the discussion on the basis of common solutions rather than the more normal procedure of negotiations between competing parties that were often seen in zero-sum terms. Thus Monnet's approach was clearly élitist, but non-confrontational.

One commentator who is critical of Monnet's federal credentials is Burgess. While acknowledging Monnet's central influence on the development of the Community, Burgess argues that this effect has not necessarily been beneficial to the federalist cause. In contrast, he extols the federalist credentials and contributions of Altiero Spinelli and Leo Tindemans to developing the idea of European Union (1989, p. 5). Monnet is criticized on a number of grounds. He is accused, albeit implicitly, of contributing to the confusing diversity of principles that underpin the Community. These founding principles are 'often incompatible and sometimes contradictory' producing a 'conceptual enigma' that 'defies simple categorisation' (p. 20). While federal ideas were instrumental, they did not form the exclusive ideological base on which the Community was to be founded. Monnet's incremental strategy precluded this single-mindedness and sought to balance, for pragmatic reasons, federalism with intergovernmentalism.

Burgess argues that the initial success of Monnet's élite bargaining functional strategy disguised a fundamental flaw in his approach as it 'did not provide Europe with the effective means to go beyond what existed' (p. 32). National governments retained their pivotal role; the opportunity to create a new central federal level of authority was surrendered as political authority was not fundamentally transformed. This was because, Burgess argues, Monnet's ideas lacked a clear ideological base and depicts him not as 'a champion of the federal cause in Europe' but, somewhat disparagingly in comparison with Spinelli's consistent federalist principles, as a 'functionalist' or 'incremental federalist'. His view of human nature stressed rationality and benevolence derived from mutual interest and he sought through the Community to transform the context and eradicate the historical reasons that lead to conflict and human rivalry (p. 46).

Burgess quotes Spinelli's damning praise that 'Monnet has the great merit of having built Europe and the great responsibility to have built it badly' (pp. 55–6). His deep-rooted confidence in the ability of institutions to shape human behaviour has been shown, it is argued, to be unjustified. While federalists acknowledge the significant role that can be played by institutions, the Community's Monnet-inspired institutional structure is seen as an impediment to a federal constitution. The rigid structures that reflect intergovernmental power and only pay lip-service to popular representation and the principle of executive accountability have 'frustrated federalists' attempts to alter the basic construction of Europe' (p. 57).

Whether Monnet qualifies for the accolade of a Community federalist, or the designation as practical visionary, his imprint on the structure of the Community is incontestable. It is perhaps a fitting testimony to Monnet's ideas that almost half a century later his basic principles should still be relevant to the current debate about the development of the Community. He is unquestionably the Community's most original and important thinker, and his enduring legacy is the belief in the central role of institutions in determining the future shape of European integration. However, as Monnet concludes towards the end of his *Memoirs*,

> the Community we have created is not an end in itself. It is a process of change ... It is impossible to foresee today the decisions that could be taken in a new context of tomorrow. The essential thing is to hold fast to the few fixed principles that have guided us since the beginning: gradually to create among Europeans the broadest common interest, served by common democratic institutions to which the necessary sovereignty has been delegated. This is the dynamic that has never ceased to operate ... I have never doubted that one day this process will lead us to the United States of Europe; but I see no point in trying to imagine today what political form it will take. (1978, pp. 522–3)

How, then, do Monnet's general approach and 'federalist-functionalist' ideas help to shape our understanding of theories of integration? What theory, if any, can best explain the development of post-war Europe?

Theories of integration

Integration theory flourished during the 1950s and early 1960s; since then the record has generally been disappointing. The inability to predict or explain the development of the Community adequately – either in practice or in theory – led to 'the collapse both of the political commitment to European integration and of the conceptual framework that had supported it' (Wallace, 1990, p. ix). As Chapter 2 illustrates, the Community's history has been chequered, with periods of significant progress towards integration, and other periods of stagnation and disintegration. The earliest conceptual approach that was used to provide a framework for Community integration was the theory of functionalism as first constructed by David Mitrany in the inter-war years. The underlying assumption was very close to the idea

of subsidiarity introduced into the Community's intergovernmental discussions of 1991. For Mitrany 'the functional approach emphasises the
common index of need. There are many such needs that cut across
national boundaries, and an effective beginning could be made by providing
joint government of them' (1970, p. 72). This approach was 'not a matter of
surrendering sovereignty, but merely of pooling so much of it as may be
needed for the joint performance of the particular task' (p. 73). While
Monnet was often broadly described as a functionalist, this approach contains a number of contradictions as well as similarities with his ideas. For
example, a parallel between functionalist theory and Monnet's practice
was their shared belief in functional agencies that would assume supranational authority across a range of specific policy areas. Thus, for example,
coal and steel production or agriculture could be removed from national
control and decision-making authority given to a functional agency separate
from any nation-state. In contrast, while both were concerned with establishing conditions which would eliminate war and rejected nationalism as
the basis for political organization and decision-making, functionalists
(unlike Monnet) did not regard regional unification as superior to the
existing system of nation-states (George, 1985, p. 20). For Mitrany, the
creation of new regional groupings would merely 'change the dimensions
of nationalism, but not its nature' (1970, p. 67). Consequently, Mitrany
argued for a series of independent though complementary international
functional agencies, not for the creation of a single supranational body
with functional authority across several sectors. Functionalism, by definition,
was to be a flexible mechanism or process that could accommodate both
expansion and contraction in its scope depending on need (Pentland,
1973, p. 70), a characteristic that was not compatible with the purely
integrationist federal aspirations of Monnet: as Mitrany explains, functional schemes

> ... have the invaluable virtue of autonomous existence, and likewise of autono-
> mous development. A scheme started by a few countries for transport, or for oil,
> and so on could be later broadened to include belated members, or reduced to
> let reluctant ones drop out. Moreover, they can vary their membership;
> countries could take part in some schemes and perhaps not in others, whereas
> in any political arrangement such divided choice would obviously not be tolerable.
> (1970, p. 73)

Monnet's 'political arrangement' (the prototype Community) was more
than a series of technical functional agencies, and it was the combination of
functionalist principles with the political objective of a form of federal government that prompted the development of theories that more closely
reflected the Community reality.

Taylor suggests that functionalism has made two significant and enduring
theoretical contributions to the understanding of integration: its expansive
logic of enmeshment or interdependencies, and its emphasis on attitudinal
change (1990, p. 133). This first aspect of functionalism – the assumption
of its expansive logic – suggests that once the process of functional organization began, the power of nation-states to act independently would be, it

argued, progressively reduced as a web of functional interdependent relations developed. This logic held true whether there were several independent or just one joint functional authority. Critics of functionalism have argued that any such systems of interdependence have not reduced disputes, but rather that functional integration has simply politicized more issues within and between states: intergovernmental disputes have come to focus on functional problems, such as the international economic system, rather than on traditional topics such as territory or sovereignty. However, many have argued that functional integration has been no more successful in eliminating these tensions than was the previous system of autonomous states (p. 135).

The second aspect of functionalism as a process identified as central to integration is the gradual change in popular attitudes through the experience of co-operation transcending national borders. In Pentland's words, individuals 'are gradually weaned away from their allegedly irrational nationalistic impulses toward a self-reinforcing ethos of cooperation' (1973, p. 84). This attitudinal change comes about through the experience of co-operative activity and through the conscious application of education and the media. It is the importance placed on mass attitudinal change that most clearly distinguishes Mitrany's work from the later neofunctionalists such as Haas and Lindberg. This commitment to attitudinal change by functionalists has been forcefully criticized; Taylor notes that there is a lack of empirical evidence that can support the claim 'that international institutions are capable of becoming the focus of loyalties at the expense of the state' (p. 133). Here again, a divergence of opinion between functionalists and Monnet is clear: while Monnet was a vigorous advocate of a democratic Community, he saw the emergence of loyalties to the Community institutions developing as a *consequence* of élite agreements for the functional organization of Europe, not as an essential *prerequisite* to that organization. The negative result of the Danish referendum in 1992 illustrates that the emergence of any such loyalty cannot be taken for granted.

The practical reality of the Community drew critical attention to the inadequacy of the general theory of functionalism as an appropriate explanation of the process of integration. The response to this conceptual crisis was the development of the theory of neofunctionalism by Ernst Haas which was specifically designed to address the Community experience. The basic tenets of Haas's neofunctionalism have been summarized as follows by Harrison. Neofunctionalism contains a normative objective – a European federation; central institutions with supranational authority are to provide the mechanism for achieving this; the process of integration is to begin with the economic sector and is dependent on interest group involvement; and the incremental creation of 'de facto' solidarity would lead automatically, if by stealth, to integration (1990, pp. 139–41). Importantly, Haas abandoned the central integrative role conferred on attitudinal change by Mitrany: integration is not *initially* dependent on mass support, although such support would, over time, become associated with its development. It was a new application of the 'expansive logic of integration' that constitutes Haas's most significant theoretical contribution and remains the 'hallmark' of his neofunctionalist theory. Haas argued that successful integration was dependent on the idea of 'spillover'. By this he means that integration by sector cannot be achieved in isolation: as one sector is integrated there will be consequences, both advantageous as well as disadvantageous, for related sectors and a 'spillover effect' will occur, suggesting a kind of inevitability to the process (Pentland, 1973, p. 119). Indeed, it is argued that even the original objective can only be realized through such spillover. Spillover is also reflected in the typical Community bargaining process whereby agreements across disparate areas are tied together: decision-making does not take place in sectoral isolation, but rather concessions or agreements in one policy area will have implications and often direct consequences for other policy areas. Thus the logic of neofunctionalism was relevant, it was suggested, to both the general integration across functional sectors and to the functional and political aspects of Community decision-making.

Attention has also been focused on the 'positive' and 'negative' aspects of the neofunctionalist view of integration. Negative integration refers to the removal of all forms of barriers to the creation of a single Community, but does not in itself imply that the member states have to forgo any of their national sovereignty and control over policy. It is a necessary but far from sufficient characteristic for integration. However, the progressive removal of these barriers does 'impair the management capabilities of governments' and raises the question 'of the need for an economic and monetary union – or what may be termed "positive" integration' based on supranational institutions (Harrison, 1990, pp. 143–4). This 'positive' spillover impacts directly on the political sphere leading to a process of élite socialization and eventually to the development of new Community-focused loyalties. As Pinder suggests, the dichotomy between these aspects of integration should not be made too distinct: the linkage between the two is essential to the dynamic of the integration process (Pinder, 1989, p. 108).

However, just as functionalism was discarded because of its poor 'fit' with reality, the events of the 1960s undermined confidence in the explanatory ability of neofunctionalism and led to 'a crisis not only in the EEC but in neofunctionalist theory' (Pentland, 1973, p. 141). More contemporary commentaries support this view; for example, Harrison's conclusion that 'it must be conceded in the light of experience that many of the expectations have been disappointed' is typical of this disillusionment with the utility of neofunctionalist theory (1990, p. 144). The initial expectations associated with the Community institutions were largely unfulfilled and spillover and progressive integration did not seem to be occurring; rather, the persistence of national self-interest indicated that the Community was closer to an intergovernmental grouping than any putative federation. The Commission appeared unable to fulfil its neofunctionalist role as the instigator of spillover due to the institutional imbalance that provided the Council with decision-making dominance. The Commission adopted a 'mediatory conciliatory role rather than a creative one', arguably as a result of the inadequacies of the Treaty of Rome that placed it in conflict and at a disadvantage to the Council (p. 145).

In his seminal account of European integration written at the beginning of the 1970s, Pentland lamented that 'events in Europe continue to outpace academic theory' (1973, p. 146). Harrison provides an extreme example of this view in his assessment of the limitations of neofunctionalist theory: 'there is no evidence in the Community experience of the beguiling automaticity of step-by-step economic integration, leading eventually to political integration. What has been achieved within the Community has depended upon political leadership by national élites and by political agreements between national governments.' (p. 146) While the pace of events since the mid-1980s have been almost as frantic as those of the founding years of 1957–63, this recognition of the role of political élites and the absence of the inevitability of spillover has led integration writers in the 1990s to reconsider neofunctionalist theory in the light of practical experience. With the passing of the Single European Act (SEA) and the creation of the Single Market of 1992, the need for an adequate integration theory is more pressing than ever: as William Wallace has recently argued, 'the greater the complexity of the processes of European integration, the more important it becomes to rebuild acceptable conceptual frameworks with which to order the mass of information' (1990, p.x). Two of the contributors to the Wallace volume, Robert Keohane and Stanley Hoffmann, offer such a reconstruction based on neofunctionalism and it is to this conceptual approach that this chapter now turns.

As noted above, early neofunctionalist theory was dependent on the notion of spillover, both functional and political. The idea that gradual integration by sector would lead towards a political union through the process of interdependence echoed quite accurately Monnet's own prescription for a united Europe. Monnet believed that successive functionalist forms of integration would inevitably create a type of federalism: this process would be gradual, but cumulative, as economic sectors were transferred from national to a Community level of competence. Consequently, central to neofunctionalist theory, as well as to Monnet's assumptions, was the *automatic* effect of the spillover process.

Keohane and Hoffmann argue that the Community exhibits (at least since the SEA) a supranational style of decision-making (based on compromise and common interests) (1990, p. 277). This idea directly corresponds to the approach of Ernst Haas who they quote as defining a supranational decision-making style as 'a cumulative pattern of accommodation in which the participants refrained from unconditionally vetoing proposals and instead seek to attain agreement by means of compromises upgrading common interest' (p. 280). The importance of their reformulation of neofunctionalism is the recognition that a prerequisite to any form of spillover (economic or political) is a successful intergovernmental bargaining process. Thus spillover *per se*, is not an automatic procedure as commonly argued by neofunctionalist theorists. Once the inevitability of spillover is denied and the limitations on the process acknowledged, the disappointments of the 1960s and 1970s and the resulting theoretical disillusion can be overcome.

Keohane and Hoffmann argue that the appropriate initial focus of analysis should, therefore, be at the intergovernmental level. Contemporary experience supports this approach: the deeper integration promoted by the SEA and the Maastricht Treaty had their origins in intergovernmental conferences. What is then achieved is a synthesis between intergovernmentalism and integration theory, replacing the antagonistic tension that has typified the debate since the 1960s. The expectation that spillover could be a sufficient explanation or stimulus for integration was unrealistic: the missing catalyst, it is contended, is the bargaining process characteristic of intergovernmentalism. To guide research, Keohane and Hoffmann provide a working hypothesis 'that successful spillover requires prior programmatic agreement among governments, expressed in an intergovernmental bargain' (p. 287). Thus the process they outline specifies external catalysts leading to an intergovernmental bargain, which in turn will result in task expansion for the Community and sectoral (political or economic) spillover internal to the EC. Spillover is stripped of its previously implied causal role and becomes a secondary, conditional consequence.

Mutimer has also contributed to the contemporary rehabilitation of neofunctionalism as 'the most useful theoretical context for discussing integration' and the Single Market of 1992 (1989, p. 78). Neofunctionalist theory stresses three elements relevant to the current debate. Firstly, it hypothesizes that there is a connection between economics and politics in the process of integration with economic integration given the causal role in producing a form of political integration (although the precise form of political union is left intentionally ill-defined); secondly, as noted already, the process of spillover provides the necessary, but not automatic, link between economics and politics; and thirdly, spillover acknowledges and promotes the importance of institutionalization in the integrative process. Such a 'non-deterministic' view of neofunctionalism and particularly of spillover can provide an important focus for evaluating the impact of the Single Market of 1992 on the broader process of European integration. Indeed, Mutimer 'suggests that 1992 is a useful test case of the validity of the neofunctionalist insights into the links between economic and political integration' (p. 100).

What insights do the approaches of these contemporary neofunctionalist commentators provide for understanding the Community in the 1990s? The question is whether the intergovernmental bargaining of 1991 will produce spillover, and if so how far will its effect spread? Certainly, spillover from the IGCs into Political Union cannot be predicted, but at least at a theoretical level the possibility exists. History has shown that it is wise to be cautionary with regard to the development of the EC. The process of spillover is a gradual one, but perceptible. For the first time since the heady days of Euro-optimism in the mid-1970s key qualitative issues central to European integration are on the agenda. Like the agreement on the SEA in 1986, these issues 'resulted less from a coherent burst of idealism than from a convergence of national interests' (Keohane and Hoffmann, 1990, p. 288). The theory of a supranational-style of decision-making, where compromises enhancing common interests have superseded the veto principle of national protection, appears to be of utility once again.

The case for the re-evaluation of neofunctionalism is strong: with the reported demise of the Luxembourg Compromise and the *saut qualitif* of the SEA, 'European decision-making has quite suddenly become more decisive, expeditious and effective' (Keohane and Hoffmann, 1990, p. 284). The reality of Community politics has once again begun to resemble the predictive elements of neofunctional theory (after an absence of some two decades). However, while spillover ought to be rehabilitated, its role has to be clearly delimited and 'the conditions under which spillover can be expected to operate must be kept in mind' (p. 289).

With these theoretical ideas as a background, Chapter 2 focuses on the historical development of the Community towards Political Union and federation in the post-war period. Neofunctionalist theory is used to distinguish between those periods of sustained integration in the Community and those of stagnation or even fragmentation. However, as Jean Monnet observed, theory must always take second place to opportunity and circumstance in the construction of Europe: '[T]he unification of Europe, like all peaceful revolutions, takes time – time to persuade people, time to change men's (sic) minds, time to adjust to the need for major transformations. But sometimes circumstances hasten the process, and new opportunities suddenly arise. Must they be missed simply because they were not expected so soon?' (1978, p. 432)

The challenge that faces all the Community's actors – the European Council, the Commission, the Council of Ministers as well as the European Parliament – is to grasp the current opportunities for reconstructing the architecture of Europe within a revised Community framework. At stake is the future of European integration and the shape and content of the Community of the next century: the task could not be of greater importance or magnitude.

References

Burgess, M., 1989, *Federalism and European Union: political ideas, influences and strategies in the European Community, 1972–1987*, Routledge, London.

Cardozo, R., 1987, 'The project for a political Community, (1952–54)' in Pryce, R. (ed.), *The dynamics of European integration*, Croom Helm, London, pp. 49–77.

Duchêne, F., 1990, 'More or less than European? European integration in retrospect' in Crouch, C. and Marquand, D. (eds), *The politics of 1992: beyond the Single European Market. The Political Quarterly*, Basil Blackwell, Oxford, pp. 9–22.

Duroselle, J-P., 1970, 'General de Gaulle's Europe and Jean Monnet's Europe' in Cosgrove, C. and Twitchett, K. (eds), *The new international actors: the UN and the EEC*, Macmillan, London, pp. 187–200.

George, S., 1985, *Politics and policy in the European Community*, Clarendon Press, Oxford.

Groeben, H. von der, 1987, *The European Community the formative years: the struggle to establish the Common Market and the political union (1958–66)*, Office for Official Publications of the European Communities, Luxembourg.

Haas, E., 1964, *The uniting of Europe: political, economic and social forces 1950–57*, Stanford University Press, Stanford.

Harrison, R.J., 1990, 'Neo–functionalism' in Groom, A.J.R and Taylor, P. (eds), *Frameworks for international co-operation*, Pinter, London, pp. 139–50.

Keohane, R.O. and Hoffmann, S., 1990, 'Conclusions: Community politics and institutional change' in Wallace, W. (ed.), *The dynamics of European integration*, pp. 276–300.

Mayne, R., 1966, 'The role of Jean Monnet', *Government and Opposition*, 2, pp. 349–71.

Mitrany, D., 1970, 'The functional approach to World organisation' in Cosgrove, C.A. and Twitchett, K.J. (eds), *The new international actors: the UN and the EEC* Macmillan, London, pp. 65–75.

Monnet J., 1978, *Memoirs* (trans. R. Mayne), Doubleday and Company, New York.

Mutimer, D., 1989, '1992 and the political integration of Europe: neofunctionalism reconsidered', *Journal of European Integration*, 13, pp. 75–101.

Patijn, S. (ed.), 1970, *Landmarks in European unity*, Sijthoff, Leyden.

Pentland, C., 1973, *International theory and European integration*, The Free Press, New York.

Pinder, J., 1989, 'The Single Market: the step towards European Union' in Lodge, J. (ed.), *The European Community and the challenge of the future*, Pinter, London, pp. 94–110.

Pryce, R., Wessels, W., 1987, 'The Search for an ever closer Union: a framework for analysis' in Pryce, R. (ed.), *The dynamics of European Union*, Croom Helm, London, pp. 1–34.

Taylor, P., 1990, 'Functionalism: the approach of David Mitrany' in Groom, A.J.R. and Taylor, P. (eds), *Frameworks for international co-operation*, Pinter, London, pp. 125–38.

Treaties establishing the European Communities (abridged edn.), 1979, Office for Official Publications of the European Communities, Brussels.

Wallace, W. (ed.), 1990, *The dynamics of European integration*, Pinter/RIIA, London.

2 The Community experience: from civil war to interdependence

For students of integration it is difficult to identify the exact beginning of the Community idea. Somewhat erroneously, Winston Churchill's frequently quoted reference to 'a kind of United States of Europe', is often adopted as the origin of post-1945 European integration. As noted in Chapter 1, Churchill certainly focused on similar themes to those also being articulated by Monnet: in this 19 September 1946 Zurich speech Churchill advocated that

> the first steps in the re-creation of the European family must be a partnership between France and Germany. In this way only can France recover the moral leadership of Europe. There can be no revival of Europe without a spiritually great France and a spiritually great Germany. The structure of the United States of Europe, if well and truly built, will be such as to make the material strength of a single state less important. (Patijn, 1970, p. 33)

However, Churchill's notion of a 'United States of Europe' was never specified in any detail and, more importantly, it was seen as an appropriately 'continental' solution that did not demand British participation. This characteristic was in contrast to the aspirations of Monnet who attempted to secure British involvement in the European Coal and Steel Community (ECSC) Treaty. For Monnet in the immediate post-war years a British-Franco union was as important as Franco-German reconciliation as the former was regarded as 'the first step towards a European federation' (1978, p. 280). Britain's reluctance throughout the 1950s to become engaged in the Community process led Monnet, reluctantly, to concentrate on building a Europe without British membership if necessary.

The history of the European experience can be catalogued in a number of different ways; most typically, the process has been divided into stages of dynamic integration, plateau and stagnation. An alternative dichotomy is to examine the Community in relation to the process of deepening (integration) and that of widening (enlargement), although these two conditions are not necessarily mutually exclusive. In this survey of the Community's history the idea of federalism is the organizing principle. The tension between the intergovernmental and *communautaire* elements within the Community are used to delineate specific periods of integration. Six periods have been isolated: pre-1950 and the search for a new European structure; 1950–57 and the creation of functional organizations; the 1960s and the assertion of intergovernmentalism; 1970–79 and neofunctional progression;

1979–84 and the danger of a 'two-speed' Europe; and 1985–92 and the communautarization of the Community towards Political and Monetary Union. Each historical juncture is examined in relation to its intergovernmental or *communautaire* contribution, providing the historical record with an evaluation of the integration process.

Pre-1950: the search for a new European structure

While acknowledging the contributions made by various international military forces and governments, within the context of the Community's development it is instructive to regard the 1939–45 war as primarily a European civil war. Just as in 1914–18, the main protagonists were European nations. For those generations born after the last major military battle on European soil, it can be difficult to appreciate the appropriate historical perspective. It remains remarkable that within five years the enmities between European peoples had dissipated to the extent that Franco-German reconciliation could be cemented through a supranational plan. The psychological and material effects of intra-European conflict concentrated the minds of politicians in the 1945–50 period.

The resultant Schuman Declaration of 1950 was not an isolated attempt to secure European peace and co-operation; rather, it was just one example, albeit an extremely successful one, of a series of initiatives designed to reconstruct Europe and restore it to its former status as a leading global power. François Duchêne, one of the original participants in Monnet's European idea, has recently written of the 'central paradox in the history of the European Community': namely, the failure to produce political union (1990, p. 9). This aspiration to build more than a series of purely functional economic agencies blossomed in the immediate post-war period. As Duchêne reminds us, this objective was not a purely European affair: the USA was instrumental in helping to relaunch Europe's shattered economy and in providing political support for the idea of integration.

These early attempts at restructuring Europe reflected the intergovernmental–supranational debate. The prime example of intergovernmental co-ordination was the establishment of the Organization for European Economic Cooperation (OEEC) in 1948. Initially constituted to help direct funds provided through the American Marshall Aid scheme, the OEEC was instrumental in encouraging the idea of co-operation between Europe's 16 recipient states. However, this organization did nothing to challenge the sovereignty of individual governments. There was, as Monnet at the time commented, an 'intrinsic weakness of a system that went no further than mere cooperation between Governments . . . the idea that sixteen sovereign nations will cooperate effectively is an illusion' (1978, pp. 271–2). As Nicoll and Salmon have suggested, 'it was a classic intergovernmental operation, acting by consensus or not at all' (1990, p. 8). The virtue of co-operation was extolled, not the principle of integration. To complement this economic intergovernmentalism, in the following year the Western European Union (WEU) was developed to counter possible military aggression in Europe. Again, the guiding principle was the independence and sovereignty of each of the member states, although the Brussels Treaty establishing the WEU calls for 'd'encourager l'intégration progressive de l'Europe (Schoutheete, 1990, p. 118). Despite neglect and its seeming irrelevance to the construction of Europe through the Community method, the contribution and credibility of the WEU *vis-à-vis* the post-Single European Act constitutional debates of the 1980s and 1990s illustrate the resilience of intergovernmental ideas within the Community's history. Despite successive reforms and the progressive communautarization of European activity, intergovernmentalism has remained the real alternative and challenge to the Community experiment.

In contrast, the Benelux agreements of the 1940s provided an alternative model based on the concept of integration that was to be instructive for the restructuring of intra-European relations. These agreements between the Belgian, Dutch and Luxembourg Governments in exile covered monetary policy (1943) and the establishment of a customs union (1944). These initial agreements were supplemented by a common commercial policy in 1950, the liberalization of capital movements in 1954 and the free movement of workers two years later: as de Schoutheete has remarked, 'in the difficult years immediately after the war they constituted a pioneering effort on the road to economic integration of sovereign states' (1990, p. 116). Indeed, throughout the history of the Community, the level of integration between these three countries has been higher than that exhibited by the EC as a whole, creating what de Schoutheete has called a privileged Community 'sub-system par excellence!' (p. 117). This differentiation should not be viewed as detrimental to a wider Community affiliation, but rather the Benelux states see themselves as more European, more *communautaire* than any other EC member states and the guardians, albeit informal ones, of the Community idea and heritage of Monnet.

As the decade of the 1940s drew to a close, alternative plans for the architecture of Western Europe were in competition: a natural consensus, be it intergovernmental or integrationist, did not exist. As Chapter 1 suggests, it is not an overstatement to conclude that the commitment of a single man coupled with the authority and ambition of a leading politician, was the important catalyst that capitalized upon the opportunity to shape the second half of the twentieth century. Given the intergovernmental forces that were arraigned at the time, the success of the Monnet-Schuman initiative was remarkable.

1950–57: the creation of functional organizations

Monnet rejected the modest intergovernmentalism of the OEEC as it embodied 'the opposite of the Community spirit': while it could provide useful technical machinery which facilitated the liberalization of economic trade, it was unable to 'ever give concrete expression to European unity' (1978, p. 273). The key to such unity was the rejection of 'mere cooperation' and the adoption of a legal, formal agreement to create new functional authorities that superseded the sovereignty of existing nation-states. Sovereignty had only succeeded in producing destructive national rivalries. By the end of the 1940s potentially the most harmful emerging rivalry was again between France and Germany, this time over modernization and the fate of the crucial industrial and coal producing regions of the Ruhr and the Saar. The Schuman Plan of 1950 addressed this problem directly and laid the foundations for the development of the European Community.

Responding to the need to resolve this political and economic impasse, during April 1950 Monnet and his associates revised a series of draft documents that sought to transfer the ownership of certain vital coal and steel resources to a common supranational body. The eventual version became the 9 May Schuman Declaration which envisaged a limited economic Franco-German union; however, from this limited idea to pool sovereignty over iron, coal and steel production, the very basis of European Union has flourished. Clearly, 'Europe was on the move' (p. 306).

The Schuman Declaration was, in the context of post-war Europe, revolutionary and provided a basis for building a new Europe beyond the inherent limitations and dangers of nationalism. The idea was startling for the time; but it was essentially an idea. There was no detailed technical operational plan on how it would be implemented: it was, as Schuman is reported to have remarked, 'a leap in the dark' (p. 305). The seemingly technical and sober content of the proposal (coal and steel production hardly seemed the stuff of ideological fervour) belied the radical and fundamental implications suggested in the declaration: *'By the pooling of basic production and the establishment of a new High Authority whose decisions will be binding on France, Germany and the countries that join them, this proposal will lay the first foundations of the European Federation which is indispensible to the maintenance of peace'* (p. 298).

It was the accusation of vagueness that contributed to the decision of the United Kingdom to decline participation, despite personal representation by Monnet and Schuman on behalf of the French Government. More specifically, irrespective of the eventual details, the British Government was implacably opposed to the supranational commitment which lay behind the idea of pooling resources and authority. Britain was not simply declining to participate, she was against any states entering into such a new international arrangement: as an official response from London stated, Britain 'would greatly regret such an outcome' (p. 312).

While Britain's refusal was unfortunate (and to prove a major historical error by Britain's policy-makers), it could not be allowed to preclude possible European integration. As Duchêne has remarked, despite the experience of collaboration during the war and the *entente cordiale*, 'Britain had to be disconnected. Even more breath-taking, it had to be replaced by Germany' (1990, p. 10). While the proposal could survive with just Franco-German support, the wider application of these ideas depended upon other European states becoming signatories and accepting the principle of supranational co-operation. Britain's reluctance was not shared by the Benelux countries or Italy. Amid quite frantic diplomatic activity and after many redrafted communiqués, in a remarkably short time it was agreed by these six nations to convene a conference to develop the Schuman proposal. These talks began on 20 June 1950 in Paris: by April 1951 the European Coal and Steel Community had been established. Britain's response to the convening of the conference highlighted the diplomatic impasse that had disassociated the UK from European affairs. The British Embassy in Paris issued the following elliptical statement: 'There are precedents of international organizations set up with fanfares of trumpets which encounter only difficulties and disappointments when the time comes to put them into practice.' (Monnet, 1978, p. 314) Thus Europe would be built without British commitment, or even goodwill.

The signing of the Treaty of Paris on 18 April 1951 created the ECSC and laid the foundation for the future Community. The formal Treaty provisions called for the ECSC to contribute 'to economic expansion, growth of employment and a rising standard of living' while ensuring 'the most rational distribution of production at the highest possible level of productivity' (Article 2). This was to be achieved within the context of a common market for coal and steel which precluded State aid or special subsidies, outlawed restrictive practices and ended other 'measures or practices which interfere with the purchaser's free choice of supplier' (Article 4(b)) irrespective of which member state was the country of origin.

The provisions of the Treaty while limited in their economic application, contained the central principles and institutions that were to form the structure of the European Economic Community some six years later. The guiding principle was supranationalism (containing implicit ideas of federalism). National sovereignty and control was to be exchanged by common agreement for joint control of a specific area of a state's economic autonomy. This commitment was more than an economic means, it constituted a political statement, what Monnet called 'the first move towards a federation' (p. 328). Thus the ECSC was based upon neofunctionalist logic: the transfer of national competences in iron, coal and steel production to a supranational level was just the forerunner to task expansion into other related economic areas of nation-state activity. What, then, were the ECSC's supranational institutions?

Monnet placed great emphasis on the importance of institutions; for him 'only institutions grow wiser; they accumulate collective experience' (p. 393). His influence is reflected in the Paris Treaty which established four principal institutions: a High Authority (assisted by a Consultative Committee); a Common Assembly; a Special Council of Ministers; and a Court of Justice. The central institution, and the greatest innovation, was the creation of a High Authority. This body was the focus of the ECSC's supranational responsibility and was charged with the duty 'to ensure that the objectives set out in (this) Treaty are attained' (Article 8). It was originally composed of nine members who were to be 'completely independent in the performance of their duties' (Article 9.2). The appointment of Jean Monnet as the first President of the ECSC High Authority ensured that the neofunctional supranational objectives were honoured and enhanced at every opportunity. Monnet's success in translating the idea of supranational co-operation into a practical reality provided the necessary stimulus and confidence for the member states to agree to construct a wider Community within a few years.

The ECSC was not a parliamentary regime; the powers of the Common Assembly were clearly circumscribed and supervisory. It had authority to question members of the High Authority, to debate general reports, and in extreme circumstances to dismiss the High Authority as a body through a motion of censure carried by a two-thirds majority (Article 24). This lack of parliamentary control was compounded by the non-elected nature of the Common Assembly's composition. Membership was drawn from delegates designated by their respective national parliaments, not directly elected representatives who could claim democratic legitimacy and corresponding legislative powers.

The inclusion of a Council of Ministers in the institutional framework illustrates the intergovernmental–supranational tension that existed at the time. Monnet's original plan intentionally did not provide an institutional home where national interests could be represented. The insertion of national sovereignty into the Treaty via the Council of Ministers was the practical concession that had to be offered to the still hesitant founding members during the first two months of the Schuman Plan conference of 1950. Monnet was not unaware of the implications of such a compromise, but in keeping with his general philosophy he believed it necessary to work within political realities rather than to maintain the 'purity' of his federal scheme and in doing so risk its implementation. In his text of the Schuman Declaration, Monnet acknowledged this necessity: 'Europe will not be built all at once, or as a single whole: it will be built by concrete achievements which first create *de facto* solidarity.' (Monnet, 1978, p. 300)

Article 6 of the Treaty of Paris provided the ECSC with the legal personality necessary to fulfil its functions. The Court of Justice was specifically empowered to ensure that the implementation of rules, their application and interpretation, were made according to the Treaty provisions. The Court had jurisdiction to declare any High Authority action void on the 'grounds of lack of competence, infringement of an essential procedural requirement, infringement of this Treaty or of any rule of law relating to its application, or misuse of powers' (Article 33). The High Authority was obliged to enact the Court's decision in these matters. In addition, the Court could be used to bring proceedings against the High Authority if it failed to fulfil an obligation required of it by the Treaty. Reciprocol rights rested with the High Authority (and with member states) to appeal to the Court to declare any act of the Common Assembly or of the Council void on the grounds of a lack of competence or serious procedural infringement (Article 38). Thus the institutional structure from its origins was constituted within a legal framework and provided the ECSC, as well as the future Community, with a clear written constitution through which to develop its political and economic personality.

The importance of the ECSC far transcended the immediate economic benefits, although these in themselves were considerable. The creation of this Community marked a historical juncture in European history where two kinds of sovereignty – national and supranational – collided. For

Monnet, the ECSC was simply the beginning: his first address to the Common Assembly as President of the High Authority was candid in its ambition. 'We can never sufficiently emphasize that the six Community countries are the fore-runners of a broader united Europe, whose bounds are set only by those who have not yet joined. Our Community is not a coal and steel producers' association: it is the beginning of Europe.' (Monnet, 1978, p. 392)

The international crises of the early 1950s proved a serious challenge to this aspiration and provided a stark reminder of the fragility of Europe's experimental architecture. War in Korea and concern about rearmament demanded an immediate European response; while the ECSC's originators had envisaged the development of supporting political and defence arrangements within a Community, such developments were to be gradual and by choice, not a consequence of crisis management. The introduction, albeit reluctantly, of the idea of a European Defence Community (EDC) came too soon. The fledgling ECSC had not had sufficient time to establish itself as an effective body and the supranational procedures on which it was premised had yet to become normal practice. While the EDC appeared to be a logically consistent neofunctional consequence of supranationalism, the political context was unsuitable. With hindsight, the EDC came remarkably close to realization. The gamble fell prey to the vicissitudes of parliamentary politics endemic in the chaos of the French Fourth Republic.

In October 1950, before the Paris Treaty had been formulated, the then French Prime Minister Pleven in an address to the French Assembly, launched the idea of two parallel Communities: the EDC and the complementary European Political Community (Duchêne, 1990, p. 12). The EDC proposal was 'the creation, for common defence, of a European Army under the authority of the political institutions of Europe' (Wistrich, 1989, p. 29). Again, the supranational and federal implications of this proposal alienated the United Kingdom; undeterred, on 27 May 1952 the six member states of the ECSC signed the Treaty creating the EDC. This was less than two months after the ECSC had effectively begun. To add a 'political' dimension to this defence co-ordination, a parallel organization, the European Political Community, was proposed. In many ways this was an early imitation of what was to be known in the 1970s as European Political Cooperation (EPC). The function of the Political Community was to create a common foreign policy by co-ordinating the individual policies of the member states. Its institutional structure was ambitious and attempted to balance intergovernmental with supranational requirements by creating a directly elected 'Peoples' Chamber', an intergovernmental Senate, an Executive Council, a Council of Ministers and a Court of Justice (Monnet, 1978, p. 394).

This Europhoria was short-lived. Each member state parliament had to ratify the Treaty before the EDC could be established. Despite positive votes in the other five countries, on 30 August 1954 the French Assembly refused to accede. A new government, dependent like its predecessors on a volatile coalition for its survival (a distinguishing, but not distinguished, feature of the Fourth Republic) and an alliance between right-wing Gaullist nationalist forces and left-wing Socialist and Communist opposition to

German rearmament, resulted in a defeat by 319 votes to 264. Thus the ECSC was stripped of its supporting Defence and Political Communities. Commentators are in agreement that 'the failure of the EDC had a decisive effect on the direction of integration' (Hackett, 1990, p. 7). Duchêne goes as far as to argue that 'From that moment on, political federation as such, has never been on the Community agenda. In fact, the federal element in all European integration plans was cut to the bone.' (1990, p. 12) Without doubt, for the rest of the decade political objectives were marginalized and an emphasis was placed on the more inclusive and less contentious approach of economic integration. However, those sceptics who predicted that the fate of the EDC spelt the end of the European idea were confounded within a year. Having failed to create European union comprehensively, Monnet and the member states returned to a neofunctionalist sectoral approach to integration. The intergovernmental conference of Messina in June 1955 represented a relaunching of the European concept and its expansion into a wider structure of a common market. The seeming paradox between the collapse of the EDC and the phoenix-like rise of the Messina conference has been explained in two ways. The question of German rearmament remained on the agenda and there was still a need to develop pan-European rapid economic growth. A free trade area appeared to become the most effective way of achieving this (Duchêne, 1990, pp. 12–13).

In contrast to the earlier ECSC which was largely shaped by Franco-German interests, the agenda for the Messina conference was significantly influenced by the Benelux countries (Nicoll and Salmon, 1990, p. 11). Monnet's invisible hand was also at work; during the spring of 1955 he met with members of the Benelux delegations on a regular basis, in particular with the leading Belgian statesman, Paul-Henri Spaak. The Messina conference resolution of 2 June provided a new and more realistic framework within which to work towards European integration. The economic objectives were stipulated as: the free movement of trade and the creation of a common market free from tariff barriers; the establishment of a European Investment Fund; the harmonization of social and employment policies; a collective approach to the production and consumption of power; and the peaceful joint development of atomic energy. The commitment of the six ECSC member state governments at Messina was reflected in their joint resolution:

> It is necessary to work for the establishment of a United Europe by the development of common institutions, the progressive fusion of national economies, the creation of a common market and the progressive harmonization of (their) social policies.
>
> Such a policy seems (to them) indispensable if Europe is to maintain her position in the world, regain her influence and prestige and achieve a continuing increase in the standard of living of her population. (Patijn, 1970, p. 101)

The conference selected Paul-Henri Spaak to chair a committee of delegates and members of the High Authority with a brief to devise a new treaty in accordance with the Messina resolution leading to European economic integration and a complementary organization for atomic energy.

The experience of the EDC failure promoted caution; significant concessions to intergovernmentalism were accepted which subtly shifted the balance away from federalism and towards national governments. It was this compromise that formed the basis of the institutional structure and policy competences of the future European Economic Community.

Within a year the Spaak Report was issued forming the basis of the intergovernmental negotiations for the new communities that began in June 1956. Perhaps, surprisingly, given the subsequent history of the Community, during this period greater attention was given to creating an atomic community (by both the governments involved and by Monnet and his recently established Action Committee for the United States of Europe) rather than an economic common market. However, in what was to become a typical Community policy-making style, the success of these developments was mutually dependent: the discussions continued in parallel with concessions in one sphere being traded against progress in the other. Of central importance was the counterbalance of French enthusiasm for an atomic community with Germany's preference for an enlarged economic zone. It was not coincidental that the resultant two treaties were signed simultaneously. Singly, neither new community would have been acceptable; only by a joint agreement could the member states persuade their domestic parliaments that the benefits of membership were significant enough to outweigh the perceived, if illusory, disadvantages.

The Suez crisis of 1956 persuaded the Six of the necessity of developing a common energy policy. As George has commented, it is somewhat ironic that their response was to create an atomic energy community to complement the existing coal community, but to ignore oil production and supply. Arguably, this decision to establish Euratom (the European Atomic Energy Community) rather than a common comprehensive energy policy, 'may actually have hindered the development of one . . . whatever the reasons for the neglect of oil, it was disastrous from the point of view of a common energy policy' (George, 1985, pp. 106–7). This omission was to be to the Community's cost throughout the 1970s and even into the 1990s.

The debate concerning the common market focused, on French insistence, primarily on the inclusion of agriculture. The principle of the market was to establish common external tariff barriers for imports from third countries and to remove all internal trade barriers between member states. Agriculture was politically sensitive for three reasons. First, the agricultural work-force in a number of member states represented a significant electoral bloc. Governments that alienated the farming lobby were precariously placed. Second, more than for any other sector of the economy, agriculture was heavily protected by national subsidies and tariffs. Third, agriculture was more than a commodity: it reflected individual social and cultural values that were of great significance, especially in France. Thus the debate could not be simply a technocratic or strategic one (as for Euratom), but had to accommodate political concessions. The final package placated the various national concerns by safeguarding the position of Europe's rural population while providing German industry with the prospect of a customs union of goods, services, and capital.

On 27 March 1957 the two Treaties of Rome were signed establishing the European Economic Community and Euratom. These, together with the ECSC Paris Treaty and latterly, the Single European Act and the Maastricht Treaty on European Union, are tantamount to the constitution of the European Community. Within the Rome Treaties intergovernmental and supranational elements are evident, again reflecting the sobering experience of the earlier aborted federal schemes. It was far from guaranteed that the development of the Community would follow integrationalist aspirations; with a concerted political will, an intergovernmental Community could easily emerge, as the experiences of the 1960s, and to a lesser extent the early 1980s, were to illustrate. But, likewise, the Treaty Articles provided for the possibility, if not probability, of the dominance of supranationalism. The often quoted preamble only calls for 'an ever closer union among the peoples of Europe', it does not stipulate categorically a federal option. Unlike the EDC, the ratification procedures were soon completed in each of the domestic parliaments and the common market began functioning at the beginning of 1958. Although it approved the Rome Treaties, the French Assembly proved again to be the least enthusiastic signatory.

The Treaty of Rome establishing the European Economic Community followed the Monnet-inspired ECSC model which emphasized the importance of institutional relations. The two dominant supranational bodies are the Assembly (subsequently known as the European Parliament) and the Commission (comparable to the ECSC High Authority). Article 137 establishes the Assembly which was to 'exercise advisory and supervisory powers'; Article 138 authorizes the Assembly to 'draw up proposals for election by direct suffrage in accordance with a uniform procedure in all Member States'; and Article 144 gives the Assembly the exclusive power to censure and dismiss the pivotal supranational body, the Commission. The Commission is responsible for the proper functioning of the common market, for the general application of the Treaty provisions, and for making recommendations and the implementation of decisions (Article 155). Commissioners are appointed 'by common accord' by the governments and must be member state nationals (with at least one and a maximum of two from each state). On their appointment, Commissioners 'shall, in the general interest of the Communities, be completely independent in the performance of their duties . . . they shall neither seek nor take instruction from any Government or from any other body' (Article 157.2).

Two supplementary institutions that have in practice contributed to the supranational content of the Community are the Court of Justice and the Economic and Social Committee (ESC). The Court is charged with ensuring that 'in the interpretation and application of this Treaty the law is observed' (Article 164). Historically, the Court has interpreted the Treaty in a manner favouring integration, expanding the powers of the Community to the limits of the Treaty rather than offering a narrow reading of the Community's legal competences. The Community institutions (Commission, Council, Assembly), the member state governments and individuals have the right of redress through the Court to challenge a Community decision or to petition for compliance with the provisions of the Treaty where these are being flouted. The ESC is composed of representatives from interest groups that are directly affected by Community competences: while it only has 'advisory status', it 'must be consulted by the Council or by the Commission where this Treaty so provides' (Article 198). The ESC adds an important transnational complexion to policy-making by institutionalizing the concept that European interests take precedent over national interests, and that organization at a Community level is the most effective and appropriate mechanism. As was the case in the ECSC, the intergovernmental tension within the Treaty of Rome is represented by the Council of Ministers. Federalist aspirations had to be balanced by the recognition of national sensitivities if the Community was to be accepted and endure. Although the Council is responsible for Community-level decision-making, there are significant concessions or omissions in the Treaty that can facilitate an intergovernmental style and permit national interests to take precedence over Community objectives. The clear intention of Spaak and his committee was progressively to enable the Council to operate by qualified majority decisions (Article 148) rather than by unanimity. But, the Treaty is far from clear on this matter and provides considerable scope for member states to invoke unanimity rules by reference to specific Treaty Articles. It has been suggested that this political concession in order to gain member state ratification (particularly in France), while necessary, was a fundamental flaw in an otherwise ambitious supranational document. However, as Monnet remarked in relation to the Draft Treaty, what is politically possible will dictate the outcome:

> Myself, I never bothered to speculate on whether the new Community Treaties might have been improved. I think they embodied as much as possible at that time and at that stage in men's (sic) thinking . . . If experience has shown that too little power of decision was initially transferred to the European level, it is up to the men (sic) of today to do what those of yesterday dared not to propose. (1978, p. 423)

The non-participation of the UK in the Messina conference and the Spaak committee prevented the British Government from having any influence on the emerging Community. That the UK applied for Community membership within four years indicates the magnitude of Britain's miscalculation. Successive British governments had received persistent invitations to take a leading role in the new European architecture: had they accepted, in all likelihood the Rome Treaties would have been more intergovernmental in style. The UK rejected active involvement in the Community building process largely because the experience of the EDC suggested that such an endeavour was doomed to failure. It was then with considerable surprise and unpreparedness that the UK witnessed the creation of a rival economic market and its own potential isolation from Europe (Wistrich, 1989, p. 31). Britain's response was to participate in a rival organization based on the principle of intergovernmentalism and excluded the idea of supranationalism – the European Free Trade Association (EFTA). Thus, at the very birth of Europe's supranational Community, intergovernmental alternatives were being canvassed. As the first decade of the Community experience was to reveal, these intergovernmental pressures were not exclusive to non-members, but were to be found in the political centre of the Community itself in the form of French President Charles de Gaulle.

The 1960s: the assertion of intergovernmentalism

If the Community was to be the core of European co-operation, the EFTA enterprise brought together the reluctant periphery. Launched on 3 May 1960, EFTA set up a free trade area between seven OEEC states that were not Community members – three Nordic countries (Denmark, Norway and Sweden), Austria, Portugal, Switzerland and the United Kingdom: Finland became an associate member in 1961 (Pedersen, 1991, p. 16). This provided for the removal of customs duties over a ten-year period for industrial goods between member states (free trade in agricultural goods was specifically excluded); the institutional framework was to be minimalist, and in direct contrast with the principles of the Community's common market, there was no common external tariff barrier. Each state retained the right and independence to set its own external duties and tariffs for non-member third countries. In this way, the United Kingdom could maintain privileged access for its Commonwealth partners. Of equal importance was the ability of EFTA to provide the United Kingdom with a political alternative to 'the creation on the Continent of a French-led political entity from which the UK was excluded' (p. 15). The resolution establishing EFTA argued optimistically that these two competing alternatives for European co-operation were 'inspired by different but not incompatible principles' (Patijn, 1970, p. 117). Experience was to prove otherwise. The federal content implicit in the Community idea could never be reconciled with the purely intergovernmentalist arrangement of EFTA. There was a fundamental difference 'between the Community, which is a way of uniting peoples, and the Free Trade Area, which is simply a commercial arrangement' (Monnet, 1978, p. 449).

Although EFTA has lasted into the 1990s, the attraction of the Community's larger market has been overwhelming. Indeed, several EFTA states had always viewed it as a transitional body that would help facilitate negotiations with the EC to create a wider free trade area (Pedersen, 1991, p. 16). By the summer of 1961, the already clear economic success of the Community and the collapse of any prospects for an EFTA-EC common accord, persuaded the United Kingdom together with Denmark and Norway to apply for full membership. Ireland had made an independent application just prior to this. Given the overtures made by Monnet, Spaak, Schuman and other leading European figures during the 1950s to secure British participation in the European experiment, the British Government could reasonably have expected to receive a favourable response to their application. The anticipated welcome failed to account for Charles de Gaulle, the first President of the recently established Fifth Republic in France. It is perhaps ironic that French nationalism and commitment to intergovernmentalism was to exclude the enlargement of the Community, given that the applicant states themselves had previously been criticized for their intergovernmental preferences and lack of Community spirit.

De Gaulle's conception of Europe was the antithesis of that envisaged by Monnet: it was to be a Europe of sovereign states, independent of the United States of America, open to the East and 'a Europe in which the dominant power in foreign policy would be France' (Duroselle, 1970, p. 191). A federal Community was an anathema, and while in opposition in the Fourth Republic he consistently opposed establishing supranational authorities. On his return to government office de Gaulle's preference was for a 'union of states', as suggested in the 1962 draft proposals for the Fouchet Plan on political co-operation, based on consultation and cooperation between states. The rejection of this French scheme by the more Community-minded member states provoked a contemptuous reaction from de Gaulle to an alternative federal proposal for integration formulated by Monnet's Action Committee. In a press conference on 15 May 1962 in which de Gaulle apportioned blame for the failure of the Fouchet Plan, he clarified his view of European Union: 'at present there is and can be no Europe other than a Europe of the states – except, of course, for myths, fictions and Pageants' (Monnet, 1978, p. 441). The Community was faced with a political impasse; as the former German Commissioner at the time has recorded, 'There can be little doubt that this French action was of enormous significance to the future development of the European Community. The differences in attitude on the objectives of integration and the methods to be used to achieve it were thrown into sharp relief.' (Groeben, 1987, p. 112)

During his decade as French President, de Gaulle opposed the extension of Community competences and attempted to thwart all efforts to realize this federal 'fiction'. Rather than emphasizing supranationalism, de Gaulle's strategy was to make the Community an intergovernmental instrument through which to further French interests (Pedersen, 1991, p. 16). De Gaulle's irreconcilable intergovernmentalist views were instrumental in the collapse of the Fouchet Plan. From this point on until his resignation as President in the summer of 1969, de Gaulle was responsible for obstructing Community development in a further three major ways: through opposition to enlargement, via the 'Luxembourg Compromise', and by refusing to extend the powers of the Community's existing institutions.

Although there were four independent applications made to the Community between July 1961 and April 1962, the question of enlargement hinged principally on the French attitude to British membership. After more than a year of negotiations and with most of the contentious issues resolved, quite unilaterally de Gaulle announced at a press conference on 14 January 1963 that Britain's application was not acceptable to France (Monnet, 1978, p. 459). The reasons had very little to do with the Community *per se*, but rather national rivalries, the very antithesis of the Community principle. Analysts are in agreement that it was the decision to purchase American rather than French nuclear weapons, and a disinclination to establish Anglo-French co-operation on nuclear technology, that precipitated the French veto (albeit an unconstitutional veto) (Nicoll and Salmon, 1990, p. 24; Pedersen, 1991, p. 17; Groeben, 1987, p. 131; Monnet, 1978, p. 458). More generally, France had assumed the leadership of the Six; British membership in an enlarged Community would significantly dilute French authority and challenge de Gaulle's 'ideas on the organization, role and policies of a European "Europe"' (Groeben, 1987, p. 132). Publically, other rationales were given. Somewhat ironically, de Gaulle accused Britain of not having the 'political will' to become committed to the Community idea and it was suggested that Atlantic ties were more important than those with Europe. At an economic level, the United Kingdom's industrial base was viewed as incompatible with the principle policy concern of the EC – agriculture; to further complicate matters, British agriculture was highly protected and preferential access was given to Commonwealth countries. Consequently, de Gaulle concluded that 'the nature and structure, the very situation that are England's (sic), differ profoundly from those of the continentals' (Patijn, 1970, p. 137). History of enlargement being blocked

Despite this political rebuff, in 1967 the United Kingdom together with the three other original applicant states reapplied for membership. Again, despite a favourable response from the Commission, de Gaulle was implacably opposed. Without unanimous agreement among the Six, even preparatory negotiations could not begin and it became evident that while de Gaulle remained as French President enlargement of the Community would be blocked. French opposition focused on the weak state of the British economy (the pound sterling was devalued in November 1967). Anglo-French relations were further impaired by the disagreement over de Gaulle's concept of Europe which led to a serious diplomatic incident – the so-called 'Soames Affair' (Nicoll and Salmon, 1990, p. 27). Thus the four applications fell into abeyance and Community enlargement was postponed until the 1970s.

Understandably, the French position on enlargement had a detrimental impact on Community relations in general. It became increasingly obvious that de Gaulle's vision of Europe was in fundamental contradiction with that of France's Community partners. The central issue of majority voting versus unanimity exposed this incompatibility. As a transitional agreement, for the first eight years major Community decisions were to be taken by unanimity; as of 1 January 1966, these exceptions were to end and the Community was to operate according to the weighted majority principle set out in Article 148 of the Treaty of Rome. In addition, the customs union for industrial goods, a common external tariff, a Community budget and agricultural policy were all planned for the following year (Wistrich, 1989, p. 32).

Matters came to a head at a Council meeting of 15 June 1965. Faced with an integrationist agenda (which included extending the EC's institutional powers and providing the Community with its own financial resources via agricultural levies), France ignored its Treaty obligations and responsibilities as the incumbent presidency, abandoned the meeting and boycotted future Community meetings. Effective decision-making ground to a halt and the Community's future seemed in jeopardy. Despite this typically

Gaullist assertion of French sovereignty, and the re-election of de Gaulle as President in December 1965, French popular opinion was surprisingly critical and in January 1966 France finally agreed to attend a meeting of the Community's Foreign Ministers in Luxembourg to resolve the dispute (Groeben, 1987, p. 188). The Commission, however, was specifically excluded from this Community Council meeting. The result, the 'Luxembourg Compromise', solved the immediate problem of French participation, but inadvertently created the Community's most debilitating long-term problem: the continued use of unanimity as the basis for decision-making. The 'Compromise' drafted by Spaak, set out the following procedure:

> Where in the case of decisions which may be taken by a majority vote on a proposal of the Commission very important interests of one or more partners are at stake, the Members of the Council will endeavour, within a reasonable time, to reach solutions which can be adopted by all the Members of the Council, while respecting their mutual interests and those of the Communities . . .
>
> the French delegation considers that where very important interests are at stake the discussion must be continued until unanimous agreement is reached. (Nicoll and Salmon, 1990, p. 26)

Rather than herald the institutionalization of majority decision-making as the normal Community procedure, January 1966 witnessed the successful defence of national sovereignty within the Community. Although not a formal Treaty amendment, the 'Compromise' had the force of convention and remained an effective intergovernmental weapon to retard the Community's supranational development for the next two decades. However, it would be incorrect to state that majority voting was rejected by the 'Compromise'; no *de jure* changes were made and majority decisions were still possible within the Community structure, except where these were against the explicit wishes of any member state (Groeben, 1987, p. 189). The experience, however, set the tone for the rest of the decade; progress towards integration was to proceed with slow caution and wherever possible avoid direct confrontation with national sensitivities.

This first constitutional crisis for the Community was broader in its impact than the principle of majority decision-making: it embodied French opposition to a series of Commission proposals for institutional and procedural reform. The early 1960s had seen the Community develop at a remarkable pace and by 1965 a majority of member states were in agreement with the Commission that the next step towards a common market and institutional authority was needed. In compliance with its Treaty obligations, in March 1965 the Commission proposed that the Community be given its own financial responsibility and resources as provided for under Article 201. Funds for the new Community budget were to be raised through agricultural levies and customs duties (which had previously gone to the member states) and all expenditure relating to the Common Agricultural Policy (CAP) was to be borne by the Community. Both these measures were to be effective from 1 July 1967. To provide a degree of democratic accountability over the budget, the Commission proposed that the European Parliament be given new powers to amend the budget. Although the Council retained the final word on budgetary matters, for those member states such as France who were committed to an intergovernmental Community, parliamentary and Commission involvement in the budget was a matter of principle which they fundamentally opposed (p. 180). To exacerbate matters, the Commission chose to announce these proposals before the European Parliament rather than the Council as was normal practice, incensing those member states who suspected the proposals were designed to marginalize the role of the Council.

France objected to both the idea that the EC should have its own resources and to the strengthening of the Parliament's powers. De Gaulle was the most outspoken critic of the Commission's proposal; but the majority of other member states also had reservations about the Commission 'package' and there was general agreement that a further five-year transitional arrangement for financing agriculture was preferable. It was somewhat unexpected then, when the French delegation walked out of the Council meeting of 29–30 June 1965 on the pretext that negotiations had irrevocably broken down. Although there were policy differences, the principle issue was that of declining French sovereignty through the gradual extension of supranational powers. In this sense, the conflict between France and the *communautaire* member states and the Commission was inevitable sooner or later (p. 185). The eventual solution that was accepted in tandem with the 'Luxembourg Compromise' delayed giving the Community its own resources until 1970; consequently, the issue of extending Parliament's budgetary powers was suspended. Indeed, the only constitutional change that was achieved during the decade was the signing of the Merger Treaty in 1965 which rationalized the institutions of the three separate Communities, the EEC, the ECSC and Euratom. This established a single Council of Ministers (differentiated according to business), and merged the High Authority with the Commissions of the Community and Euratom (Nugent, 1989, p. 44).

The 1960s can lay claim to being the most volatile and precarious period in the Community's history of integration; as we saw in Chapter 1, the reality of everyday events undermined the theoretical assumptions of neofunctional integration to the point where intergovernmentalism appeared the dominant approach for understanding the Community process. Against this background of political calamities there were economic and policy developments that promoted the common market, albeit cautiously and within certain constraints. Most importantly, and ahead of schedule, the customs union was completed on 1 July 1968 abolishing intra-Community duties and establishing a common external tariff, and progress was made on the principle of the free movement of workers, but not on the free transfer of capital. More ambitious attempts to establish a common and comprehensive Community economic policy leading to economic union were unsuccessful. The Commission produced a series of monetary, regional, energy and transport policy initiatives which in general failed to gain substantive member state support; the general effect was to freeze the integration process. Even agriculture, the one economic area where a common policy was established as 'the driving force behind integration – proved, for economic and psychological reasons, to be the greatest obstacle in the way of a balanced development of the European Economic Community' (Groeben, 1987, p. 202).

Articles 38–47 of the Treaty of Rome outline the objectives of the Common Agricultural Policy (CAP). These are to increase productivity; ensure a fair standard of living for agricultural workers; to stabilize markets; to guarantee the availability of supplies; and to ensure reasonable prices for consumers (Article 39.1). Any seeming incompatibilities between these objectives should not be surprising. The agricultural policy was the 'price' that the predominantly rural member states, notably France, demanded for integration. It is important to remember that a significant percentage of the Community population were engaged in agriculture in the 1950s, and that their support was important to social cohesion and to the political success of political parties (Marsh, 1989, p. 148). Based on these guidelines, the Commission was charged with the responsibility of developing the appropriate regulative system for producing a common market for agriculture. After extensive consultations, the mechanisms of fixed prices and product guarantees became the basis of the agricultural policy, and the CAP began operating in January 1962 (Groeben, 1987, pp. 70–8).

Supranationalism, when applied to the agricultural sector, was strongly supported by all states, including France; however, the principle of unanimity became the *de facto* rule, producing a situation that was detrimental for specific policy decisions. The agricultural market was organized at the Community level, but national interests and vetoes dominated the levels of individual product support. The 'Luxembourg Compromise' deferred the decision on the self-financing of the agricultural budget and the existing system of national contributions was extended until the end of the transitional period in 1970. As George has commented, 'agriculture, which appears at first sight to be the one example of the success of the EC in establishing common policies, appears at second sight to be both a partial success and a partial failure' (1985, p. 115). In the second half of the 1960s agriculture presented the very worst aspects of supranationalism; a dirigistic and interventionist policy-style constrained by national self-interest. It was hardly an attractive advertisement for the Community ideal. And yet, agriculture was a success in that it indicated that a common approach could be engineered and that the Community's competences could expand, mirroring the neofunctionalist belief in spillover.

Neofunctionalist progression: 1970–79

On 28 April 1969 de Gaulle resigned from the French Presidency after losing a referendum on regional devolution and reform of the Senate. With his departure, Europe was diverted from its intergovernmentalist cul-de-sac and re-routed back on to the *communautaire* road. His replacement as President, Georges Pompidou, was no less a French nationalist; however, he saw a successful Community as being central to the revival of the French economy, not its rival. With the election of Willy Brandt as West German Chancellor in October 1969 and of Edward Heath as British Prime Minister in June 1970, in a little over twelve months the Community experienced a remarkable transformation in the *communautaire* spirit of Europe's political élite.

This relaunch of the Community was formally recognized at The Hague Conference of the Heads of State and Government of December 1969 which was convened on a French initiative. The new agenda was ambitious in its crusade against intergovernmentalism: the supranational issues that had divided the Community throughout the 1960s became the focus for consensus. In the final communiqué it was agreed that the Community should be given its own financial resources (including for agriculture) in accordance with Article 201 of the Treaty of Rome; a plan for economic and monetary union (EMU) should be drafted within the next twelve months; negotiations for membership should be commenced 'as soon as practically and conveniently possible'; and, that the European Parliament should be given greater powers. Seeking to establish a new political commitment, the Six declared that

> the Community has now arrived at a turning point in its history . . . paving the way for a united Europe capable of assuming its responsibilities in the world of tomorrow and of making a contribution commensurate with its traditions and its mission.
>
> The Heads of State or of Government therefore wish to reaffirm their belief in the political objectives which give the Community its meaning and purpose. (Hague Conference, 1970, pp. 10–11)

Additional areas where a new direction was sought included co-ordinating industrial research and development, a research programme for Euratom and reform of the Community's Social Fund. The communiqué also revived one of the Fouchet Plan proposals, the development of a Community foreign policy. There was agreement 'to study the best way of achieving progress in the matter of political unification, within the context of enlargement'; this decision was to lead to the 1970 Davignon Report which established European Political Cooperation (EPC), the Community's nascent collective foreign policy (see Chapter 5).

The enlargement of the Community was its most significant development in the 1970s. The negotiation process, which began in June 1970 between the Community and the four applicant states (the UK, Ireland, Denmark and Norway), was not without its difficulties, however. Again, the British application was potentially the most contentious; initial negotiations floundered on the nature of transitional arrangements, budgetary contributions and access for specific Commonwealth products. It was only after a bilateral meeting between Heath and Pompidou in May 1971 that these outstanding issues were resolved, and by October of that year the British Houses of Parliament gave their assent to membership. Irish, Danish and Norwegian negotiations developed in parallel, and these states together with the UK signed the Accession Treaties on 22 January 1972 providing for membership on 1 January 1973. The ratification process resulted in favourable referenda results in Ireland and Denmark; in Norway a slim majority voted against membership and consequently Norway revoked its accession preferring to remain an EFTA state. Thus after two aborted attempts, the original Community of the Six became the Community of the Nine. And yet within eighteen months this new beginning was again threatened by further British prevarication.

Between 5 March and 19 May 1974, political leadership in the Community's dominant three states – Britain, France and West Germany – changed: Heath and Brandt lost office and Pompidou died. This transformation had a significant impact on the balance of authority within the Community; whereas Helmut Schmidt and Valéry Giscard d'Estaing were committed Europeans, the new British Prime Minister, Harold Wilson, was decidedly reserved. As a consequence, the Franco-German alliance within the Community became ascendant largely at Britain's expense. In its February 1974 election manifesto, the British Labour Party committed Britain to renegotiating the terms of entry agreed to by the former Conservative Government of Edward Heath and to holding a referendum on continued membership. It argued for changes to the CAP, the way the Community was financed and to the European Parliament's power. This acrimonious process resulted in sufficient concessions being negotiated to allow the British Government to support membership in the referendum held on 5 June 1975: the result produced a majority in favour of the Community (Nicoll and Salmon, 1990, pp. 148–53). The expectation was that the UK was finally a committed Community partner, even if this was by force of circumstance rather than conviction:

> The June 1975 referendum, in which two-thirds of the voters endorsed British membership of the European Community, set the seal on what was already obvious: Great Britain had no choice, now, except solitary decline or integration into a larger grouping. To tell the truth, that had been obvious for twenty five years; but it takes a good quarter-century to efface the illusions that dead realities leave in the minds of nations and of men (sic). (Monnet, 1978, p. 497)

Experience was to show that this expectation was somewhat premature.

Heath is rightly regarded as the most *communautaire* of any British Prime Minister; from his days as Macmillan's chief Brussels negotiator in 1961, until his replacement as leader of the Conservative Party by Margaret Thatcher in 1975, his personal conviction was fundamental in resolving the UK's membership dilemma. In the short period he had as Prime Minister he successfully negotiated entry into the Community and was instrumental in creating the new quasi-Community institution, the European Council. During the summer of 1973 Monnet discussed his idea of a 'Provisional European Government' with Heath, Brandt and Pompidou. All were in agreement that there needed to be a central body to provide the Community with an overall political direction, and in October 1973 Pompidou unveiled a system of regular Heads of State and Government meetings 'with the aim of comparing and harmonizing their attitude in the framework of political co-operation'. The concept of the European Council had been born, although its inaugural meeting was delayed until 10 December the following year, by which time none of the three leaders were still in office. (pp. 503–10).

Although a seemingly intergovernmental construction, the creation of the European Council has provided the Community with the mechanism for enhanced decision-making and facilitated a deepening of the supranational process. Neofunctionalist assumptions, if interpreted indulgently, can be seen to have validity in the early 1970s. Spillover was evident, not in the classical economic sense, but rather politically through the process of enlargement and institution building. It was the *communautaire* idea that was spreading rather than sectoral economic functionalism. Despite these considerable incremental achievements, the ambition of the Community, as stated at the 1972 Paris Summit, to transform the 'whole complex of their relations into a European Union' by 1980, seemed unlikely to be fulfilled. Reflecting this trend, the European Council meeting of December 1974 instructed one of its participants, Belgian Prime Minister Leo Tindemans, to produce a report by the end of 1975 on progress made towards European Union and how the integration dynamism could be given impetus. The subsequent Tindemans Report outlined an integrated and neofunctionally organized Community that encompassed both economic and political affairs.

The *communautaire* spirit of the Report was unquestionable, but as a way of implementing European Union it was to prove inadequate: unlike the original proposals of the Spaak Report for integrating the Community, it did not offer a timetable of progressive stages to achieve Union. Without this necessary discipline, the Report failed to have an immediate effect, although several of its ideas were reactivated and adopted during the 1980s, and the focus of the Intergovernmental Conferences (IGCs) of 1991 mirrored the issues raised by Tindemans fifteen years earlier. Arguably, its bold suggestions remain a blueprint for a future federal European Union (see Chapter 3). Tindemans made far-reaching recommendations advocating economic and monetary integration, rights of European citizenship, regional and social policies, institutional reform, the role of the European Council and the development of the Community's global relations and foreign policy. The extra-Treaty European Council was given primacy in the Tindemans version of European Union; it was the only body capable of providing a comprehensive assessment of EC policies and of establishing general policy guidelines. To enhance consistency, Tindemans called for the Presidency of the Council of Ministers and of the newly created European Council to be extended from six months to one year. The experiences of the 1973 Yom Kippur war and the ensuing oil crisis had exposed the inadequacies of the Community's fledgling European Political Cooperation (EPC). To resolve these, Tindemans argued for a common defence policy and a common foreign policy. The existing *ad hoc* co-ordination was criticized as insufficient and called for an 'obligation to reach a common point of view' (Tindemans, 1976, p. 15). It was suggested that the European Council would define the broad parameters for a common foreign policy and that unanimity would be replaced by majority decision-making.

Echoing the debates of the early 1960s, institutional reforms were proposed to strengthen the democratic role of the European Parliament. Parliament was to be given the right of initiative, its competences extended to cover all aspects of the new Union, and the European Council was to be obliged to consider parliamentary resolutions. These reforms complemented the decision of the Paris European Council meeting of December 1974 which endorsed the principle of direct elections and set the date of June 1978 for their implementation. Direct election of the Parliament was seen as essential to 'reinforce the democratic legitimacy of the whole European institutional apparatus' (p. 29). A delay in passing the necessary UK domestic legislation required to implement the elections (more political than practical in nature) resulted in a twelve-month postponement. Consequently, the first direct elections were held on 7–10 June 1979, although not under a uniform electoral procedure as required by Article 138.3 of the Treaty of Rome (Butler and Marquand, 1981, pp. 30–44).

According to functional theory, popular support for the idea of the Community was believed to be a necessary condition for integration to occur (see Chapter 1). Consequently, the direct elections were expected to demonstrate an awareness and support for the Community among the peoples of Europe, thereby providing a *saut qualitif* in the level of Community integration. In practice, these 'second order' elections provided only a modest advance towards European Union (Reif and Schmitt, 1980). The supranational aspects of the election were partially camouflaged. Transnational party co-operation was at a rudimentary level and the decision to run each of the nine European elections independently and according to national electoral rules did little to persuade voters that the elections were any different from their respective national elections. The election issues were not European ones, but reflected national concerns and parochialism: as a result, turn-out was disappointingly low, averaging just 62 per cent, despite compulsory voting in two Community countries. In two member states turn-out was below 50 per cent, with the UK having the lowest figure at 32.6 per cent (Nugent, 1989, p. 123). Faced with this apparent popular disinterest, the first direct elections failed to provide the anticipated springboard for accelerated integration; rather, as the Community entered the 1980s, the popular legitimacy and future development of the Community came into question and a renewed trend towards more modest intergovernmental co-operation emerged.

In contrast to this popular disinterest, incremental progress towards integration was achieved in a number of spheres: further enlargement, external relations and monetary policy. Since 1961 Greece had had an association agreement with the EC providing for a customs union and policy harmonization; in 1975 full membership of the EC was applied for. Negotiations commenced the following year and 1981 was set as the date of accession. Two years later Spain and Portugal applied; in view of the disparities between these applicant states and the Community level of economic development, a minimum seven-year transition period to full membership was agreed to. In the event, Spain and Portugal only became Community members in 1986.

1975 also saw the signing of the first Lomé Convention on commercial co-operation and trade between the Community and 46 African, Caribbean and Pacific (ACP) countries. This five-year Convention replaced the Yaoundé agreements of 1963 and 1971 between the EC and 18 former French and Belgian colonies. The new Convention was necessary because of the 1973 enlargement and Britain's existing Commonwealth relationships. Lomé II was signed in October 1979, extending these trading privileges to 58 ACP states. Thus UK membership in the 1970s had an impact on the global role of the Community as well as upon internal institutional developments. Other types of trade agreements were also signed during the decade. In 1973 the Community signed preferential trade agreements with the EFTA states, and during 1976–7, international trade agreements were also signed with a number of countries and groups of states: for example, with the Maghreb countries (Algeria, Morocco and Tunisia), the Mashreq countries (Egypt, Jordan, Lebanon and Syria) and Israel, establishing a comprehensive Mediterranean trade policy.

This external economic activity was matched internally by the Community's attempts to establish a European Monetary System (EMS). Responding to the failure to create European Monetary Union by the end of the decade, EMS was proposed in late 1977 by then President of the Commission, Roy Jenkins, and the subject dominated the three European Council meetings of 1978. The system was eventually launched in March 1978 due largely to Franco-German commitment. Britain endorsed the EMS in principle, but deferred the decision to join at this time, and the weaknesses of the Greek, Portuguese and Spanish currencies excluded them from initial membership. The EMS had two major objectives: to create a European zone of monetary stability and to encourage convergence in national economic policies to promote internal Community stability (Hackett, 1990, p. 135). It created the European Currency Unit (ECU) whose value was based on a basket of national currencies, and established exchange-rate, credit and intervention mechanisms. Despite its limited initial participation and its role as substitute for real Economic and Monetary Union, the EMS has been judged a relative success even by the Community's critics (George, 1985, p. 133). If nothing else, it produced the practical and necessary conditions from which EMU was relaunched in the 1990s.

The Europhoria that began the decade and the expectation that a full European Union could be achieved by 1980 diminished as the Community struggled with familiar problems: the attitude of the UK, institutional reform, and transition from the security of intergovernmental co-operation premised on consensus towards a *communautaire* federal notion of integration. As Duchêne has conjectured, 'When Britain joined in 1973, the Community had in many ways lost its impetus. In such a context, constant expansion of membership was akin to running to seed' (1990, p. 17). Significant progress was achieved, but it was largely incremental and opportunistic. No overall plan for the next stages of integration was developed; indeed, the question of what integration might be and what the endpoint might constitute seemed studiously avoided. In that respect, rather than concentrating the minds of Europe's political élite, the Tindemans Report led to a form of collective amnesia. However, such procrastination has been a typical feature of Community history as Monnet's emphasis on practical achievements and 'everyday realities' indicates. Even those such as Monnet who professed to know the eventual destination of the European idea were unable to predict how long the journey to European Union would take. It was dependent on political and economic factors at both the Community and national level and, as was soon to be apparent, the election of Mrs Thatcher as British Prime Minister in May 1979 undoubtedly prolonged Monnet's anticipated journey.

1979–84: Two-speed Europe

At the June 1979 European Council meeting, the first Margaret Thatcher attended as Prime Minister, Britain's budgetary contribution was raised as an agenda item; this subject, which was supposedly resolved in 1975 and approved by referendum in Britain, was to dominate Community business into the mid-1980s. Successive European Councils became obsessed with what was known as 'the British problem'; the depth of the conflict was such that on one occasion (the December 1983 meeting) no joint communiqué could be issued on behalf of the Heads of State and Government. The core of the 'British problem' focused on the Community's financial contributions and the funding structure of the CAP. Britain's relatively small agricultural sector meant that its contributions to the Community budget had always exceeded funds accrued through agricultural subsidies. Only two Community countries were net contributors rather than net beneficiaries, the UK and West Germany; while the Federal Republic was the strongest European economy during this period, Britain was clearly one of the less prosperous Community nations. Consequently, Thatcher lobbied for a permanent reform of the budgetary mechanism and of the CAP.

The Community's initial response was an incremental one. The Venice European Council meeting of June 1980 produced a short-term adjustment covering the financial years 1980/1–1981/2. The UK received a rebate of roughly two-thirds of its contribution (£2,062m); this resulted in Germany and France becoming the leading net contributors to the Community budget. At the Athens, December 1983, European Council Britain again pushed for a long-term solution; this meeting and the subsequent one in Brussels in March 1984 under the French Presidency ended in deadlock. The Community seemed poised on the edge of a disastrous abyss; only after feverish diplomatic activity was a basis for agreement finally reached in time for the June 1984 Fontainebleau European Council (Taylor, 1989, pp. 4–5). The new 'formula' linked raising the ceiling for the EC's value added tax (VAT) from the existing 1 per cent to 1.4 per cent and giving the UK a 66 per cent rebate on the difference between British VAT contributions and Community funds going to the UK. Applied retrospectively, this gave the UK a rebate of £631m for 1983. This mechanism became effective from 1985 and was a permanent arrangement provided that the VAT rate stayed at 1.4 per cent: if this level of Community resources changed, as happened in 1988, the rebate and the structure of Community funding were open to renegotiation (p. 6).

As Taylor has argued, during this period 'the EC had been taken to the brink of disaster' for what were relatively paltry sums given the scale of national budgetary expenditure, engineering 'probably the lowest point in relations between the British and the others, especially the French, of the 1970s and 1980s' (p. 5). The division within the Community had become so acrimonious that the idea of a two-speed Europe – one for the states favouring deeper integration, the other for those tied to intergovernmentalism – became a possibility and, some would have argued, the most likely and preferable alternative. The prospects for any significant extension of supranational authority appeared bleak. As bizarre as it may appear, Thatcher represented the reincarnation of the Gaullist tradition; just as de Gaulle had stymied any concessions that encroached on French sovereignty during the 1960s, Thatcher was committed to opposing any federal attack on British national independence. The extent of this opposition was to become both increasingly apparent, but also increasingly ineffectual within the Community. Britain's marginalization was once again becoming a reality.

It was in this context that the second direct elections to the European Parliament took place. The Community's shabby image and record of internecine bickering did nothing to inspire new loyalties to the European idea among the voters of Europe. The elections took place between 14–17 June 1984, one week before the Fontainebleau compromise was achieved, and it was not surprising that turn-out fell below its 1979 level to 60 per cent; in only two Community states did support increase during this first five-year period. Once again, the UK had the lowest level at 32.4 per cent. More worrying was the low turn-outs exhibited in a number of staunchly *communautaire* original member states: France and West Germany recorded figures of 56.7 and 56.8 per cent respectively, whereas in The Netherlands turn-out fell to just 50.6 per cent, (Nugent, 1989, p. 123). As in 1979, the elections lacked a Community focus and were again characterized as 'second order' elections (Reif, 1984).

Throughout the history of the Community there have been regular proposals to reform the European Parliament, such as the Fouchet Plan, the Vedel Report, the Tindemans Report and the Report of The Three Wise Men (Lodge, 1986a, pp. 4–6). Both the advocates for greater parliamentary powers and those who wished to limit Parliament's legislative influence saw the poor result as vindicating their respective positions. Without any evidence of popular legitimacy intergovernmentalists concluded that it was inappropriate to extend the powers of the European Parliament in any significant way. Proponents for a stronger legislative role for the Parliament countered that popular support for the institution would only be forthcoming when it was given the legislative authority that its current status vitally lacked. The first five years of the elected Parliament had been fairly tumultuous, with the new parliamentarians seeking every opportunity to interpret their constitutional powers to the full. For example, one of the Parliament's first acts had been to reject the Community budget in December 1979: this defiance was permissible constitutionally, but had never been done before when the Parliament was composed of national delegates. From this moment on, the battle for institutional authority and a reform of the Community's 'democratic deficit' became a dominant Community theme, and one at the very heart of the intergovernmental – federal debate. The European Council contributed to the discussion through the Stuttgart Solemn Declaration on European Union of 1983 and the Dooge Committee which was established at the 1984 Fontainebleau meeting. However, the most ambitious proposal came from the Parliament in the form of the overtly federal Draft Treaty on European Union which it adopted in February 1984 (Lodge, 1986a). This Draft Treaty was 'designed to take a qualitative step forward in the process of European integration; to update and expand upon the existing treaties; to set up an existing institutional framework for the Union; and to render the institutions established by the Community more democratic, effective and accountable than hitherto' (p. 8). Thus, drawing on the assumptions of pluralist democracy, the Treaty was seen as part of the process for the 'democratic unification of Europe' in accordance with federal principles, especially that of subsidiarity. The ambitions of the Parliament were not shared by all the member states and the Draft Treaty was not implemented: however, the experience did persuade the Community to consider the issue of institutional and policy reform, and the Draft Treaty can be seen as the catalyst behind the more modest and more intergovernmental Community response, the Single European Act (SEA).

The strains upon the Community caused by its internal budgetary disputes and debate of institutional reform were matched by the challenges of international relations during this period: the Iranian hostages crisis; the Soviet invasion of Afghanistan; the introduction of martial law in Poland; and the Falklands war. It is perhaps somewhat remarkable given the disunity within the Community domestically, that as an international actor the EC was able to sustain its collective policy of EPC. The appearance of unity belied the underlying difficulties of achieving and implementing a collective foreign policy; too often the content of effective policy was delayed and diluted by the lowest common denominator in order to maintain an international image of joint action.

The seizing of the US Embassy and taking of American hostages in Tehran on 4 November 1979 provoked immediate Community condemnation, but agreement on specific joint action was delayed until 22 April 1980. The Community adopted a two-stage approach: immediate diplomatic and limited military and economic sanctions were imposed; with Iran's refusal to release the hostages, on 17 May full economic sanctions on contracts signed between member state companies and Iran after 4 November 1979 were adopted. These stayed in place until 20 January 1980, one day after the release of the American hostages. For the Community, the importance of these sanctions was not their economic significance, but the fact that this was the first EPC action that had invoked a Treaty competence (Article 113 and 223) (Holland, 1988, p. 6).

The Community's diplomatic response to Soviet intervention in Afghanistan was similarly unequivocable. Condemning the invasion as 'a serious violation of the principles of international relations enshrined in the Charter of the United Nations' and 'a threat to peace, security and stability in the region' (Council of Foreign Ministers, 1980), the EC suspended food-aid and specific export subsidies (under Article 113) and agreed not to replace the grain shortfall caused by the comprehensive American embargo. While the Community's policy was confined to limited economic measures and not military action, the Nine acted in concert. In contrast, the Community response to the introduction of martial law and violation of human rights in Poland in December 1981 was fragmented; the new member state, Greece, could not agree to the Community's decision to support the American policy of sanctions against the USSR while maintaining humanitarian aid for the Polish people. The trade sanctions applied by the remaining nine Community states were extremely modest in nature and affected only 150m ECU in Soviet exports to the EC, and these were only agreed, after three months, in March 1982.

An attack on a sovereign territory of a member state is construed as an attack upon the whole Community. Consequently, the Argentinian invasion of the Falkland Islands in April 1982 was not exclusively a British foreign policy issue; there was a legal as well as EPC dimension that required a Community response. However, that response could only draw upon the economic instruments available under the Treaty of Rome; military action was outside the Community's competence and remained a unique national foreign policy tool. On 2 April, one day after the occupation of the Islands, the Ten issued a joint statement calling for Argentinian withdrawal; one week later using Article 113 to invoke a Council Regulation, all Argentine trade with the Community was suspended. This embargo was agreed to by all Community states for an initial one-month period: after this date, however, EPC consensus was fractured, albeit by common consent drawing on a Treaty basis (Article 224), when the Irish and Italian Governments withdrew from the sanctions package which was extended indefinitely by the remaining eight member states (Edwards, 1984, p. 304). The Falklands war illustrated both the strengths and weaknesses of EPC. At a minimum a European 'reflex' to consult was confirmed as normal EPC procedure. Collective action had proved possible, but the consensus was a fragile one whose impact in economic terms was muted and slow. The experience showed that EPC was not a 'common' foreign policy (minority positions could exist), and while EPC could play an active supporting role, 'collective' policy was not a substitute for national foreign policy (Holland, 1988, p. 7).

The experience of the Iran and Afghanistan crises had exposed the cumbersome nature of existing EPC mechanisms, particularly the inability of the Community to respond quickly even at a diplomatic level. The 1981 London Report went some way to resolving these procedural inadequacies. It introduced the idea of 'Gymnich' type ministerial meetings (confidential, excluding officials), an extension of the Troika procedure and a 48-hour procedure for calling ministerial meetings in a crisis at the request of any three member states. This procedure was used for the first time to convene an emergency Council meeting to discuss the Falklands crisis. Ambitiously, the Report called on the Community to 'seek increasingly to shape events and not merely to react to them' (London Report, 1981, p. 14). This cautious progress in developing a pro-active *communauté de vues* within EPC reflected a common Community commitment to extending its relations with the developing world through the Lomé Convention. Lomé II was signed in October 1979 between the EC and 58 ACP states and Lomé III between the Community and, by now, 66 ACP states, five years later, in December 1984.

The Community's domestic agenda was not completely overshadowed by the 'British' problem. Greece formally became the tenth member state in January 1981 beginning the important process of the southern enlargement that was to be completed during the 1980s. In contrast, in February 1982, the semi-sovereign Danish territory of Greenland voted to leave the Community, the only part of the EC ever to do so. This secession reduced the Community's landmass by 50 per cent, but had virtually no impact on the Community's institutions: Greenland was only allocated one MEP and was represented in the other institutions by Danish representatives. The Community also made policy developments. The scope of a Common Fisheries Policy that had been developing since 1970 was finally agreed in 1983; and in the following year, a free-trade area between the Community and EFTA was established and a multilateral dialogue between the two organizations formalized at ministerial and political level (Pedersen, 1991, p. 20). This experience of this new structure for Community-EFTA co-operation was to lay the foundations for the creation of a 'common European area' and contributed to the decision by the majority of EFTA states to apply for full Community membership during the 1990s.

The Dublin European Council of December 1984 symbolized the closing of a chapter of Community conflict. Having removed the distraction of the 'British problem' (although events were to see it reappear before the end of the decade in a different guise), which had occupied such a high proportion of European Council time since 1979, progress on two substantive policy matters was imperative: the CAP and budgetary discipline. The complexities of both these areas, however, meant that they were to remain significant issues for the next decade. Despite these specific structural long-term constraints a consensus emerged, albeit a fragile one, on the reform of Community institutions and the extension of policies, and the Community entered its most dynamic phase of integration since the launching of the Treaty of Rome in the 1950s. Although a full treaty revision as envisaged in the Draft Treaty on European Union was not accepted by the Community, this European Parliament initiative provided the necessary stimulus for the launching of the intergovernmental conference on treaty reform that was eventually to lead to the SEA and the contemporary discussion of Political, Economic and Monetary Union of the early 1990s.

1985–92: Towards Economic, Monetary and Political Union

The long crisis of 1979–84 had placed the Community 'on the brink of failure'; the remedy was to reform the procedures and decision-making methods of the Council of Ministers (Noël, 1989, p. 4). The appointment of Jacques Delors as the President of the new European Commission in January 1985 provided the Community with a renewed commitment to European Union; under his guidance the Commission was to regain its role as the engine of integration. If Thatcher was the inheritor of the Gaullist tradition, Delors can reasonably be seen as a guardian of Monnet's Europe.

The SEA was the first formal amendment to the Community's constitution and its impact affected four distinct areas of Community activity: it modified the decision-making process by introducing majority decisions for a significant number of Articles; it created a co-decision procedure with the Parliament; it set a programme and deadline for the completion of the internal market; and, it incorporated and codified EPC within the Treaty framework (see Chapter 3 for a fuller discussion of these reforms). The success of the SEA lay in linking institutional questions to economic progress. Those countries who were committed to the internal market had to concede institutional reform in order to gain consensus – the decision to realize these goals had to be by unanimity. After considerable debate, the June 1985 Milan European Council meeting agreed to convene an intergovernmental conference (invoking the authority of Article 236) with a wide mandate to revise and amend the Treaties of Rome. This decision, in contrast, was a procedural one and only required a simple majority (the UK, Denmark and Greece were outvoted) (Noël, 1989, pp. 5–6). It was hoped that this process would be completed before the end of 1986; however, a legal debate and eventual referendum in Ireland delayed this process and the SEA was only finally ratified as a binding Community document as of 1 July 1987.

The SEA represented a necessary contribution to building integration, but it was not in itself sufficient and did not constitute the final construction of European Union. It also provided a further example of the 'central paradox in the history of the European Community' (Duchêne, 1990, p. 9). The objective of European Union is political, yet once again the means chosen were primarily economic. This dichotomy was again evident at the June 1989 European Council discussions which led to the decision to convene a new Intergovernmental Conference on Economic and Monetary Union to reflect the economic momentum created by the prospect of 1992. Only at the later date of 28 April 1990, and after intense lobbying, did the European Council agree to convene a parallel IGC on Political Union with the intention of achieving ratification of both IGCs simultaneously before the end of 1992. With due pomp and ceremony, the two IGCs opened in Rome on 14 December 1990. This linkage was more than a calendar convenience; the success of each IGC was mutually dependent. As the history of the Community illustrates *ad nauseam*, package bargains are fundamental to institutional progress. Despite the desire to avoid a potentially precarious disequilibrium, progress on EMU was not matched by developments towards Political Union. Whereas the EMU agenda was commonly agreed to, the topics for discussion under Political Union were wide-ranging and matters of dispute: if the EMU resembled a table d'hôte menu, the IGC on Political Union was undoubtedly à la carte.

Despite this consensus on the issues, agreement on the principles of Monetary Union proved difficult to negotiate, with the UK resisting the idea of a single European currency being implemented by a set date. Different, but equally difficult, reservations were raised by Germany over the role of a European Central Bank to oversee monetary policy (see Chapter 3). The obstacles in the IGC on Political Union focused on three separate issues: first, reform of the Community institutions and decision-making structure to redress the 'democratic deficit'; second, the transformation of EPC into a Common Foreign and Security Policy; and third, a Treaty commitment to the 'federal nature' of European Union. The debate focused on the Luxembourg Presidency's *Draft Treaties Articles with a View to Achieving Political Union*. Discussion continued into the second half of 1991 under the Dutch Presidency. Significant concessions were made at the final European Council meeting by the Dutch Presidency in order to gain unanimous approval of what was to become the Treaty on European Union signed by the Heads of State and Governments in Maastricht on 7 February 1992. As is discussed in Chapters 4 and 8, the federal language of the original Draft had to be removed to appease British political sensibilities; parliamentary reform was limited and the common foreign policy retained considerable intergovernmental features.

During the SEA negotiation phase, both Spain and Portugal signed accession treaties; both countries attended the IGC and other Community meetings as non-voting participants and fully accepted the evolving *acquis communautaire*. This third enlargement was completed in 1986 although extensive transition periods for key economic sectors were permitted so as not to distort existing Community policies and markets. Thus the simultaneous process of deepening and widening integration was relaunched. Further enlargement presented the Community with a dilemma; the lure of economic prosperity promised by the single market and the collapse of East–West confrontation combined to make the Community an irresistible magnet for diverse and numerous states. Turkey was the first to apply in 1987, followed by Austria in 1989, Malta and Cyprus in 1990, Sweden in July 1991 and Finland in March 1992. With the exception of Turkey who were advised that the application was premature, faced with a potential deluge of applications, the Community chose to suspend any decision on the next stage of enlargement until after the completion of the single market in 1993. This prevarication has not been a disincentive to the EFTA countries of Switzerland and Norway, and the new East European democracies of Hungary, Czechoslovakia and Poland, all of whom began to consider possible future application for membership during the 1990s. Accommodating enlargement constitutes the Community's greatest challenge to successful integration during the remainder of this century: such an enlarged Community may revert to intergovernmentalism, albeit in a formalized setting, at the expense of integration along federal or *communautaire* lines.

The potential disequilibrium of enlargement was illustrated in 1990 by the unification of Germany. The Community was faced with the unique situation of how to incorporate the territory of the German Democratic Republic (GDR) within the Community framework. Three options were possible. The GDR could have had an independent association agreement with the EC; the GDR could have signed a treaty of accession and officially become the Community's thirteenth state; or, as did happen, the GDR could accede to the Federal Republic requiring no legal alterations *vis-à-vis* Community membership. The problems associated with German enlargement were of a different nature to those of Spanish or Portuguese membership (focusing as they did on amalgamating fundamentally different economic and political systems), and the whole process was considerably contracted (it was less than a year between the fall of the Berlin Wall and unification) (Langguth, 1991, pp. 139–40). Consequently, many of the economic problems were not addressed as there was no negotiation and accession process. On 3 October 1990, in theory, EC law became applicable throughout the whole of Germany, with limited transition exemptions only where completely necessary. In practice, in major areas such as pollution, the environment and agriculture 'there is no hope that standards established by the Community can be immediately complied with' (Tomuschat, 1990, p. 429).

Although not an example of enlargement in a legal sense (as there was no new treaty of accession with the Community), the social, economic and political difficulties that emerged through the experience of unification suggests that incorporating the less-developed East European economies into the EC will be a difficult and lengthy process. The enormity of the task should not be underestimated. In a limited sense, the GDR was already the Community's unspoken thirteenth member; in a Protocol attached to the Treaty of Rome, trade between the two German states was given the special status of 'German internal trade' confirming that this intra-German trade was not regarded as trade with a third country. Despite these existing provisions, the integration of the former *Länder* of the GDR into the Federal Republic, and thereby into the Community, has been more difficult than even the most cautious of observers had estimated.

In another sense, German unification cannot be seen in isolation from the European process: as was clear to European integrationists such as Monnet for the 'German Question' to be resolved, 'a peaceful solution can be found only within the Community, whose aim is not to make coalitions of States but instead to unite peoples' (1978, pp. 478–9). The unification of Germany also removed any doubt as to the future *Ostpolitik* intentions of the Federal Republic. The future of Germany and of the Community was inextricably entwined. Arguably, German unity has strengthened the process of Community integration, even if the impetus behind such efforts comes from a fear of German domination on the part of certain member states: only the Community method and treaty obligations are able to restrain the new German colossus, producing a European Germany rather than a German Europe (Langguth, 1991, p. 144).

Although Title III of the SEA did not provide EPC with a *saut qualitif*, the contemporary period has witnessed an increased emphasis on the Community's role in international affairs: collective positions were developed on a variety of issues ranging from sanctions against South Africa and mediation in the Yugoslavian civil war, to the Community's recognition of the independence of the three Baltic states of Estonia, Latvia and Lithuania. Two catalysts were responsible for this development, one internal, the other external to the Community. Externally, the new global and European political cartography of the late 1980s, symbolized by the crumbling of the Berlin Wall, forced a new international role on the Community. Internally, EPC had to match the impressive strides taken by the EC in economic and monetary spheres with a commensurate commitment to fuller integration at the level of foreign policy. Economic and political integration had to develop in parallel (Holland, 1991, p. 1). Without denying the importance of this linkage, as the following examples illustrate, the credibility and effectiveness of the Community's foreign policy has not gone unquestioned.

One of the Community's earliest and most long-standing EPC policies has been on the issue of apartheid and South Africa. In 1979 the EC introduced a *Code of Conduct* designed to monitor the employment practices of EC firms in South Africa; between 1985 and 1987, a range of trade sanctions were introduced, new direct investment prohibited, and aid given to anti-government organizations and to 'the victims of apartheid'. While the Community was able to maintain a collective policy, both the limited effectiveness of the measures in realizing the EC's policy objective (the removal of apartheid), and the public acrimony and divisions within the Twelve over their implementation led most observers to conclude that the prospects for a comprehensive common Community foreign policy were bleak. The principle of the lowest common denominator seemed as disruptive to the implementation of Community foreign policy as the 'Luxembourg Compromise' had been to effective decision-making (Holland, 1988, pp. 29–48). With the release of Nelson Mandela and the unbanning of the African National Congress in early 1990, the Community's foreign policy underwent a transition and the sanctions introduced during 1985–86 were gradually removed. Once again, this collective agreement was marred by disagreement, but a collective response was maintained and the spirit of the SEA to 'refrain from impeding the formation of a consensus' was honoured (Article 30.3.c).

The Middle East has often confronted the EC with difficult foreign policy choices, for example, the 1980 Venice Declaration, the Israeli Occupied Territories and the Islamic Revolution in Iran. These difficulties continued during the late 1980s and early 1990s with the Iran-Rushdie affair, and the Gulf war providing the Community with new challenges. The Rushdie affair illustrated that an attack upon a national of a member state was an attack upon a Community citizen and demanded a collective European response at the diplomatic level. The ability of the Community to do more than deliver diplomatic *démarches* was exposed by the Gulf war. The initial response was a collective one with EC embassies in Kuwait co-operating to protect all Community citizens and uniform sanctions being imposed. However, EPC had no military competence and such an option was not available; as the crisis progressed even the Community's joint diplomatic response began to evaporate. Alternative British and French initiatives to prevent war replaced a concerted Community-level approach. It was widely argued that the crisis exposed both the inherent weaknesses of EPC, as well as the impossibility of the Community developing a common foreign policy. Even the federalist Commission President Delors was moved to acknowledge that 'the Gulf war has provided an object lesson – if one were needed – on the limitations of the European Community' (1991, p. 1). Criticism of the Community's policy on the Gulf war resulted in the IGC on Political Union debating at considerable length how a Common Foreign and Security Policy might replace the flawed EPC. The commitment to a common, binding approach, irrespective of a federal content, again proved to be too great a concession for key Community states to accept. The eventual compromise accepted at the final December 1991 IGC European Council meeting provided modest procedural reforms and very little in the way of substantive progress in the content and expression of the Community's foreign policy.

The Community's response to the Yugoslavian crisis of mid-1991 was a striking contrast. Rather than becoming divided internally and marginalized by American and bilateral action, the Community became the dominant international actor – and a unified one. The outbreak of hostilities took priority over the IGC agenda planned for the Luxembourg European Council meeting of 28 June; the meeting discussed the report of the first of several Troika missions that visited Yugoslavia to seek out an agreement for a cease-fire. Subsequently, the Community sent a team of unarmed observers to monitor the situation and over the following months Brussels assumed the responsibility for facilitating negotiations. On 7 July on the Yugoslavian island of Brioni the Community succeeded in producing a joint declaration between all the parties which was to serve as the basis for a cease-fire and future negotiations of Yugoslavia's future. The experience confirmed, perhaps for the first time, that the Community was capable of a rapid collective foreign policy response, and that EC action could be effective irrespective of a military capacity. It was not coincidental that this new commitment to common action developed during the Community's Intergovernmental Conferences: the linkage between internal and external aspects of European Union were becoming increasingly apparent.

The failed Soviet coup of late August 1991, the subsequent fragmentation of the Soviet Union and rush to achieve independence by the Republics tested the Community's ability to adapt its response to a quickly changing international environment. The Community was one of the first international actors to take action against the coup: the Council met immediately (20 August) and agreed to suspend all technical and economic aid that had been granted in December 1990 (worth ECU 1,150m) until normal constitutional government was restored. With the restoration of order and the return of President Gorbachev to office on 22 August this decision was revoked. The Community's response to the ensuing demands for independence by eight Soviet Republics was more cautious and allowed for bilateral action to undermine the Community's newly asserted image of collective action. Denmark was first to recognize the Baltic Republics unilaterally; however, by 29 August unity was restored with the Community collectively recognizing the independence of Estonia, Latvia and Lithuania. The Soviet crisis illustrated both the strengths and the continuing weaknesses of EPC. On the positive side the Community reacted swiftly, incisively and jointly; furthermore, the words of condemnation were matched by economic action. On the negative side, this cohesion did not replace independent bilateral foreign policy; again, the Community's collective response was pre-empted and compromised by member states devaluing the Community's perceived global role to some degree.

Other areas where the Community's international image was enhanced included the United Nations (UN) and the Conference on Security and Cooperation in Europe (CSCE). Increasingly, the Community was becoming a single unanimous actor in its voting record at the UN (Regelsberger, 1988, p. 48); but the degree of consistency was less important than 'the conviction of the member states that they have the ability to act collectively on major foreign policy questions confronting them' (Rummel, 1988, p. 140). At the CSCE the Community's record is even more cohesive and provided the EC with a venue for discussing security issues beyond the limitations of EPC discussions (Rummel and Schmidt, 1990, p. 270). Further evidence of the Community's growing international stature was the decision of the G-24 countries in 1990 to ask the Commission to be responsible for the 'Phare' programme dedicated to the economic reconstruction of Eastern Europe. Lastly, Lomé IV was signed in December 1989 providing for a new ten-year preferential trade convention linking 69 ACP countries to the Community.

Domestically, the Community held the third set of direct elections to the European Parliament in June 1989. The strengthened powers of the Parliament by the SEA and the significance of 1992, appeared to have little impact on its popular appeal. Turn-out fell to an average of 58.4 per cent (despite the fact that in three countries the direct elections were held in tandem with national elections) (*Bulletin*, 1989, p. 18). The experience of the first decade showed a consistent overall decline in support at each successive election. Within this general trend there were some particularly worrying specific cases; turn-out fell in five of the six original member states (by as much as 8 per cent in France); participation in the two newest members, Spain and Portugal, fell by 14 and 21 per cent, respectively; and in four Community countries, turn-out was below 50 per cent (the UK, Denmark, France and The Netherlands) (Schmitt, 1990, p. 120). The awaited transition from second-order to first-order elections failed to materialize creating a potentially destabilizing dichotomy between an integrated single economic market and an institutional structure lacking in representative legitimacy.

Policy development focused largely on implementing the necessary directives to achieve the single market, budget reform and the perennial concerns over the CAP. The 1984 Fontainebleau budgetary 'solution' proved short-lived as the Community soon exhausted the new ceiling set for its own resources. A more ambitious reform was adopted in 1988 which expanded the Community's ability to raise its own funds and provided a new type of own resource in the form of national contributions linked to a percentage of the EC's overall gross domestic product GDP) (Nugent, 1989, pp. 260–1; Shackleton, 1989, pp. 131–2). From 1986 onwards, the Community has sought to eliminate the persistent agricultural problems of surpluses, increased budgetary costs, unstable markets, declining farm income and the deterioration of the environment through intensive production. Agriculture has proven remarkably impervious to fundamental change; too often, the consensus for reform has been based on diametrically opposed assumptions which have led, typically, to compromise package deals that fail to address the structural problems. The list of reform proposals offered by the Commission is extensive: price reductions, quotas and co-responsibility levies, supply control measures, Social Policy support, diversification, afforestation and retirement incentives; all have met with national self-interest and at best led to incremental success and acceptance.

Another domestic issue that the Community believed had been resolved in the mid-1980s re-emerged, albeit in a revised form, during 1988 (Taylor, 1989, pp. 14–23). The notorious 'British problem' changed its focus from a budgetary complaint to a fundamental policy and ideological dispute. The essential arguments were laid out in Thatcher's well-known address to the College of Europe in Bruges on 20 September 1988. She argued that while the Community was a manifestation of the European identity, it was not the exclusive institutional option for Europe. Rejecting supranationalism by stealth, this apparent *communautaire* heresy was based on the principle that a successful European Community could only be built on the 'willing and active co-operation between *independent sovereign states*' (*Survey*, 1988, p. 336, emphasis added). The federal direction of the Community as espoused by President Delors was an anathema to the UK who saw further integration and British sovereignty as incompatible. Until her forced resignation as British Prime Minister in November 1990 progress towards Economic and Monetary Union (with the implied single currency and European Central Bank) threatened to split the Community, with the effect, once again, of sidelining the UK and distracting the Community's own internal dynamic at the expense of integration. Despite the UK's belated membership of the EMS and exchange rate mechanism and the election of the less anti-Community John Major as Prime Minister, the commitment to European integration by the British Government remained the dominant issue of the IGCs throughout 1991.

This ideological debate crystallized around the wording of the preamble to the Draft Treaty submitted by the Luxembourg Presidency of the IGC which noted the eventual 'federal objective' of the Community. As Dunn has noted, 'Arguments among European leaders over federalism may indeed go beyond the immediate concerns of 1992, but they do emphasize real differences of approach to the EC and are symptomatic of the obstacles still in the way of common policies' (1989, p. 2). British opposition met with German insistence; at the June 1991 European Council meeting the Presidency conclusions on Political Union euphemistically described this division, noting 'discussions have gone into greater detail on some issues for which a solution is crucial to the success of the negotiations'. However, a principle of Union was to be 'the evolving nature of the process of integration or union' (European Council, 1991, p. 1). Irrespective of the outcome, the federal option was again at the centre of the European political debate. What was particularly surprising was that the UK saw these words as being more sinister than the commitment to 'an ever closer union among the peoples of Europe' as stipulated in the 1957 Treaty of Rome. Arguably, accession in 1973 had committed the UK to the Community path and whether this federal aspiration was explicit or implicit within a treaty revision seemed disingenuous. As an editorial in *Agence Europe* argued, the phrasing of the original Treaty

> is far more menacing, to anyone concerned with preserving national sovereignty, than a 'federal union'. An 'ever closer union' must mean, if it means anything, that no matter how far we have gone in linking the member states to each other, we must strive to go further still. A federal union, by contrast, usually means one in which the respective spheres of competence of the union and its component parts are defined in a manner intended to be permanent. (12 July 1991, no. 5533, p. 1)

The major issues of dispute in the IGC on Political Union that emerged during the first six months were identified by the outgoing Luxembourg President Santer as foreign and security policy, the Parliament's co-decision power, and the social dimension and cohesion. Overall progress in the IGC on EMU seemed less controversial; all states had indicated a willingness, in principle, to participate in EMU and accepted that no single state could block the transition of the majority to the next stage of EMU. However, at this mid-point in the IGC discussions there was no decision on a single currency, or on a timetable for the introduction of the next stage of union. These matters, like the contentious issues concerning Political Union were left until the December 1991 Maastricht European Council for final resolution (*Agence Europe*, 30 June 1991, no. 5524, pp. 1–2).

Conclusion

1992 signifies more than the realization of the Community's internal market. It may prove to be the year in which the Community finally takes the long-awaited *saut qualitif*, or perhaps more aptly, the plunge from the precipice of national sovereignty into the unknown waters of progressive federalism. As this account of the Community experience has tried to illustrate, the key to comprehending the different periods of progress, stagnation or regression in the post-war period is to be found in the debate between supranationalism and intergovernmentalism.

An evaluation of the supranational progress made by the Community must recognize the enormity of its achievements: within a decade the nations of Europe had relinquished hostilities for economic co-operation and interdependency. That armed conflict between the member states is now inconceivable, confirms the remarkable progress and sense of collective interests that have come to permeate the Community. The cautious initial integration in specific economic sectors has spilt-over into a range of economic activities culminating with the inclusion of Economic and Monetary Union. This neofunctional effect has also been transmitted into the political arena; EPC has matured within two decades into a recognizable Common

Foreign and Security Policy and a commitment to Political Union, if imprecisely defined, has been accomplished. But intergovernmentalism has proved resilient and its announced demise greatly exaggerated. From the failure of the EDC, the imposition of the 'Luxembourg Compromise', through to the 'British problem' of the 1980s and the Bruges rejection of a federal Community, national sovereignty has been the focus of significant conflict, at times jeopardizing the very existence of the Community's unicity. And yet, while these two interpretations of events may seem conflicting and even mutually exclusive, the underlying theme has been the realization of an integrated Europe. To survive the challenges of enlargement, reform and Union over the next decade, the Community needs to regain the vision of Europe contained within the ideas of Jean Monnet.

It remains to be seen whether the political élites of today, and those of tomorrow, will have the ability and commitment to continue the European idea. As Monnet wrote, the Community is part of, and responds to, the changing world order; consequently, its final destination cannot be known:

> The sovereign nations of the past can no longer solve the problems of the present: they cannot ensure their own progress or control their own future . . . Yet amid this changing scenery the European idea goes on . . . Where this necessity will lead, and toward what kind of Europe, I cannot say . . . The essential thing is to hold fast to the few fixed principles that have guided us since the beginning. (1978, pp. 523–4)

References

Bulletin of the EC, 1989, 'Results of the European elections', 22–6, pp. 18 *et seq.*

Butler, D. and Marquand, D., 1981, *European elections and British politics*, Longman, London.

Council of Foreign Ministers, 1980, *Declaration by the Foreign Ministers of the Nine on Afghanistan*, 15 Jan., European Community, Brussels.

Delors, J., 1991, 'European integration and security', Alastair Buchan Memorial Lecture, 7 Mar., International Institute of Strategic Studies, London.

Duchêne, F., 1990, 'More or less than Europe? European integration in retrospect' in Crouch, C. and Marquand, D., (eds), *The Politics of 1992: beyond the Single European Market, The Political Quarterly*, Basil Blackwell, Oxford, pp. 9–22.

Dunn, J. F., 1989, *The European Community*, Wilton Park Paper no. 16, HMSO, London.

Duroselle, J-P., 1970, 'General de Gaulle's Europe and Jean Monnet's Europe' in Cosgrove, C. and Twitchett, K., (eds), *The new international actors: the UN and the EEC*, Macmillan, London, pp. 187–200.

Edwards, G., 1984, 'Europe and the Falkland Islands crisis 1982', *Journal of Common Market Studies*, 22, pp. 295–313.

European Council, 1991, 'Presidency Conclusions', 26–28 June, European Community, Luxembourg.

George, S., 1985, *Politics and policy in the European Community*, Clarendon Press, Oxford.

Groeben, H. von der, 1987, *The European Community the formative years: the struggle to establish the Common Market and the political union (1958–66)*, Office for the Official Publications of the European Communities, Luxembourg.

Hackett, C., 1990, *Cautious revolution: the European Community arrives*, Greenwood Press, Westport.

Hague Conference of the Heads of State and Government, 1970, 'Final communiqué of the Conference', *Bulletin of the EC*, 6, pp. 10–18.

Holland, M., 1988, *The European Community and South Africa: European Political Co-operation under strain*, Pinter, London.

Holland, M. (ed.), 1991, *The future of European Political Cooperation: essays on theory and practice*, Macmillan, London.

Langguth, G., 1991, 'Germany, the EC and the architecture of Europe: the German question in the context of the EC', *AussenPolitik*, 42, pp. 137–46.

Lodge, J. (ed.), 1986a, *European Union: the European Community in search of a future*, Macmillan, London.

Lodge, J., 1986b, 'The Single European Act: towards a new European dynamism?', *Journal of Common Market Studies*, 24, pp. 203–23.

London Report, 1981, 'Report on Political Cooperation' *Supplement of the Bulletin of the EC*, 3/81, European Community, Brussels.

Marsh, J., 1989, 'The Common Agricultural Policy' in Lodge, J. (ed.), *The European Community and the challenge of the future*, Pinter, London, pp. 148–66.

Monnet, J., 1978, *Memoirs*, (trans. R. Mayne), Doubleday and Company, New York.

Nicoll, W. and Salmon, T.C., 1990, *Understanding the European Communities*, Barnes and Noble, Savage, Maryland.

Noël, E., 1989, 'The Single European Act', *Government and Opposition*, 24, pp. 3–14.

Nugent, N., 1989, *The government and politics of the European Community*, Macmillan, London.

Patijn, S. (ed.), 1970, *Landmarks in European unity*, Sijthoff, Leydon.

Pedersen, T., 1991, 'EC-EFTA relations: an historical outline' in Wallace, H. (ed.), *The wider Western Europe: reshaping the EC/EFTA relationship*, Pinter/RIIA, London, pp. 13–30.

Reif, K-H (ed.), 1984, *Ten European elections*, Gower, Aldershot.

Reif, K-H. and Schmitt, H., 1980, 'Nine second order elections: a conceptual framework for the analysis of European election results', *European Journal of Political Research*, 8, pp. 3–44.

Regelsberger, E., 1988, 'EPC in the 1980s: reaching another plateau?' in Pijpers, A., Regelsberger, E., Wessels, W. and Edwards, G. (eds), *European Political Cooperation in the 1980s*, Martinus Nijhoff/TEPSA, Dordrecht, pp. 3–47.

Rummel, R., 1988, 'Speaking with one voice – and beyond' in Pijpers, A., Regelsberger, E., Wessels, W. Edwards, G. (eds), *European Political Cooperation in the 1980s*, Martinus Nijhoff/TEPSA, Dordrecht, pp. 118–42.

Rummel, R. and Schmidt, P., 1990, 'The changing security framework' in Wallace, W. (ed.), *The dynamics of European integration*, Pinter/RIIA, London, pp. 261–75.

Schmitt, H., 1990, 'The European elections of June 1989', *West European Politics*, 13, pp. 116–23.

Schoutheete, P. de, 1990, 'The European Community and its sub-systems' in Wallace, W. (ed.), *The dynamics of European integration*, Pinter/RIIA, London, pp. 106–24.

Shackleton, M., 1989, 'The budget of the European Community' in Lodge, J. (ed.), *The European Community and the challenge of the future*, Pinter, London, pp. 129–47.

Survey of Current Affairs, 1988, 18–10, HMSO, London.

Taylor, P., 1989, 'The new dynamics of EC integration in the 1980s' in Lodge, J. (ed.), *The European Community and the challenge of the future*, Pinter, London, pp. 3–25.

Tindemans, L., 1976, *European Union: report to the European Council, Bulletin of the EC*, 1/76, supplement.

Tomuschat, C., 1990, 'A united Germany within the EC', *Common Market Law Review*, 27, pp. 415–36.

Wistrich, E., 1989, *After 1992: the United States of Europe*, Routledge, London.

3 The United States of Europe: catalysts of reform

> Have I said clearly enough that the Community we have created is not an end in itself? It is a process of change . . . I have never doubted that one day this process will lead us to the United States of Europe. (Monnet, 1978, pp. 523–4)

The idea of the Community was never a static conception; reform and progressive refinement are both characteristics of the Community's history and of its constitutional framework, the Treaty of Rome. This chapter compares the Community's most significant reform proposals, identifying common themes as well as the unique contributions each has made. The three examples chosen are the 1975 Tindemans Report; the Single European Act (SEA) of 1985; and, the Intergovernmental Conferences (IGCs) of 1991. Although the immediate fate of each of these reforms was different (for example, the legal recognition and application of the SEA compared with the informal influence of the Tindemans Report), all three have sought to focus the debate on the future shape of the Community, reflecting again the pervasive intergovernmental and supranational tensions inherent to the Community. Each of these reform initiatives can be compared thematically for their respective contributions to European Union and a vision for Community development; citizenship and a people's Europe; a global role and a common foreign policy; policy expansion and cohesion; and institutional reform and the democratic deficit.

The Tindemans Report

Since associating themselves in the Treaty of Rome to the idea of 'an ever closer union among the peoples of Europe', Community member states have periodically attempted to define the meaning of this commitment and establish a European Union. The first attempt, and possibly the most ambitious to date, occurred in the wake of the Community's relaunch of the early 1970s and just as the Community was coming to terms with economic recession. As noted in Chapter 2, the Tindemans Report was instigated by the Paris European Council meeting of December 1974, with the brief to evaluate progress towards the objective of European Union as agreed to at the previous Heads of State and Government Conference of October 1972 (and reaffirmed at the 1973 Copenhagen meeting). Tindemans was instructed to submit a comprehensive report to the European Council before the end of 1975 on the basis of recommendations received from the Community institutions, member states and public opinion. The final Report was presented to the European Council on 29 December 1975 and was published on 7 January 1976. The Report pursued a dual objective: it defined the general approach and framework for action to realize European Union by 1980; and it suggested specific practical measures that had to be adopted to promote this overall goal. That the IGCs of 1991 set themselves similar tasks should not detract from the importance and prescience of the Tindemans Report.

In his preamble, Tindemans noted the potentially debilitating dichotomy between the commitment espoused by Europe's political élite to European Union and the scepticism at the level of public opinion. Consequently, the Report sought to address a perceived 'crisis in Europe' and advocated 'drastic measures to make a significant leap forward' (1976, p. 6). Tindemans viewed European Union as a continuous process dependent on the ability of institutions and individuals to adapt to its objectives. To have specified a date whereby the completion of European Union would be achieved was seen as inappropriate. This decision stood in contrast to the specific deadlines found in earlier proposals, such as the Spaak Report or the Treaty of Rome. This omission of any timetable has been criticized for providing the member states with an alibi to prevaricate and delay European Union (Wistrich, 1989, p. 36). Tindemans' approach was that of a committed European and a federalist, although this did not protect him from criticism from more outspoken federalists, particularly Commissioner Altiero Spinelli (Burgess, 1989, p. 83). Tindemans argued that the very success of the EC had meant that the Community had become an everyday reality and complacency had begun to dissipate the dynamic of further integration – 'Europe today is part of the general run of things; it seems to have lost its air of adventure' (1976, p. 11). Furthermore, the Community structure was incomplete and new challenges of the 1970s had found the limited nature of the 1950s Treaty somewhat wanting. What was missing was an explicit political content and popular appeal. This reliance of mass support for Europe was reminiscent of earlier functional theory. Tindemans called for the technocratic achievements of the Community to be supplemented by a democratic commitment to integration at the popular level – 'We must listen to our people. What do Europeans want? What do they expect from a united Europe?' (p. 11) In the context of the 1970s, this proposal was radical; the democratic content of the EC typically had taken second place behind economic harmonization. Tindemans wanted to build Europe in the fullest sense, and not limit integration to a series of functional economic agreements. As the Report's ambitions stated:

> No one wants to see a technocratic Europe. European Union must be experienced by the citizen in his (sic) daily life. It must make itself felt in education and culture, news and communications, it must be manifest in the youth of our countries, and in leisure time activities. It must protect the rights of the individual and strengthen democracy through a set of institutions which have legitimacy conferred upon them by the will of our peoples. (A.3, p. 12)

To complement this democratization of the Community, Tindemans advocated a greater global voice for Europe and the dissemination of European ideas internationally to challenge the hegemony of the superpowers.

Europe, it was argued, 'must recover some control over its destiny. It must build a type of society which is ours alone and which reflects the values which are the heritage and the common creation of our peoples.' (A.1, p. 12)

Tindemans did not attempt to define European Union unilaterally, but rather acknowledged this was the task of the European Council. The Report did, however, identify six components that collectively represented the basis for European Union:

> (1) European Union implies that we present a united front to the outside world.
> (2) European Union recognizes the interdependence of the economic prosperity of our States . . .
> (3) European Union requires the solidarity of our peoples to be effective and adequate.
> (4) European Union makes itself felt in people's daily lives.
> (5) In order to achieve these tasks European Union is given institutions with the necessary powers to determine a common, coherent and all-inclusive political view, the efficiency needed for action, the legitimacy needed for democratic control.
> (6) Like the Community whose objectives it pursues and whose attainments it protects European Union will be built gradually. (p. 13)

It was stressed that European Union depended equally upon all these interconnected factors; only with their mutual development could Union be attained. Implicit in this scheme was the necessity of transferring further competences to common institutions and redistributing resources from the prosperous to less prosperous regions of the Community.

Europe in the World

An external policy was seen as essential to European Union and the Tindemans reforms were both practical and revolutionary in nature. First, it was proposed that the increasingly unworkable distinction prohibiting EPC from being discussed at EC meetings (due to its extra-treaty status) be removed, and further that 'the institutions of the Union can discuss all problems if they are relevant to European interests and consequently come within the ambit of the Union' (II.A, p. 15). These reforms were aimed at ensuring policy coherence by encouraging the development of a single Community decision-making centre. Aspects of these procedures became informal practice, but the formal recognition of EPC in the Treaties had to wait until the SEA.

The revolutionary ambitions concerned the voluntary nature of EPC. In order to secure European Union, Tindemans argued that it was necessary to substitute the existing political co-ordination of EPC by common policies derived from a legal 'obligation to reach a common point of view': the stated implication was 'that the minority must rally to the views of the majority at the conclusion of a debate' in the Council (II.B pp. 15–16). This commitment to produce a common foreign policy was to be applied across a diverse range of international topics, covering relations with the developing world, between Europe and the USA, security issues and the Community's position as the embodiment of the then existing East–West political divide. Specific recommendations were made: with respect to the developing world, the Community sought to 'present a united front at multilateral negotiations', gradually transfer 'to the Community a substantial part of national appropriations intended for development cooperation', adopt 'a common stand on general political problems which could arise in our relations with the Third World' (II.C.1. pp. 16–17). Cumulatively these initiatives would lead the Community to pursuing a common external policy *vis-à-vis* developing nations. With respect to EC-US relations, Tindemans advocated a regular and direct dialogue at the Presidential-Head of Government level with the Community delegating its authority to a single member: this proposal has resulted in a formal meeting between the US President and the Community President every six months. While acknowledging the sensitive nature of the issue, the Tindemans Report argued that European Union would not be complete without an eventual common defence policy: to facilitate this long-term objective, it was recommended that member states regularly 'hold exchanges of views on our specific problems in defence matters and on European aspects of multilateral negotiations on security' with a view to reaching 'a common analysis of defence problems' which will take account of each others' respective positions before proposing any action (II.C.3. p. 18). Much of the Community's activity in the CSCE has reflected this broad recommendation as did the Community's response to the changing post-1989 security regime in Europe. A more detailed proposal was to establish a European armaments agency to achieve the standardization and joint manufacture of armaments. Finally, the Report proved itself to be especially prescient and particularly radical in discussing potential crises in the European region. It proposed the Community 'should from now on be united, that is to say, that we should accept the constraints imposed by a common policy'; this was not to be a continuation of the existing voluntary concertation, but involved a 'general rule . . . to lay down a common policy and act together within this framework . . . wherever important problems or crises arise in Europe or in the Mediterranean' (II.C.4. p. 18).

In short, Tindemans defined European Union in terms of 'a qualitative change in the nature and intensity' of the Community's external relations, gradually leading to binding commitments that were enshrined as legal obligations, at which point 'European Union will then have become a living reality' (p. 19). These radical 'qualitative changes' failed to generate a consensus; the rapid acceleration envisaged in EPC was too advanced for the cautious pace of the Nine and the major thrust of the Report's external relations recommendations was ignored (Holland, 1988, p. 5).

Community economic and social policies

Economic and Monetary Union (EMU) had been Community policy since being reaffirmed at The Hague 1969 European Summit; quite what this meant, however, was open to interpretation. This confusion reflected a lack of political will; this impediment, combined with international economic and financial difficulties, had resulted in little being achieved during the intervening years towards establishing EMU. The Tindemans remedy was to generate a consensus which balanced common economic and monetary policy with other sectoral policies, including Community Social and Regional policy. But this compromise was largely at the expense of a full EMU which was regarded as a fundamental requirement for achieving a European Union. Tindemans had to acknowledge that among the member states 'there is no agreement on how to achieve a common economic and monetary policy . . . In the present state of affairs, no real progress can be expected' (III.A.1. p. 20). Within this political context, the Report offered proposals that were practical rather than ideological, the first of which was to instruct the European Council to revive a very broad discussion on EMU with all Community institutions.

Reflecting these practical constraints, Tindemans supported a two-speed approach to EMU arguing that this was not, necessarily, an impediment to Union, as 'each country will be bound by the agreement of all as to the final objective to be achieved in common; it is only the timescales for achievement which vary' (III.A.2. p. 21). It was proposed that the starting-point for this variable Union should be the development of monetary stability through the 'Snake'. This involved the Community institutions taking full control of the process in order to achieve a convergence of economic and monetary policies between member states. Existing obligations on external monetary policy were to be supplemented by obligations in internal monetary policy and control of the money supply; budgetary policy and the extent and financing of deficits; and short-term economic policy such as the control of inflation. To balance these restrictions, economic support between member states was to be enhanced creating 'the embryo for a European central bank'; obstacles to the free movement of capital were to be gradually removed; and assistance given to allow those EC states not in the existing Snake to join (III.A.3. p. 21). This extension of the Snake was not in itself sufficient, but rather constituted a starting-point for the eventual formation of a common economic and monetary policy. To encourage the progressive development of EMU it was suggested that the Commission submit an annual report to the European Council on progress towards EMU and make recommendations on the next steps to take. This could also form part of the Commission's annual state of the Union address to the Parliament. As the Report conceded, 'These steps will lead to a degree of integration which is doubtless imperfect but which will make it easier to take the "large steps" which at some point will have to be taken' (III.4.b. p. 23).

A humane Community: social and regional policies and a citizen's Europe

European Union was not just a technocratic idea, but involved 'a form of economic growth which respects human values and human needs' represented through the extension of the Community's Social and Regional policies (III.C. p. 24). Regional policy was necessary to counteract the concentration of the Community's economic activity in key centres at the expense of the periphery; consequently, a transfer of Community resources from the most prosperous to the least-favoured areas was recommended on the basis of need, not of national quota. Social policy at the Community level is designed to supplement, not to replace, national social provisions. Tindemans called for the Union to stipulate common standards and generate 'a consensus in matters of social justice' for wage-rates, pensions, social security, minority and women's rights and working conditions (III.C.1. p. 25). Where possible, collective European agreements across sectors were to be promoted, as was greater worker participation in the management and control of business enterprises. Cumulatively, Tindemans was advocating what was to be described during the late 1980s as a European 'Social Charter', designed to produce 'a more humane and just society' (p. 25).

This social face of European Union was reinforced by a commitment to produce a 'citizen's Europe'. This was to involve the protection of individual rights (including consumer rights), the environment and a general recognition of European citizenship. It was suggested that the envisaged increase in powers for the Community institutions in the proposed Union required balancing by an uncompromising commitment to fundamental economic and social rights which, if infringed, could have legal redress through the Court of Justice. The Report argued that the most important single market for the Community was the common environment which Europeans shared and an urgent European approach was required for the regulation and control of nuclear power and the disposal of radioactive and thermic waste. Freedom from pollution (whatever its origins) was a fundamental right. Positive individual rights proposed included 'the gradual disappearance of frontier controls on persons moving between member countries' to complement the existing agreement on common passports; improved transport and communication throughout the Union; reciprocal health rights; mutual recognition of national educational qualifications; and, collaboration between national media organizations to promote greater European awareness (IV.B. pp. 27–8). As the Report argued, collectively the 'proposals for bringing Europe nearer to the citizen are directly in line with the deep-seated motivations behind the construction of Europe. They give it a social and human dimension' (p. 28). In this respect the recommendations were in keeping with Monnet's belief in the Community as a moral idea and 'a way of uniting peoples' (1978, p. 449).

Institutional reforms

Tindemans did not seek to deconstruct the existing Community structure, but accepted as the basis of European Union the institutional framework created by the Treaty of Rome. The relationship between institutions and their respective roles could, however, be reconstituted where necessary, by Treaty amendment. A qualitative change in favour of supranational decision-making and rejecting intergovernmental co-operation was viewed as central to achieving Union: this could only be assured by reinforcing common institutional machinery. Four criteria were used to outline the principles of institutional reform: authority, efficiency, legitimacy and coherence.

Working from the presumption that the European Parliament was soon to be directly elected and would therefore derive greater authority and democratic legitimacy, the Report offered the following reforms. First, the Councils of Ministers should be required to consider Parliament's resolutions; second, with experience this procedure should become a legal Treaty obligation giving Parliament 'a real right of initiative'; and third, Parliament should be immediately given the power to consider all areas covered by the Union irrespective of their Treaty basis (V.A.1. p. 29). In addition, it encouraged the Parliament itself to heighten its public profile by convening a state of the Union debate under each EC presidency to which all leading politicians would be invited to participate.

The creation of the European Council was an illustration of the inability of the Treaty of Rome's institutional structures to provide sufficient 'political momentum' to create a European Union. Tindemans recommended that the European Council must provide 'coherent general policy guidelines' and provide clear decisions directed at specific institutions with instructions on how and when policy should be enacted. When dealing with EC matters, decision-making should follow Treaty procedures and the Commission should attend all European Council meetings (V.B. p. 30). Thus while not explicitly calling for the incorporation of the European Council within a treaty framework, Tindemans suggested an informal agreement for the European Council to act as if it were bound by Treaty requirements.

Reforms of the Council of Ministers were, perhaps, the most radical. As noted above, the Report called for the ending of the distinction between EPC and EC business. Majority voting for Community business was to become 'normal practice', replacing the existing principle of consensus and unanimity; this implied that minority views should 'rally to the view of the majority at the end of the discussion', thereby revoking the veto of the Luxembourg Compromise. To provide enhanced continuity and to strengthen its authority, Tindemans proposed that the presidency term (for the European Council and Council of Ministers) be extended to one year and, where appropriate, specific Community tasks (such as negotiations) be delegated to individuals, member states or the Commission. Although these proposals were procedural rather than substantive in content, they touched on some of the most delicate supranational/intergovernmental sensitivities and their reception was decidedly mixed. However, these fundamental issues were introduced into the Community agenda, and were to remain there during the EC's next two stages of internal reform between 1985 and 1992.

To facilitate European Union, the powers of the Commission were to be extended utilizing Article 155 of the Treaty of Rome which empowers the Commission to act widely in pursuit of 'the proper functioning and development of the common market'. To add to the Commission's authority, a Treaty amendment was sought whereby the President was to be appointed by the European Council and confirmed by vote in the European Parliament, after which the new President, in consultation with the Council, will appoint the remaining Commissioners (V.D. p. 31). Finally, in order to secure legitimacy for these various reforms, Tindemans insisted that all new sectors and powers derived from the Union would be covered by the Court of Justice whose legal authority would remain paramount. All Community institutions, member states and individuals would be subject to its rulings, as was the existing practice under the Treaty of Rome (V.E. p. 32).

The Tindemans Report was not a static depiction of the European status quo, but reflected upon the impact of enlargement on European Union. It concluded that 'other European states will want to join the undertaking. This will be open to them, on condition that they accept the overall view of the European Union as well as the constraints imposed by its gradual creation. New accessions must not slow down the development of the Union nor jeopardize it.' (VI. p. 34) These comments bore a remarkable similarity to the July 1991 Commission response to Austria's application for membership which stated that 'applicant countries should accept the *acquis communautaire*, not as it was at the time of their application for membership, but *as it will be at the end of the two Intergovernmental Conferences*' (Europe Documents, 1991, p. 1). A clear consistency in not jeopardizing integration (deepening) through *ad hoc* enlargement (widening) had become part of the Community's reform strategy.

The concluding thrust of the Report called for 'a single decision-making centre supplemented by the principle of the delegation of executive power' (V.G. p. 33). As already noted, the demolition of the existing EC institutional structure was not considered, but rather specific reforms to enhance its legitimacy, authority, efficiency and coherence. The desire to achieve European Union was based on the recognition that in the post-war era the power of individual states had declined significantly, and for any meaningful sovereignty to exist European states had to co-operate collectively. For Tindemans the future was federal, an aim that was consistent with the ambitions of the Community's founding fathers. Mirroring the words on Monnet, the Report perceived the existing Community structure as just the first stage of an 'historic undertaking': the transition to a European Union would be the next step on the road to federalism. And yet, Tindemans' recognition of the political constraints within which his proposals had to operate led some federalists to scorn his pragmatism. The most senior critical voice was that of Spinelli who remarked that the Report 'had the consequence that it remained without consequence' (Burgess, 1989, p. 90).

In summary, Tindemans opted for the political high ground, laying his Report bare for the anticipated intergovernmental parry. As he clearly demonstrated, there was 'the price of Union' . . . 'But what price would we pay for inaction? The crumbling away of the Community, voices isolated and often going unheard on the world stage, less and less control over our destiny, an unconvincing Europe without a future.' (p. 14) This warning epitomized Tindemans' dilemma – how to demystify and make practical the idea of European Union, while avoiding a too detailed and explicit exposure of its federal and supranational connotations. While the concept was shrouded in imprecise definition and vacuous commitment, it remained acceptable to the then Nine: once the contours of Union became focused, then the implications – economic, social and political – were too ambitious for their time and Tindemans' warning largely went unheeded, at great cost for the Community, for a further decade.

The Single European Act

The Single European Act (SEA) can be regarded as a vital contribution to the reform process within the Community; indeed, as already noted, the contrast between the first and second halves of the 1980s with respect to integration and Community cohesion was remarkable. Unlike the Tindemans Report which relied solely on an informal and non-legal based authority, the discussions leading to the SEA invoked a formal legal authority derived from a decision of the June 1985 European Council to apply Article 236 of the Treaty of Rome. This difference in status was significant: Article 236 allowed for the convening of an intergovernmental conference, the conclusions of which were to constitute a Treaty amendment once ratified by each member state. Although the conference kept to its timetable (meeting between July and December 1985) and the text of the SEA was agreed to in February 1986, the ratification process delayed the introduction of the SEA for a further 17 months (see Chapter 2).

The SEA was a far more sober document than the personal integrationist appeal of Tindemans. None the less, the preamble states a commitment on the part of the member states 'to transform relations as a whole among their States into a European Union, in accordance with the Solemn Declaration of Stuttgart of 19 June 1983', and Article I.1 defined the Community's objective as 'to contribute together to making concrete progress towards European Unity'. A critical reading of the SEA reveals, however, that the content of this unity was primarily economic and not political in nature. Title II of the SEA extends the EC's policy competences to cover the internal market, monetary policy, social policy, economic and social cohesion, research and technology and the environment. The most immediate consequence of the SEA, and arguably its *raison d'être* was the completion of the Community's Single Market. Colloquially known as project '1992' (31 December 1992 being the date set for implementation), the SEA provided for an internal market comprising 'an area without internal frontiers in which the free movement of goods, persons, services and capital is ensured' (Article 8A). This was to be achieved through the implementation of some 282 Directives which would serve to liberalize trade. It would be naïve to expect this abolition of trade barriers in themselves to establish a single market; without further reforms the European market will remain a fragmented collection of twelve national markets (Campbell, *et al.*, 1990, p. 138). Similarly, while the internal market provides the necessary economic base on which to construct a fuller economic and political Union, its acceptance did not imply a consensus among the member states to progress towards further integration. While the objective of Economic and Monetary Union was incorporated into the SEA, opposition from the reluctant integrationists, principally the UK, resulted in the provision being made that any further monetary changes would require a formal Treaty amendment. Such an amendment would require unanimity. As Nevin has observed, these 'reluctant integrationists probably believed that this provision would make further progress towards monetary union more rather than less difficult' (1990, p. 283).

Title II of the SEA also introduced important procedural changes (such as majority voting), institutional reform (the co-operation procedure with Parliament), whereas Title III codified and improved the operation of EPC. Qualified majority voting was not unknown prior to the SEA; majority decisions had always been acceptable in relation to the budget, for example (Nugent, 1989, p. 322). The SEA gave a renewed impetus and legal recognition for majority decisions to be extended to specific Treaty articles, principally those concerned with establishing the internal market. A comprehensive extension of the principle was unrealistic; consequently the SEA limited majority decisions to the market in goods and services within the EC and to commercial policy with third countries. It was specifically not extended to include the more sensitive topics of taxation and monetary policy, the free movement of individuals and employee rights (Nevin, 1990, pp. 37 and 341). Despite this legal delimitation, the effect on behaviour has become far-reaching: as Noël argues, this reform 'serves as a political signal: the clear indication that systematic recourse to unanimity voting in the Council must be abandoned' (1989, p. 10). As evidence, Noël records that since 1985 voting has become increasingly evident in Council business, and claims that the 'Luxembourg Compromise' (which was explicitly invoked on thirteen occasions between 1973 and 1985 (p. 11)) has lost its former authority as a Community convention. An opposite interpretation is given by Nevin who concludes that the conspicuous absence of any mention of the 'Compromise' from the SEA, indicates that it remains unaffected by the Act: consequently, 'while governments may endure the experience of being outvoted on issues of relatively minor importance, it may prove to be a different matter when the national stakes are high' (1990, p. 341). Whichever of these interpretations eventually proves correct, there is general agreement that in a formal sense, under the SEA those areas where member states have retained the *de jure* power to veto policy has been narrowed to 'fundamental, constitutional-type questions within the Community, such as enlargement, any redistribution of power among the institutions and any move to new, unchartered areas of policy' (Nicoll and Salmon, 1990, p. 233).

To complement the effect of majority voting, the SEA extended Parliament's involvement in the legislative process via the co-operation procedure. However, this involvement was limited to only those areas where majority decisions were permissible under the SEA (namely, the internal market, social policy, economic and social cohesion and research and development) (Nevin, 1990, p. 51). A system of two readings was introduced (Lodge, 1986a, p. 214; Fitzmaurice, 1988, p. 390). First, the Parliament examines the draft legislation submitted by the Commission (as was the case prior to the SEA). The Council then adopts 'by a qualified majority . . . a common position' (Article 149.2.a); this is then reconsidered by the Parliament. At this second reading stage the Parliament can either amend or reject the legislation provided that it comes to a decision by an absolute majority within a period of three months (149.2.c). However, this procedural reform fails to give the Parliament any final authority over the legislation, as the amended proposal is then reconsidered by the Commission who may adopt all or only some of the Parliament's proposals before this composite version is sent to the Council for final deliberation. At this stage the Council can adopt the legislation by qualified majority; if it wishes to reject the Parliament and Commission amendments then unanimity is required in the Council (149.2.d,e) (Lodge, 1986b, p. 193).

For all but those intergovernmental member states, the Parliament's new 'powers' were disappointing and fell far short of what the parliamentarians had lobbied for. The Parliament could still do little on its own; it required support from other Community institutions (the Commission and an ever changing alliance of minority member states) to be assured of having some influence (Nevin, 1990, p. 51). The extent of parliamentary involvement and the appropriate institutional procedures first raised by Tindemans, remained contentious matters throughout the 1980s. The SEA failed to resolve the issue of democratizing the Community's legislative procedures, and did not even attempt to address how to reconcile the 'inescapable conflict of interest' between the authority of the European Parliament and the powers of national parliaments (p. 51). At most, it provided 'a lever to prise open new windows of institutional debate' (Fitzmaurice, 1988, p. 390). In this indirect manner, the SEA did contribute to maintaining the process of reform that was to lead to the 1991 IGC on Political Union. It was difficult to see, however, how this contribution could be compatible with Tindemans' view of the Parliament being central to the construction of European Union (V.A.1. p. 29). The Parliament's role remained marginal, hardly the most inspiring epitaph for a successful reform.

The intergovernmental appendages that had grown as the Community matured were addressed in the SEA. First, reflecting the sense of the Tindemans Report, the European Council was brought into the Community system under the Common Provisions of Title I: its composition was defined (to include the President of the Commission) and a minimum number of meetings specified (at least two per year) (Article 2). Second, and again echoing Tindemans, the communautarization of EPC was viewed by integrationists as an essential step towards European Union. EPC had been established as an intergovernmental procedure that operated explicitly outside the Community's formal Treaty provisions. The SEA finally removed this distinction (which Tindemans noted already a decade before had become increasingly difficult to defend) and symbolized the EC's graduation from a purely economic to a potentially political organization: as the 'Common Provisions' of Title I state, 'The European Communities and European Political Cooperation shall have as their objective to contribute together to making concrete progress towards European unity' (Article 1). Thus the linkage between the EC and EPC was formally established. Article 30 of Title III stipulated that member states 'shall endeavour jointly to formulate and implement a European Foreign Policy' (30.1); 'ensure that common principles and objectives are gradually developed and defined' (30.2.c); and 'shall, as far as possible, refrain from impeding the formulation of consensus and the joint action which this could produce' (30.3.c). Arguably, the SEA provided at least the opportunity for 'the progressive development of political co-operation to the eventual detriment of national foreign policy autonomy' (Holland, 1988, p. 8); the practical constraint was the necessity for EPC to remain a consensus based procedure. The detailed changes to EPC contained in Title III cover the 'closely' and 'fully associated' roles of the European Parliament and Commission which were clarified and enhanced; EPC was 'crowned' with its own Secretariat (modest in size and function); and, the scope of EPC extended for the first time to include limited 'political and economic aspects of security' (30.6.a).

The intergovernmental conference that produced the SEA consisted of two separate working groups, one for EPC, the other for Treaty reform, reflecting the then existing demarcation between these two Community activities (Nicoll and Salmon, 1990, p. 116). This, together with the choice of the title, Single European Act, and its division into discrete sections, signified a considerable debate concerning the legal status of these reforms. In particular, the relative position of EPC has been discussed within the context of a shift from 'soft to hard law' by Dehousse and Weiler. They suggest that despite the modesty of Title III the SEA has the force of a binding international agreement thereby strengthening the underlying legal effect of EPC. This is not, however, the same as fully integrating EPC into the Community framework: the character and functioning remained largely intergovernmental and unanimity remained the basis for decision-making. And yet, its revision of what had previously been 'political commitments to the status of legal rules' had been opposed by many states for several years (1991, p. 137). Any concession to an exclusively intergovernmental regime produced, in some member states, 'a feeling that by casting their relationships into a legal mould, they ran the risk of being dragged into an evolution they might not entirely be able to master' (p. 137). The SEA became the first step on the slippery slope to a common foreign policy and a federal Community.

The legal recognition of EPC within the Community framework was an important reform; however, the impact on behaviour was the more important effect. According to Wessels, in the two-and-a-half years after the ratification of the SEA there was 'a trend towards greater cooperation among member countries, greater differentiation of the EPC procedures themselves, and greater coherence between EC and EPC activities' (1991, p. 157). Ginsberg has recorded a significant increase in EC foreign policy actions in the 1986–90 period compared with the previous five years before the SEA (188 and 121 respectively) (1991, p. 1). But this quantitative increase is not tantamount to 'a common foreign policy likened to that of a single nation-state. Member states pursue their own foreign policy actions and will continue to do so' (p. 9). Consequently, the search for a *communauté d'action* to supplement the existing *communauté de vues* and *communauté d'information* was not significantly improved by the SEA; while the member states did move closer to a 'common European foreign policy' (as required by Article 30.1), the speed towards achieving this goal did not accelerate noticeably as a result of the Act (Wessels, 1991, p. 158).

Despite these improvements and encouragements to find common positions, the requirement of an obligatory common foreign policy as outlined by Tindemans a decade earlier, was once again absent. The opportunity to communautarize EPC fully was compromised to placate specific member state reservations; what was preferred was an admittedly improved, but essentially identical form of intergovernmentalism which had historically limited the development of an integrated Community collective foreign policy. As Article 1 of the Common Provisions makes clear, Title III 'shall confirm and supplement the procedures agreed in the reports of Luxembourg (1970), Copenhagen (1973), London (1981), the Solemn Declaration on European Union (1983) and the practices gradually established among the member states'. No radical departure was sanctioned. As with reform of the European Parliament, the issue of a common foreign policy was to resurface during the 1991 IGC debates.

Given its broad scope, it is not surprising that opinion is divided whether the SEA was a significant constitutional reform or a somewhat unnecessary procedural refinement. A leading critic, Pescatore, has concluded 'that the putting into force of the Single Act will be a setback for the European Community' (1987, p. 17). This assessment argues that the 'reform' of the SEA is 'fundamentally deceptive': it ignores the progress made towards a common market which was already 'practically operative' by the mid-1980s; and it downgrades the Community objective from a 'common market' to 'the one-sided notion of an internal market' and 'heralds a new era of protectionism in the Community' (pp. 11–12). A more balanced criticism was offered by Nugent, who viewed the SEA package as 'rather modest, reflecting the unwillingness of most governments to commit themselves firmly to political integration' (1989, p. 174). Similar reservations were expressed by Lodge who unfavourably compared the limited proposals of the SEA with the more radical ideas embodied in the European Parliament's Draft Treaty. She suggested it 'is difficult to avoid the conclusion that the SEA is little more than a charter to safeguard and preserve national interests in the face of pressures for greater EC action in new and old areas' (1986a, p. 221). Be this as it may, it was the SEA that gained unanimous support through its realistic pragmatism, whereas the ideals of the Draft Treaty were discarded. Again, Monnet's incrementalism appeared the better strategy.

This early pessimism has been ameliorated by the experience of the SEA in operation. Writing in 1989, Noël argues that the SEA deserves neither exalted honour nor the indignity of derision, but should be recognized as containing 'important innovations, which might lead to significant changes in the behaviour of institutions and in the way in which the Community itself will develop' (1989, p. 3). Far from being revolutionary, the SEA constituted a recommitment to the Community ideal espoused in the preamble to the Treaty of Rome and provided a much needed relaunch in the wake of the disunity evident within the Community during the first half of the 1980s. That a new series of intergovernmental conferences were convened within five years of signing the SEA should not be taken as indicative of its failure, but rather of its contribution to accelerating and stimulating the debate on the Community's future. The question of European Union was once again at the forefront of the Community agenda.

The 1991 Intergovernmental conferences

Contrary to the limited aspirations of the 'reluctant integrationists' (Nevin, 1990, p. 283), the economic momentum generated by the Single Market established by the SEA encouraged the Community to convene a new Intergovernmental Conference (IGC) dedicated to examining the broader implications of Economic and Monetary Union (EMU). The Commission's working document on EMU was presented on March 20 1990 and tabled for Community deliberation at the 28 April Dublin European Council summit. This Commission initiative had been signalled as early as the June 1988 Hanover European Council meeting which reaffirmed the progressive realization of Economic and Monetary Union: the subsequent Report by the Delors Committee provided the June 1989 Madrid European Council with a three-stage plan for achieving EMU. This debate led to the 1990 decision to launch an IGC which was formally ratified at the June 1990 Dublin European Council.

As noted in Chapter 2, the second IGC on Political Union did not have such a long gestation period: it was not independently planned, but developed in response to the EMU decision. Key Community states thought it imperative to balance economic integration with political integration (or perhaps more realistically to link the latter to the more dynamic performance of the former). An economically integrated Europe without a comparable political dimension seemed the antithesis of the Community ideal. Consequently, at the Dublin European Council it was agreed that a second IGC would be convened to run in parallel with the EMU IGC, both commencing on 14 December 1990 and concluding (it was hoped) in June 1991 (this date for both IGCs was subsequently extended to the end of 1991).

Thus, almost unintentionally, the Community committed itself to a further fundamental examination of its institutional relations and expansion of policy competences. As the Luxembourg Presidency Draft Treaty indicated, the very essence of the Community was once again on the agenda; the Pandora's box of federalism which had been firmly locked since the Tindemans Report was reopened, the consequences of which no one could predict. What was clear, however, was that the Community had reached the crossroads; it could no longer avoid having to make a choice between the road to deeper integration or the route to enhanced intergovernmentalism. Whether this choice could be taken on the basis of consensus was debatable.

Economic and Monetary Union

The agenda for the EMU discussions was clearly defined, although there were serious divisions among the member states on the various alternative solutions. The basic profile was set out in the April 1989 Delors Report on Economic and Monetary Union. The Report built on the principles of the Single Market programme; a three phase process was defined, although a specific timetable for implementation was not stipulated. Significantly, the exercise was seen as a unified process and the decision to embark on the first stage presumed a whole-hearted commitment to realize the entire objective (*Bulletin*, 1989a, p. 9). There was no half-way house; once begun EMU had to be completed. As Keohane and Hoffmann have suggested, the Delors Report provides a good illustration of the dual supranational and intergovernmental processes that work jointly within the Community and offers a negative commentary on the logic of spillover: '[p]erceptions of functional linkages between the single market and exchange rate arrangements led to a process that was both supranational – the report of April 1989 prepared by the Delors Committee – and intergovernmental – the adoption of its first phase by the Council in Madrid two months later' (1990, p. 291).

The Report suggested that stage one could be commenced at any time up until July 1990. This involved improved economic and monetary co-operation and co-ordination leading to a strengthening of the European Monetary System (EMS) and the role of the ECU. This, in turn, would stimulate a convergence of economic policies and performance among the Twelve. A necessary condition for the second stage was the agreement on a new treaty outlining EMU; once this was in force, there would be a transition period whereby national powers were transferred to the Community level according to the principle of subsidiarity. The most important innovation would be the 'creation of a federal-type European System of Central Banks (ESCB)', independent from national governments and Community institutions as regards monetary policy and exchange-market intervention. The third stage would institute 'irrevocably locked exchange rates' and the full application of the new Treaty leading, eventually, to the 'adoption of a single currency' (Commission, 1990a, p. 85).

The June 1989 Madrid European Council produced some important unanimous conclusions. The Delors Report was accepted as the basis for discussions leading to EMU and 1 July 1990 agreed to as the date for the commencement of stage one (although its length was not determined). To balance these economic initiatives, the European Council called for the complementary development of a social dimension drawing on the existing proposal for a Charter of Fundamental Social Rights. Most importantly, the Commission was asked to co-ordinate the preparatory work for an Intergovernmental Conference to lay down the subsequent stages of EMU (*Bulletin*, 1989b, p. 11). The spectre that haunted the 'reluctant integrationists' of monetary reform leading to a Treaty revision, had become a reality.

One of the fundamental issues that had to be addressed was the relationship between the existing European Monetary System (EMS) and EMU.

The assumption underlying the Madrid European Council decision was that there would be the progressive linking of member state currencies; in the late 1980s four national currencies – those of Greece, Portugal, Spain and the UK – while part of the ECU basket, were not tied to the EMS through the Exchange Rate Mechanism (ERM) (Nevin, 1990, pp. 282–3). The problem was one of economic sovereignty and the ability and political right of a member state to set its own currency value. Spain responded immediately and placed the peseta into the ERM in June 1989, and the decision by Mrs Thatcher to take the pound sterling into the ERM in the Autumn of 1990 effectively cleared the stage for the move towards monetary union, despite her protestations and those of her immediate successor, John Major. A fully inclusive EMS and ERM would not be tantamount to effective monetary union. The greatest flaw in the EMS was that it did not fix the value of Community currencies *vis-à-vis* third currencies, particularly the US dollar. This created the opportunity for currency fluctuation; for monetary union to proceed there was 'the need for some single central authority to determine and maintain the rate of exchange between the Ecu (and thus all its component currencies) and other major currencies of the world' (p. 283).

The Madrid European Council signified a fundamental change in the context of European integration; the Delors Committee Report transformed the ongoing Community dispute over the desirability of monetary union into an acceptance of this in principle: the debate was now focused on the form and timing that such a union should take (p. 285). For integrationists, the dilemma was how to achieve Treaty reform which by its constitutional nature required unanimous approval; the 'reluctant integrationists' had an implied veto. The Commission continued to refine its view and submitted further ambitious proposals as discussion documents for the Community institutions. The culmination of this process occurred at the April 1990 European Council meeting in Dublin where the Commission's reformed working document on EMU was discussed. The proposal was more detailed in a number of respects. It outlined the creation of a new Community institution (EuroFed) that would be independent and responsible for directing the common monetary policy (with a legal obligation to maintain price stability), but also democratically accountable to the Parliament and European Council. The EuroFed was to have a federal structure consisting of a Council responsible for general policy composed of the twelve governors of the national banks and a board of appointed experts to oversee the day-to-day implementation of a common monetary policy. Consistency between internal monetary policy and external exchange rate policies was emphasized based on the ECU as an eventual single currency. The principle of subsidiarity should guide EMU and economic diversity within the Community should be accommodated. A single monetary policy did not, necessarily, demand a single economic policy, although a 'sufficient degree of convergence and consistency' was essential (*Bulletin*, 1990, pp. 8–9). Lastly, a timetable for EMU was proposed – stage two was to begin in 1994 and stage three as early as 1996.

The opening of the IGC in December 1990 adopted the Commission's draft treaty on EMU as the basis for discussions; this acceptance, however, did not confer legitimacy on the Commission's plan. The Luxembourg Presidency's Draft Treaty on the Union of June 1991 established the framework within which the debate would be conducted during this penultimate phase leading to the conclusion of the IGC at the Maastricht European Council meeting of December 1991. The consolidated Draft Treaty was a synthesis of the progress made in both IGCs and covered a wide range of topics such as the principles of Union; citizenship; institutions; foreign policy and relations with third countries; as well as specific Treaty revisions required to achieve EMU.

Most controversially, the 'Common Provisions' outlining Union stated that '[T]his Treaty marks a new stage in a process leading gradually to a Union with a federal goal' (Article A). Consequently, EMU was clearly aligned with, and seen as instrumental to, realizing this objective. More specifically, the new Union's aims were to develop the existing *acquis communautaire* 'to promote economic and social progress which is balanced and sustainable in particular through the creation of an area without internal frontiers, through the reinforcement of economic and social cohesion and the establishment of economic and monetary union including, finally, a single currency' (Article B).

The individual policy measures needed to realize a common market and EMU were stipulated in Article 3 and many of the ideas of the Delors Committee Report were directly incorporated: for example, there was provision for 'the irrevocable fixing of exchange rates between the currencies of the Member States and the introduction of a single currency, the ECU, the definition and conduct of a single monetary and exchange policy the overriding objective of which shall be to maintain price stability' (Article 3a). The European System of Central Banks (ESCB) is given legal personalty (Article 106) and its competences codified: the ESCB is responsible for exchange transactions and holds and manages official exchange reserves; it is expected to ensure 'the prudential control and stability of the financial system' and regulate the issue and circulation of currency (Article 105). Its composition mirrors that suggested in the Delors Report and its independence is recognized. The ESCB may not

> seek or take instruction from Community institutions or bodies, from any governments of a Member State or from any other body. The Community institutions and bodies and the Governments of the Member States undertake to respect this principle and not to seek to influence the members of the decision-making bodies of the European Central Bank and of the central banks of the Member States in the performance of their tasks. (Article 107)

The actual control and setting of price support targets was an issue that touched the nerve of EMU; to what extent would policy be determined by majority vote or by unanimity, reflecting the confrontation between supranational-federal aspirations and those of economic intergovernmentalists? While the Draft Treaty suggested specific institutional safeguards, it was unable to set out an agreed preference and this issue remained part of the EMU debate during the second half of 1991. What

was agreed was that the ESCB should begin operating on 1 January 1996 at
the latest.

Political Union

The issues contained within the IGC on Political Union were disparate and
not so obviously interconnected as those concerned with EMU. Four distinct
areas were debated: foreign policy; citizenship; new Community competences; and democratization and institutional reform. Perhaps reflecting
this mixed agenda, consensus was initially harder to achieve. The Commission were quick to respond to the April 1990 decision to convene a parallel
IGC on Political Union and their opinion was published on 21 October
1990: unlike the Delors Committee Report, however, key elements in the
Commission's proposal were challenged in the June Draft Treaty.

A fundamental characteristic for the Commission was that the Community
should remain a single Community: this so-called 'unicity' recalled the
intentions of the original Treaty framers and emphasized the supranational
interrelated wholeness of the EC. Past expediency had forced a dual
approach on the Community producing a gap 'between progress on common
policies on the one hand and advances on political cooperation on the
other': consequently, a single institutional structure and decision-making
process was required to remove this 'grey area' between supranational and
intergovernmental control (Commission, 1990b, p. 11). This assumption
did not go unchallenged; during the early months of the IGC a provisional
version of the Draft Treaty rejected unicity in favour of three separate pillars
under an overarching Community edifice (encouraging the continuation
of intergovernmental and supranational structures in tandem). After much
acrimonious and often public debate, the Draft Treaty reinstated the principle of unicity.

> The Union shall be served by a single institutional framework which shall
> ensure the consistency and the continuity of the actions carried out in order to
> reach its objectives while respecting and developing the acquis communautaire.
> The Union shall in particular ensure the consistency of its external actions as a
> whole in the implementation of its external relations, defence, economic and
> development policies. (Common Provisions, Article C)

The Commission were influential, but ultimately unsuccessful, in the 'federal'
debate. Their October 1990 Opinion acknowledged the indeterminate
shape of European Union but counselled 'in favour of keeping to the
course charted by the Treaty of Rome, leading eventually to a federal-type
organization' (1990b, p. 11). The Luxembourg Presidency response was to
reject this wording and commitment, only to see the phrase 'federal goal'
reinserted in the June Draft Treaty before being dropped in December
1991 at Maastricht.

The area where dispute was the fiercest (both between the Commission
and the member states and within the Twelve themselves) concerned the
Community's foreign policy. As illustrated in Chapter 2, the invasion of

Kuwait and resultant war had mercilessly highlighted the limitations of the existing mechanism of European Political Cooperation (EPC). There was consensus on the inadequacy of EPC, but not on how this could be solved. Of all the areas covered in the Political Union IGC, the outcome of the foreign policy debate was the least predictable. Vagueness, inclusivity and non-specific alternatives shaped, or rather failed to shape, the initial discussions. The introduction of the concept of a Common Foreign and Security Policy (CFSP) to enhance EPC again exposed the federal nerve within the Community. The Commission advocated that the new Treaty should outline the methods and procedures for creating a 'common' policy (as opposed to a single policy) which would eventually lead to a common security and defence policy (pp. 13–4). CFSP policy-making would continue to be shared by Community institutions as at present; the Commission did not argue for an exclusive right of initiative. As for the scope of the new foreign policy the Commission advised that it would be inappropriate to list specific areas where the Community could act in the Treaty. Rather, 'it would be preferable to leave it to the European Council to decide on the areas to be transferred from the scope of political cooperation to that of a common or Community policy' (p. 15). Once defined, decision-making would be by an augmented qualified majority requiring the support of at least eight member states: security issues and areas that remained under EPC would retain the consensus rule. The Commission did not call for any new extension of formal parliamentary involvement (consultation on a regular basis being the only requirement) although clarification of the existing assent procedure was supported (p. 16).

The avowed purpose of the IGC was 'to deal with *all aspects* of foreign and security policy *without exception*' (General Secretariat, 1990) (my italics). Certainly, the deliberations were frank and addressed fundamental issues. To the one extreme, the Franco-German communiqué of March 1991 represented the integrationists' aspirations: the objective of the IGC was 'to precisely define the principles and procedures of a common foreign and security policy leading in time to a common defence policy . . . [to] obtain the best content and institutional formulas for the implementation of a common foreign and security policy that will allow Europe to act effectively in the world's important affairs.' (*Agence Europe*, 23 March 1991) But as the eventual Treaty on European Union showed, this commitment was not universal and there was significant resistance to a *saut qualitif* to a higher level of foreign policy co-operation that breached the consensus principle. Three specific areas of disagreement were isolated: the question of defence; qualified majority voting; and the role of the Commission. Broadly speaking, reservations on these issues were raised by Ireland, Denmark, Portugal and the UK.

The Treaty sought to establish an agreement on the fundamental principles underpinning a CFSP as well as develop a consensus on the mechanisms for its implementation. The Common Provisions mirrored the Commission's input and called upon the Community 'to assert its identity on the international scene, in particular through the implementation of a common foreign and security policy which shall include the eventual framing of a defence policy' (Article B). The precise details of this were laid out in the Treaty on European Union Title V *Provisions on Common Foreign and Security Policy* (see Appendix in this volume): again, the considerable influence of the Commission's Opinion was clear. This CFSP was to be comprehensive and its objectives were:

- to safeguard the common values, fundamental interests and independence of the Union;
- to strengthen the security of the Union and its Member States in all ways;
- to preserve peace and strengthen international security, in accordance with the principles of the United Nations Charter as well as the principles of the Helsinki Act and the objectives of the Paris Charter;
- to promote international co-operation;
- to develop and consolidate democracy and the rule of law, and respect for human rights and fundamental freedoms. (Article A.2)

Joint action was to be gradually introduced where the Member States have essential interests in common under a single Union institutional framework, and consistency between foreign policy, external economic relations and development co-operation was to be asserted (Article J.2). The European Council retained its central position of defining the principles and guidelines for the CFSP, delegating this as appropriate to the Council. The existing Permanent Representatives Committee, Political Committee and the General Secretariat support the Council, the latter replacing the formerly autonomous EPC Secretariat which it incorporated. As for the existing EPC procedures, the Commission retains its 'full association', whereas the European Parliament was to remain peripheral to foreign policy-making (Articles J.5 and J.7).

Article J.3 concerns the major innovation regarding joint action; here, specific areas that are to be governed solely by the Union are addressed. Once agreed to the inclusion of specific foreign policy topics, 'joint actions shall commit the Member States in the positions they adopt and in the conduct of their activity', with the details for carrying out a joint action adopted by qualified majority. If not removed, the unanimity principle central to EPC has been breached. This compromise position, partially *communautairizing* the execution of foreign policy, borrows from the prescient Tindemans Report which argued for the ending of separate EC and EPC topics and for the Community method to cover all activity undertaken in the name of the EC. This departure also parallels the subsidiarity debates common to the EMU IGC. Simply, those areas not specifically assigned to the EC level (because this would not be effective or appropriate) remain in the domain of the member states. Lastly, it is important to note that the Treaty is concerned with developing a *common* foreign policy: the idea of a *single* foreign policy has been rejected. This distinction is of paramount importance. While the Treaty calls on member states to support common policies 'actively and unreservedly in a spirit of loyalty and mutual solidarity' and 'refrain from any action which is contrary to the interests of Union' (Article A.4), this constraint is not absolute. Such a common policy implies a progressive evolution in the scope and implementation of a collective Community foreign policy, while providing the possibility within the

Community's legal framework for states to be excluded from a common policy because of specific obligations. Article J.3.6 of the Treaty could be interpreted in this light and obviously the principle of unanimity required to commit the EC to joint policy remains an important defence of intergovernmentalism. While ardent federalists may be critical of this characteristic Community compromise, an expanding 'common' foreign policy can clearly be seen to be a necessary prerequisite to a single European foreign, security and defence policy. However, it has to be conceded that the current situation of common and bilateral foreign policy existing in tandem will continue for the foreseeable future.

The Draft Treaty also considered intra-Community institutional relations, particularly the role of the European Parliament. The co-operation and co-decision procedures introduced by the SEA to provide a legislative function for the Parliament were revised. However, this revision only confirmed the Parliament's negative legislative role: it could block and postpone, but it could not directly initiate legislation. The Treaty only bestowed the Parliament with an indirect form of initiative; on a majority vote, it can request that the Commission submit a proposal on any matter that the Parliament deems necessary in order to implement the provisions of the new Treaty (Article 137a).

Article 189a outlines the new procedure for creating Community law: The Council is allowed to adopt a common position on the basis of a qualified majority and this is transmitted to the Parliament. The Parliament then has four options: within three months it must chose between approving the common position, offer no opinion (in which case the proposal becomes law), reject the proposal (by an absolute majority vote) or propose amendments and send the revised proposal to the Commission and Council for consideration. The Council then has a further three months in which to either approve the Parliament's amendments (by qualified majority) or to reject or refuse to comment on the revisions. In this case a Conciliation Committee, composed of an equal number of Council and of Parliament representatives presided over by the Commission, is convened. If a joint text can be agreed to within six weeks, for the law to be approved then absolute and qualified majority decisions are needed in the Parliament and Council within a further six weeks. If either of these institutions fails to give approval, the law is not adopted. If a joint text cannot be formulated, the Council can confirm its original common position (which may possibly include some parliamentary amendments) by qualified majority: faced with this situation the Parliament can only block the proposal by a majority vote rejecting the final Council proposal. Clearly, the Parliament's negative blocking power is the more constrained, and as in the SEA Parliament has no opportunity to insist that its amendments be adopted.

It was hardly surprising that the Parliament perceived these modifications as a substitute for effective participation in the legislative process and inconsistent with the objective of removing the existing 'democratic deficit' within the Community institutional structure. The original Commission Opinion of October 1990 was even less accommodating, but this was adapted somewhat in the light of the 1990 Martin Report of the Parliament's

Committee on Institutional Affairs. This called for the Parliament to be given the right of initiative to override the Commission on those occasions where it declines to prepare a legislative proposal as requested by the Parliament; and a procedure of complete co-decision for all Community legislation to facilitate effective democratic scrutiny.

The second major institutional change considered in the Draft Treaty relates to the Commission. Article 158 proposes to remove the preference given to the five larger member states who currently appoint two Commissioners each, replacing this with one Commissioner for each member state. The appointment of the Commission President is more controversial. The Martin Report called for the presidential term to be coterminal with the five-year European Parliament term, and that after each European election the Parliament has exclusive responsibility for electing the President. The new Treaty did not concede this devolution of executive power. Rather the existing practice was modified and codified. Thus, national governments 'nominate by common accord, after consulting with the European Parliament, the person they intend to appoint as President of the Commission' for a four-year term (Article 158.2). The remaining Commissioners are then appointed by the member states in consultation with the nominated President and subject to a vote of approval as a complete body by the European Parliament. Thus the Parliament's power over the Commission replicated the original position found in the Treaty of Rome. If the Parliament wished to demonstrate its disapproval, it could only do so by dismissing (or refusing to approve) the Commission as a whole: it could not direct its opposition at a specific Commissioner or the President. History has shown that this all-or-nothing characteristic has effectively emasculated this potential parliamentary sanction.

The role of the Court of Justice was also reviewed, and two significant changes were proposed. First, a Court of First Instance was created in order to relieve the burden on the existing single Court (Article 168a). Second, the Court of Justice in concert with the Commission were, for the first time, given the authority to impose punitive sanctions. Under the existing Article 171 of the Treaty of Rome, member states who fail to fulfil their obligations may be subject to a Court of Justice judgment requiring them to take the necessary measures to ensure compliance. However, the Community had no powers to punish non-compliance: the new Treaty Article seeks to redress this impotence. Where the Commission believes that a member state has not complied with any such judgment within a specified and reasonable time limit, it can take the state back to the Court and specify a 'lump sum or penalty payment to be paid by the Member State concerned which it considers appropriate in the circumstances' (Article 171.2). If the Court finds that the state is in contravention of its earlier judgment it may impose such a penalty.

This somewhat negative legal encouragement towards integration was balanced by a more positive use of Community law. One of the strengths of the Tindemans Report had been its commitment to a people's Europe: this emphasis was given modest and somewhat tentative legal recognition under 'Union Citizenship' in the Treaty. All EC nationals were to become

Union citizens with rights and duties explicitly conferred by the Draft Treaty. These included the right 'to move and reside freely within the territory of the Member States' (Article B.1); the right to vote and stand in local elections and elections to the European Parliament on the basis of residency, not nationality (although certain derogations could be applied) (Article C.1 and C.2); where no diplomatic national representation exists in a third country, the right as a Union citizen to full and equal diplomatic and consular protection by any member state delegation 'on the same conditions as nationals of that state' (Article D); and the right to petition the European Parliament and appeal to the newly created office of Ombudsman in the Treaty (Article F). The Ombudsman was to be appointed by the European Parliament to investigate complaints by Union citizens concerning maladministration by Community institutions (excluding the Courts); the office did not have any powers of compliance, however (Article 137.c). This general commitment to European citizenship avoided some key areas, in particular the long-running conflict over a uniform electoral system for the elections to the European Parliament. Although the Treaty on European Union addressed this topic (Article 138), the amended text was no more effective in its wording than the original article in the Treaty of Rome: unanimity in the Council was still a prerequisite for a decision on a uniform electoral system for the member states.

The incoming Dutch Presidency confirmed that the Draft Treaty on the Union would remain the basis for further discussion between June and December 1991, thereby supporting the unicity of the reforms and the need to resolve the question of the Union's 'federal goal'. The final resolution agreed at the December 1991 Maastricht European Council made three major revisions to the Draft Treaty. First, the language of a 'federal goal' was deleted in favour of the less explicitly federal wording of the Treaty of Rome to create 'an even closer Union among the peoples of Europe' (Article A). Second, the British obtained a dispensation that allowed them to defer a decision on a common currency until 1996. Third, the Social Charter failed to be incorporated in the Treaty due to Britain's veto: consequently, the Eleven committed themselves to using the Community institutions and *communautaire* system in an annex to the Treaty which explicitly excludes the UK (see Chapter 7).

There was nothing unique about the IGC process: the outcome of both the Political Union and EMU debates reflected the typical Community package-deal policy-making process. As one commentator has noted previously, the compromise was 'between, on the one hand, the enthusiasts satisfied with nothing less than a full-blown United States of Europe and, on the other, the pragmatists profoundly suspicious of any changes in excess of the minimum strictly necessary for the attainment of a specified and limited end' (Nevin, 1990, p. 285).

Common themes

Despite Spinelli's opinion quoted above that the Tindemans Report had 'the consequence that it remained without consequence', there is evidence that both the SEA and 1991 IGCs inherited many of the themes and aspirations first enunciated in the mid-1970s by Tindemans. What, then, are these common strands in the Community's reform programme?

European Union and a vision for the Community

All three reform proposals have attempted to offer a goal that the Community should strive for. This objective was not in the form of a detailed definition, but rather a working principle within which future policies and institutional arrangements could be framed. As the frenetic and unpredictable nature of change in recent international politics has indicated (for example, the unprecedented events such as the fall of the Berlin Wall in November 1989 and the fragmentation of the Soviet Union in 1991), to be prescriptive as to the shape of the Community for even the 1990s would be conceited, foolish and probably inaccurate.

In their respective individual interpretations, each reform sought to promote a European Union consistent with the commitment to 'an ever closer union among the peoples of Europe'. For Tindemans, like Monnet, the Community was an embryonic federation; European Union was dependent on the mutual development of a series of interrelated factors which could only be built gradually. This evolutionary perspective can be found in both the SEA and the Maastricht Treaty. The Community vision of the SEA 'to transform relations as a whole . . . into a European Union' stipulated the need collectively to ensure 'concrete progress towards European Unity'. But these objectives were neither binding nor hardly revolutionary and mimicked earlier solemn commitments and declarations on European Union that had failed to produce a *saut qualitif*. Although not adopted, the Draft Treaty at least had the unique virtue of clearly and openly stating the 'federal goal' of European Union, though once again the emphasis was placed on the gradual process of constructing a Union. This approach confronted the two seemingly irreconcilable visions of Community development – intergovernmentalism and federalism. Despite being deleted from the final version, the 1991 IGCs made the invaluable contribution of insisting that this fundamental issue of federalism be discussed fully and publicly. If not immutable, by the end of 1991 the Community had made significant progress in designing the central elements of the long-awaited European Union.

A People's Europe

Both the Tindemans Report and the IGC on Political Union addressed the necessity to transform the popular negative image of a Brussels bureaucratic Community into a positive expression of Community citizenship that was visible and applicable to everyday life. The aspirations of Tindemans were expansive and foreshadowed many of the arguments that were to emerge in the second half of the 1980s concerning a European Social Charter to protect fundamental rights. In contrast, the SEA specifically avoided this concern with the place of the individual within the Community and stressed the economic and technological aspects of integration. The IGC had the virtue of placing the idea of European citizenship within a treaty and, therefore, a legal context. This was a necessary, but not sufficient step. The idea of the Community required more than the symbolic trappings of a flag, anthem and periodic popular elections: a new Community political culture had to be nurtured and matured if a people's Europe was to be cultivated out of the purely legal notion of citizenship.

A global role and a common Foreign Policy

All three reforms isolated the inadequacies of the Community's existing mechanisms for international action and eulogized Europe's potential to regain its historical role as a major global actor. Their respective remedies for these inadequacies were substantially different, however. The SEA was the most conservative in its position although it did introduce two crucial changes. First, an important practical development was the establishment of the EPC Secretariat (despite the intergovernmental rather than supranational nature of its organization); and second, EPC was finally brought within the ambit of a treaty (even if a communautairization of the procedure was resisted). In somewhat of an ironic contrast, the Tindemans Report advocated radical change, but had virtually no practical impact. The issues of an obligatory common policy via majority voting, defence co-operation, the joint manufacture of armaments and extending the scope of Community action were largely ignored. Any changes adopted were behavioural and procedural and did not require any formal Treaty revision.

The IGCs represent the compromise position between these two options. The obligation to reach a common position was abandoned, but a procedure for exercising majority decisions was introduced and the existing narrow EPC mechanism was jettisoned for a more comprehensive and effective Common Foreign and Security Policy. While still not yet a single policy, Maastricht represented a qualitative change: there is now a consensus on the necessity to develop a collective European response to foreign, security and, ultimately, defence policy, a development that is in keeping with Tindemans' overall prescription.

Policy expansion and cohesion

Paradoxically, Tindemans' radicalism in external relations was, with respect to EMU, cautious and deferential to the then existing political obstacles to further integration. He even endorsed a Europe *à deux vitesse*,

an intergovernmental anathema to most federalists. Yet despite these reservations, the seeds of the EMU debate were sown in 1975 making the
path towards these objectives less difficult by 1991. The Report called for
stability in internal and external monetary policy, an embryonic European
central bank, closer linking of EC currencies and the free movement of
capital throughout the Community. The SEA built upon the economic
rather than the monetary recommendations by establishing the principle
of the Single Market for 1992. The IGCs picked up the gauntlet of monetary
union directly and committed the Community to full monetary union
before the turn of the century, with the complementary development of a
central European bank, common currency and external currency stability.

While all three reports placed a premium on aspects of EMU, they all
also recognized the need to balance this with an extension of the Community's general policy competence, particularly in terms of regional and
social policies, supplementing and reinforcing the belief in a people's
Europe. Thus Tindemans prescribed the abolition of internal frontier controls
not on the grounds of an economic single market, but on the basis of individual human rights. Policy co-ordination was needed to facilitate this free
movement so that European citizens would be treated equally (socially,
politically and economically) irrespective of their nationality. This recognition
of comprehensive policy cohesion was to appear again in the Draft Treaty.
It proposed an innovative reform and possibly the most important contribution to European Union – the inclusion of the principle of subsidiarity in
the Treaty. This provided a consistent measure by which the extension of
Community competences could be evaluated. Article 3b states:

> [I]n the areas which do not fall within its exclusive jurisdiction, the Community
> shall take action, in accordance with the principle of subsidiarity, only if and
> insofar as the objectives of the proposed action cannot be sufficiently achieved
> by the Member States and can therefore, by reason of the scale or effects of pro-
> posed action, be better achieved by the Community.

Finally, there appeared to be the possibility of constructing Community
integration and federal Union according to a general principle acceptable
to all. Experience would tell whether this general principle was workable
and legally enforceable.

Institutional reform and the democratic deficit

How to revise the institutional structure has been an almost perennial
Community preoccupation. However, the basic framework established in
1957 has not come into disrepute, but rather successive reforms have
sought to accommodate new bodies and relationships within the context of
the existing unicity. Thus the existing *acquis communautaire*, derived from
the practical experience of the Treaty of Rome, remains the non-negotiable
basis for any institutional reform. The consistent reform elements have
been efficiency, supranational authority and most importantly, democracy:

as should be apparent by now, on occasions these combined characteristics have been antagonistic, even mutually exclusive.

According to Tindemans, efficiency was to be enhanced through simple procedural reforms: the abolition of the spurious dichotomy between EC and EPC business; the introduction of majority voting as the normal decision-making principle; the extension of the Council Presidency to a full year; the reinvigoration of the Commission as the engine of integration; and, more generally, a clear single Community decision-making centre. The SEA and Maastricht have incorporated all but the extended term for the Presidency in their proposals. Although restricted to specifically those policy areas delineated in the SEA, majority voting has become normal practice. The SEA legally recognized the existing informal legitimacy of EPC business and the IGCs abolished this distinction entirely. Both reaffirmed the central and exclusive role played by the Commission and supported the principle of consolidating rather than diversifying the decision-making structures.

The extension of supranational authority illustrates some of the antagonistic elements within the reform process reflecting, quite naturally, the package-deal inevitability of consensus-based change. Thus there has been the progressive acceptance of the dominant role of the European Council, and its progression from an extra-Treaty body to incorporation into the Community system, leading to its elevation in the Maastricht Treaty to defining general policy guidelines and 'to provide the Union with the necessary impetus for its development' (Article D). Arguably, the newly empowered European Council remains a bastion of intergovernmental restraint, rather than a natural ally of supranational authority. To balance this, the IGC adopted almost verbatim Tindemans' recommendation on the appointment and ratification of the President of the Commission. And yet, while this new procedure will extend the legitimacy of the Commission, this decision fails to meet the democratic requirements demanded by the Parliament.

The Community's democratic deficit concerns the limited legislative role ascribed to the European Parliament and the lack of direct accountability of key Community institutions, notably the Commission. While all the three reform proposals pay homage to this principle, none has introduced a successful remedy. Understandably perhaps, Tindemans was restrained in his vision of parliamentary powers given that direct elections had yet to take place; he called for Parliament to be given the right of initiative and full competence to discuss any Treaty matter. The SEA introduced the complex co-decision and co-operation procedures, but failed to provide the Parliament with much more than a negative legislative role, a condition replicated at Maastricht. As noted above, the accountability of the Commission is a good example of the influence (whether direct or subliminal) of the Tindemans Report on the presumed innovations of the IGC. While disappointing the parliamentarians, the proposed involvement of the Parliament in ratifying the appointment of the Commission President moves somewhat closer to removing the democratic deficit *vis-à-vis* the Community's executive. Lastly, none of the three reform packages could be expected to have an impact on what many commentators see as the fundamental issue relating to the democratic deficit: namely, the

Parliament's reduced legitimacy caused by the low turn-out at each of the three direct elections held since 1979. The dilemma remains whether to extend Parliament's authority immediately in the hope of stimulating increased legitimacy, or to wait for evidence of popular support before conferring real legislative powers.

Conclusion

The central issue underlying these various procedural and substantive reforms is the conflict over the form of Union being envisaged, a problem that has been an integral part of the Community since its origin. In the contemporary period, this discord has primarily been represented by two of Europe's leading political figures: Jacques Delors, the federalist President of the Commission from 1985–92, and Margaret Thatcher, British Prime Minister from 1979–90 and defender of the intergovernmentalist cause (Nugent, 1989, pp. 326–7). This dispute goes beyond personalities, however, and represents a serious tension within the Community. While the maximalist supporters of supranationalism (led by Mitterrand and Kohl) are a clear majority within the Twelve, intergovernmental concern is not unique to the United Kingdom; increasingly, other states questioned specific federal initiatives at the 1991 IGCs. Progress since the SEA has significantly enhanced the level of integration, but the fundamental issue of the 'federal goal' of the Community has not been adequately resolved. This negative theme is perhaps the dominant strand connecting each of the three reform processes examined here.

The conclusion should not be overly pessimistic: successive enlargements have tended to strengthen the intergovernmentalists – the UK, Denmark and Greece – but supranationalism has been resilient and made significant advances which cumulatively have progressively undermined national sovereignty. Writing prior to the decision to convene the IGCs, Nugent listed the various intergovernmental and supranational characteristics contained within the Community: those areas where intergovernmentalism was dominant were over the control of the major areas of policy-making; through the decision-making pre-eminence of the Council; via the consensus principle; the limited roles ascribed to the Commission and the Parliament; and the political authority of the European Council (pp. 321–2). In the light of Maastricht a perceptible movement in favour of supranationalism can be perceived. First, the scope for national policy-making has been reduced, most spectacularly in relation to EMU, but also in social areas and in foreign policy: this expansion of Community competence has also been given stronger legal backing through the ability of the Court of Justice to impose penalties. Second, though formally limited to specific Treaty articles, majority voting has begun to have a more pervasive effect on the prevailing political culture within the Council and has replaced the Luxembourg Compromise as the axis on which decision-making rests. Third, the new co-operation and co-decision procedures and the retention of the Commission as policy initiator have contributed, in a modest way, to rebuffing intergovernmental advances from the Council. Fourthly, although usually seen as the manifestation of intergovernmentalism, the role of the European Council as specified in the Treaty on European Union can give some comfort to advocates of supranationalism. The commitment to a federal Union can only come through political consensus in the European Council. Thus fully incorporating this body within the constitutional structure of the Community is an essential prerequisite to achieving Union. Despite the difficulties, there is no other path to federalism.

This chapter has shown the consistency in the Community's reform programme and recorded the important changes that have been adopted incrementally in recent years. The supranational dynamic is in the ascendancy, but its eventual success cannot be guaranteed as the Danish referendum on the Maastricht Treaty underlined. As the history of the Community repeatedly illustrates, the fate of constitutional reform is as dependent on political personalities and public opinion as it is upon a belief in the Community ideal. It is instructive to recall that the current EMU debate is taking place more than three decades since Monnet considered that 'the first steps towards a European currency seemed to be practicable' (1978, p. 439). There is nothing inevitable about European integration. The Community has survived the intergovernmental rebukes of de Gaulle and Thatcher, but it would be remarkable if a new heir apparent to the intergovernmental crown were not to emerge in the 1990s. Thus the tension between these two opposing visions of the Community are set to remain for the foreseeable future. Indeed, some have argued that the Community derives its own dynamic from this tension and intergovernmental criticism is essential to the development of appropriate and acceptable supranational structures for the twenty-first century.

To conclude, despite their different legal status and eventual fates as well as their clearly different intergovernmental and federal strands, the symmetry of the Tindemans, SEA and Maastricht attempts to reform the Community is striking. And yet it is sobering to record that the 'overall picture of European Union' as depicted by Tindemans remains the most informative expression of this objective (whether implicitly or explicitly federal). The task still remains:

> . . . arriving at a political consensus on the aims and main features of the Union in terms which give expression to the deep aspirations of our peoples; . . . determining the consequences of this choice in the various areas of the Union's internal and external activities;
> . . .strengthening the institutional machinery to enable it to cope with the tasks awaiting it. (Tindemans, 1976, VI., p. 34)

References

Bulletin of the EC, 1989a, 'Report of the Committee for the study of Economic and Monetary Union', 22–4, pp. 8–9.
Bulletin of the EC, 1989b, 'European Council: Madrid 26–27 June', 22–6, pp. 8–17.

Bulletin of the EC, 1990, 'The Single Market and the Community: preparations for the Intergovernmental Conference', 23–3, pp. 8–9.

Burgess, M., 1989, *Federalism and European Union: political ideas, influences and strategies in the European Community, 1972–1987*, Routledge, London.

Campbell, J., Barnes, I. and Pepper, C., 1990, 'Implementing the Internal market' in Crouch, C. and Marquand, D. (eds), *The Politics of 1992: beyond the Single European Market. The Political Quarterly*, Basil Blackwell, Oxford, pp. 138–56.

Commission of the EC, 1990a, *XXIIIrd General Report on the activities of the European Communities 1989*, European Community, Brussels.

Commission of the EC, 1990b, *Commission Opinion of 21 October 1990 on the proposal for Amendment of the Treaty establishing the European Economic Community with a view to Political Union*, European Community, Brussels.

Dehousse, R. and Weiler, J.H.H., 1991, 'EPC and the Single Act: from soft law to hard law?' in Holland, M. (ed.), *The future of European Political Cooperation: essays on theory and practice*, Macmillan, London, pp. 120–41.

Draft Treaty on the Union, 1991, presented by the Luxembourg Presidency to the 'Conference of the Representatives of the Governments of the Member States– Political Union and Economic and Monetary Union', Luxembourg, 18 June.

Europe Documents, 1991, *European Commission opinion on Austria's request for membership to the European Community. Agence Europe* No. 1730, 3 August, pp. 1–3.

Fitzmaurice, J., 1988, 'An analysis of the European Community's co-operation procedure', *Journal of Common Market Studies*, 26, pp. 389–400.

General Secretariat of the Council, 1990, 'Note: Political Union – outcome of the proceedings of the personal representatives of the Ministers for Foreign Affairs', General Affairs Council of the EC, document 10356/90, 30 November.

Ginsberg, R., 1991, *Foreign policy actions of the European Community*, Lynne Rienner, Boulder.

Holland, M., 1988, *The European Community and South Africa: European Political Co-operation under strain*, Pinter, London.

Keohane, R. O. and Hoffmann, S., 1990, 'Conclusions: Community politics and institutional change' in Wallace, W. (ed.), *The dynamics of European integration*, Pinter, London, pp. 276–300.

Lodge, J., 1986a, 'The Single European Act: towards a new European dynamism?', *Journal of Common Market Studies*, 24, pp. 203–23.

Lodge, J., 1986b, 'The European Community: compromise under domestic and international pressure', *The World Today*, 42, pp. 192–5.

Monnet, J., 1978, *Memoirs* (trans. R. Mayne), Doubleday and Company, New York.

Nevin, E., 1990, *The economics of Europe*, St Martin's Press, New York.

Nicoll, W. and Salmon, T. C., 1990, *Understanding the European Communities*, Barnes and Noble, Savage, Maryland.

Noël, E., 1989, 'The Single European Act', *Government and Opposition*, 24, pp. 3–14.

Nugent, N., 1989, *The government and politics of the European Community*, Macmillan, London.

Pescatore, P., 1987, 'Some critical remarks on the Single European Act', *Common Market Law Review*, 24, pp. 9–18.

Tindemans, L., 1976, 'Report on European Union', *Supplement of the Bulletin of the EC*, 1/76, European Community, Brussels.

Wessels, W., 1991, 'EPC after the Single Act: towards a European foreign policy via treaty obligations' in Holland, M. (ed.), *The future of European Political Cooperation: essays on theory and practice*, Macmillan, London, pp. 142–59.

Wistrich, E., 1989, *After 1992: the United States of Europe*, Routledge, London.

4 The end of the nation-state: the EC's institutional relations

Only institutions grow wiser; they accumulate collective experience. (Monnet, 1978, p. 393)

The previous three chapters have all stressed the importance of the idea of Europe, emphasized the fluidity of this concept and outlined the antagonistic tensions contained within it. Since the emergence of the Community idea some 40 years ago, a complex institutional structure has evolved, reflecting both the supranational aspirations of the Treaty of Rome as well as the intergovernmental concerns of several member states. In this chapter the principal institutions of the Community are discussed within the context of sovereignty and the decline of the independent authority of the nation-state in Western Europe in the post-war period. Increasingly, authority and decision-making are being transferred and pooled at the Community's collective level with profound implications for the traditional role of the state and national parliaments (Pinder, 1991, p. 203).

In trying to understand the European Community, the language and concepts commonly used in Western democratic societies are often inappropriate. The normal distinction between executive and legislative functions, or between bureaucratic and political roles, inadequately describes the Community's innovative and to date unique institutional structure. The only reliable similarity is in the comparison of the Treaty of Rome as the equivalent to a written constitution. Even here the neatness of the comparison is blurred as other treaties (such as the 1952 Treaty of Paris, the 1985 Single European Act or the 1992 Treaty on European Union) have to be considered as either supplements to, or amendments of, this founding document. Thus the Community is a legal system and its competences and authority are derived from these collective documents; but the equivalent to constitutional conventions also play a part in the Community's behaviour, most noticeably in relation to European Political Cooperation (EPC). In sum, the Community is based on a hybrid formal and informal system which has shown a remarkable flexibility and adaptability in its short life.

As the previous chapters have indicated, this poor match between the Community's structure and other forms of Western democracies goes beyond institutional competences: the very nature of the organization is imprecise. Is it supranational or intergovernmental? Or is it both simultaneously? As the Community experience has shown, both federalists and intergovernmentalists have interpreted the Community's legal authority prejudicially. The attempt to insert a 'federal goal' in the Draft Treaty failed to resolve this dilemma as the key institutions created to build this federal construction were intergovernmental in character. Employing a poacher as gamekeeper may be a clever ploy, but it is certainly also an extremely risky constitutional strategy. This chapter continues to use the intergovernmental–supranational dichotomy as the appropriate vehicle for analysis. Community institutions that are predominantly supranational in character are contrasted with those that represent an intergovernmental approach. The chapter concludes with an examination of the relationship between the member states and the Community and explores the transfer of sovereignty that is implied by a federal Community.

The supranational institutions

The Commission

The pivotal role assigned to the Commission replicated that of its forerunner the High Authority of the European Coal and Steel Community. Both the powers and the working procedure were largely shaped by the ideas and involvement of Jean Monnet, the first President of the High Authority. The creation of the Commission represented a radical innovation by combining a traditional bureaucratic role with a constitutional responsibility to protect and advance the objectives of the Treaty of Rome, thereby empowering the Commission with a very clear political character. In the formative years, under the strong leadership of President Walter Hallstein, the Commission sought to exploit these characteristics to the full, only to see their power curtailed by de Gaulle's rejection of the principle of the Community's own resources and the Community's acceptance of the Luxembourg Compromise. During the following decade the Commission has generally been described as being in decline. The introduction of the Committee of Permanent Representatives (COREPER), the management Committee procedure and the creation of the European Council all underscored the intergovernmental influence in decision-making and detracted from the Commission role as policy initiator (George, 1985, p. 12). Only with the appointment of Roy Jenkins in 1976 did the Commission begin to regain the important integration role envisaged in the original Treaty. His successor, President Gaston Thorn continued this rehabilitation, and from 1985–92 under President Delors, the Commission has largely regained its original political authority and has been instrumental in defining the shape of integration in the 1990s.

The 1965 *Treaty establishing a Single Council and a Single Commission of the European Communities* (the Merger Treaty) unified the separate High Authority of the European Coal and Steel Community with the Commission of the European Economic Community. The various Community treaties provide the Commission with numerous avenues through which it can influence decision-making both directly and indirectly. The Commission's responsibility for the 'proper functioning and development of the common market' is outlined in the Treaty of Rome: these are to 'ensure that the provisions of this Treaty and the measures taken by the institutions pursuant thereto are applied'; 'formulate recommendations or deliver opinions on matters dealt with in this Treaty, if it expressly so provides or if the Commission considers it necessary'; 'have its own power of decision and participate in the shaping of measures taken by the Council and by the Assembly [Parliament] in the manner provided for in this Treaty; exercise the powers conferred on it by the Council for the implementation of the rules laid down by the latter.' (Article 155)

These broad powers both provide the Commission with authority and constrain it by creating specific responsibilities. The political apex may be the European Council, but the integrative dynamic flows principally from the Commission. The independence of the Commission is demanded: as the central supranational institution, it is answerable only to the Community constitution, not to any member state. Thus Article 157 states that in performing their duties, the Commission 'shall neither seek nor take instructions from any Government or from any other body' and requires member states to respect this principle. The metamorphosis that all Commissioners are required to undertake, from national politician to public servant loyal exclusively to the Community, is remarkable and possibly unreasonable: what is even more remarkable is the extent to which past Commissioners have all been able to achieve this transformation, causing more than one government recently to complain that 'their' Commissioners had 'gone native'. However, the successful execution of the Commission's role demands this impartial approach; where Commissioners are perceived to be excessively partisan, the whole cohesion of the Commission's programme is threatened (Nugent, 1989, p. 57).

The independence of the Commission may be tarnished in an important way. Commissioners are appointed by national governments, and although the Commission as a whole has to be approved 'by common accord', there are no examples where a country's choice of Commissioner has ever been denied. In the past this procedure has required at least one Commissioner to be nominated by each member state with an additional Commissioner for the larger countries (France, Germany, Italy, Spain and the UK). It remains the exclusive right of each member state to appoint, reappoint or decide not to reappoint its Commissioner. The removal of Lord Cockfield by the UK after one term as a Commissioner is a healthy reminder of this ultimate power held by each member government. The Maastricht Treaty proposed certain changes, but left this appointment procedure intact. The choice of the President and the other members of the new Commission agreed to by common governmental accord is subject to the approval of the European Parliament. The selection of the Commission remains a national prerogative, if constrained by the qualification that Commissioners are 'chosen on the grounds of their general competence and whose independence is beyond doubt' (Article 157.1).

Commissioners are each assigned individual portfolios by the President and are responsible for policy development in these policy areas. The

President rarely has a free hand in this matter: negotiation, lobbying and concern for political balance all play important roles. It is often difficult to ignore the claims of second-term Commissioners or of particular country nominations who demand specific portfolios or recognition of seniority (Nugent, 1989, p. 58). The decision to put forward a proposal to the Council is made collectively, normally by unanimity, though majority voting can and does occur. A cohesive and effective Commission is essential for policy innovation and, by implication, for integration. The potential difficulties are considerable. The Commission itself has no control over its own composition and certainly since the first enlargement the probability that all the Commissioners would share a common political outlook is remote. Thus within the same policy-making body you will find a range of political views competing with and complementing each other. While this synergy may be dynamic and fruitful, it can also cause serious policy sclerosis, particular if political differences are overlaid with national partisanship.

The Commission's annual programme is set out by its President in the January European Parliament debate. In this address specific policy objectives are outlined and a political direction given to the integration process. The selection of President of the Commission is dependent on intergovernmental bargaining at the European Council level. While there is no strict principle of national rotation, there are clear assumptions by member states of an informal allocation of the office. The leading role ascribed to the President is crucial to the effective working of the Commission: but the President is given very few executive powers to control it. The President has no influence over the appointment of his or her fellow Commissioners; the technical freedom to assign portfolios to specific individuals is, in practice, considerably constrained by national government pressures; and the Presidency cannot remove an appointed Commissioner. Once appointed for a four-year term Commissioners can only be replaced in one of two ways: either the European Parliament can dismiss the entire Commission collectively; or individual Commissioners can be compulsorily retired from office by the Court of Justice on application from the Council or the Commission, where it can be established that the Commissioner 'no longer fulfils the conditions required for the performance of his (sic) duties or if he (sic) has been guilty of serious misconduct' (Merger Treaty, Article 13).

Current debate has focused on the democratic deficit within the Commission. Should this key Community institution continue to be selected by national political leaders, or should the European electorate have a direct say in who are to become the Community's Commissioners? As noted above, the lack of control over its composition and its non-elected nature places it in a precarious position. The Commission is collectively accountable to the European Parliament (the only Community institution that can dismiss it): in the Parliament a two-thirds majority of those voting provided that this exceeds half of those eligible to vote is required. This ultimate sanction has never been invoked and this blunderbuss approach to accountability is highly inappropriate: there is no mechanism for the censure or removal of specific Commissioners. Nugent has challenged whether it is even reasonable for the Commission to be held accountable at all in the current Community structure. Although it is responsible for policy initiatives, it has little autonomy over the fate of those proposals, the decision-making capacity is still predominantly an intergovernmental prerogative. Further, to be harangued by the Parliament is often illogical: generally, the Commission and the Parliament favour integration and the expansion of supranational authority and it is singularly inappropriate for the Parliament to censure its only institutional ally.

Despite these limitations, the Commission Presidency has attracted extremely high-calibre candidates who have generally held senior political office previously in their national governments. For example, the three Presidents to hold office between 1976 and 1992 can all be fairly described as leading national political figures. The first British President, Roy Jenkins, had been Chancellor of the Exchequer and Home Secretary in Harold Wilson's Labour governments; Gaston Thorn had served as Luxembourg's Prime Minister; and Jacques Delors was Finance Minister in Mitterrand's first administration. All three were committed Europeans, with Delors an open supporter of a federal Europe. The importance of the Presidency's commitment cannot be overstated; whether mischievous or fanciful, after her resignation the suggestion that Margaret Thatcher could be a candidate to succeed Delors as Commission President exposed the fragile basis of this key Community institution. The focus for supranational authority is, ultimately, decided according to intergovernmental demands.

The resurgence of the Commission under Delors has not gone unchallenged; some of the intergovernmental annoyance expressed was understandable given the often seeming direct provocation of President Delors. Adverse criticism was drawn in response to Delors's 1988 comment to the European Parliament that within a decade up to 80 per cent of current national economic, and possibly fiscal and social legislation would orginate at the Community level. In retaliation, Thatcher made her notorious Bruges speech in which she firmly rejected a federal Europe, a concept which she equated with a centralized state. Her disparaging remarks reflected the intensity of this division: misrepresenting the Community as seeking to achieve 'some sort of indentikit European personality' designed to remove cultural and traditional differences between countries, she declared '[W]e have not successfully rolled back the frontiers of the state in Britain, only to see them re-imposed at a European level, with a European super-state exercising a new dominance from Brussels.' (Nugent, 1989, p. 327) This caricature of the European idea refused to acknowledge the historical basis of the Community experiment; for Jean Monnet the strength and importance of the Community lay in its heterogeneity: reflecting on the 1950 Schuman proposal, he wrote 'Europe's unity will not put an end to her diversity – quite the reverse. That rich diversity will benefit civilization and influence the evolution of powers like America itself.' (1978, p. 310)

Opposition to Delors was not confined to a personal vendetta by the British Prime Minister. During the early IGC debates there was a concerted effort to reduce the traditional role of the Commission and to reinforce the intergovernmental component within the Community structure. The basic structural unity of the Community seemed under threat in an early version of the Luxembourg Presidency's treaty draft which proposed an intergovernmental-communautaire hybrid. A distinction was made between the functioning of the Community and of the new Union, with the latter being fundamentally intergovernmental and in control of the former. A three-pillared structure was proposed which separated the existing EC, foreign policy and internal and legal affairs: these three areas were not to be linked under a single treaty. The Commission was to be excluded from these purely intergovernmental activities and its role within the new Union structure limited to exclusively those affairs falling under the EC pillar. This marginalization was a direct challenge to the type of institutional structure envisaged in the founding treaties; indeed, the potential changes deprived the EC of its basic characteristic – a cohert single focus promoting full integration.

The contrast between this intergovernmental proposal and the Commission's earlier submissions on Union that emphasized the unicity of all Community activity (and the central role within this to be played by the Commission) could not have been greater. The Commission's response was immediate. A rebuttal to the Luxembourg document was issued on 21 May which appealed to the historical origins of the Community.

> 1. The Commission considers that the Intergovernmental Conference should be guided by the basic thinking which has been behind the construction of Europe for 40 years now, namely that all progress made towards economic, monetary, social or political integration should gradually be brought together in a single Community as the precursor of a European Union . . .
>
> This being so, it is somewhat paradoxical that the current trend in the Intergovernmental Conference favours a kind of revision of the Treaty of Rome that would depart from this general unification process and keep the Community no longer as the focal point but simply as one entity among others in a political union with ill-defined objectives and a variety of institutional schemes . . .
>
> 3. The Commission stands by its view set out in its opinion of 21 October 1990 that the main, indeed the central, objective of transforming the Community into a European Union should be to ensure the unity, the consistency and, as a result, the efficiency of its international activities . . .
>
> 4.b The unitary character of the European construction should be reflected in the structure of the Treaty. (Commission, 1991, pp. 1–3)

Subsequent discussion of Political Union at the Foreign Ministers meeting of 3 June in Dresden found majority support for the Commission's position. According to the integrationist Belgian Foreign Minister, Mark Eyskens, the Community had 'more or less righted the helm' by accepting the unitarian structure of any new treaty (*Agence Europe*, no. 5504, 3/4 June, 1991, p. 3), and the final version of the Luxembourg Draft Treaty preserved and reflected the unicity of the reform process.

That such a direct challenge to the role of the Commission should have even been contemplated illustrates the often precarious and disadvantaged position the Commission still holds in the Community structure. It can encourage and propose a federal communautaire structure, but the fate of the Community resides ultimately with the national governments. The symbiotic relationship between national and supranational authority envisaged in the original Community has been difficult to maintain: despite the resurgence under Delors, the Commission has become a less equal partner. While constitutionally free from national interference, the success of the Commission's policy proposals is dependent on the goodwill and support of the Council: the Treaty-based legitimacy and independent political authority of the Commission is rarely a match for intergovernmental opposition. To achieve its policy agenda the Commission has to construct favourable coalitions of support, in both the Council and Parliament.

Too often there are exaggerated reports comparing the Commission's administrative structure to some bureaucratic leviathan. In practice, the support staff of the Commission is modest when compared with the size of most national member state civil services. At the apex of this administrative structure each Commissioner has his or her own *cabinet* composed of around six individuals chosen personally. These appointments are temporary and staff can be drawn from the Commission's bureaucracy or seconded from national government service or political parties: at least one is expected to be a national from another member state. Each *cabinet* is organized by a *chef* whose is responsible for co-ordinating the weekly Commission meetings and for the preparation of the Commissioner's portfolio (Nicoll and Salmon, 1990, pp. 53–4; Nugent, 1989, p. 58). Below this elite level lies the bulk of the Commission bureaucracy totalling almost 12,000, one-fifth of whom are engaged in translation work. Recruitment to this administrative level combines selection on the basis of merit and of an equitable national balance across the member states. These administrators are assigned to specific Directorates General (DG), specialized policy agencies roughly equivalent to national ministries which are responsible for the overall work of the Commission. At the end of 1991 there were 23 Directorates General plus nine additional special units and support services. The DGs vary considerably in their size and importance: DGVI (Agriculture) and DGI (External Relations) have traditionally been the most senior, but with the expansion of the Community's competences through the SEA and thanks to the appointment of capable and ambitious Commissioners, other sectors such as DGXI (Environment, Consumer Protection and Nuclear Safety), DGIII (Internal Market and Industrial Affairs) or DGIV (Competition Policy) have recently grown in stature. Thus the Commission's bureaucratic structure is flexible and can respond to changing policy demands.

The Commission performs a range of supranational roles. Other than its policy-making function and the right of initiative (which is discussed later in this chapter), the Treaties have conferred specific powers on the Commission. It is responsible for the application of certain Community policies and participates in the policy amendment process (a combined executive and legislative function); is the guardian of the treaties with the right of redress through the Court of Justice (a supervisory function); and plays an important role in the Community's external relations (an international representation role). For specific policy areas the Commission has the authority to implement Community legislation (regulations, directives and decisions) directly. This authority is clearly prescribed and generally is confined to policy details implementing decisions already taken at the Council level. The Commission is active in exercising its powers under the ECSC Treaty, in relation to both the Community's Social and Regional development funds, the management of the budget, and most notably, with respect to the Common Agricultural Policy (Nugent, 1989, pp. 72–3). The SEA introduced a new procedure whereby the Council shared with the Commission its authority to implement decisions. Supplementing Article 145 of the Treaty of Rome, the new provisions 'confer on the Commission, in the acts which the Council adopts, powers for the implementation of the rules which the Council lays down' (Article 10). Thus the Commission's involvement straddles what in a national setting are clear lines of demarcation between administrative and executive functions underlining the unique character of the Community structure.

In its capacity as guardian of the Treaties, the Commission is responsible for ensuring that the provisions of the ECSC, EEC, Euratom and latterly the SEA and the Treaty on European Union are observed and honoured. As the Community's watch-dog, where the Commission is of the opinion that a Treaty requirement has been infringed or where there is a breach of Community legislation, the Commission possesses the authority to demand compliance and, where necessary, can subject the infringement to a Court of Justice ruling. Acting under Article 169 of the Treaty of Rome, the Commission delivers its reasoned opinion to the state involved specifying the precise infringement and requesting an explanatory report within a specified period, usually between one or two months. If the report is not forthcoming, or the response unsatisfactory, the Commission may, if it so wishes, submit the case to the Court of Justice for adjudication. The Court's findings are final and binding on all concerned. While there has been a noticeable upward trend in the number of infringement proceedings undertaken by the Commission, only a minority end in Court. Generally, compliance is forthcoming once the Commission draws a state's attention to an infringement. In 1970, only 50 infringement proceedings were begun, with just two going to the Court of Justice. By 1981 this had mushroomed to 135 reasoned opinions and 57 Court cases and by the end of the decade there were still 36 judgements that had not been complied with. This legislative impasse has been compounded since the introduction of the SEA. The Commission has been concerned with the slow transposition of the 282 Directives into national law needed to achieve the internal market: as of the beginning of 1991 just 110 Community Directives had been given effect by national legislation (EIU, 1991, p. 7).

As guardian of the treaties the Commission is as pro-active as possible within its limited personnel constraints. However, without direct powers of sanction itself, and with the compliance of Court ruling dependent on government acquiescence, yet again the tactical and practical advantages lay at the intergovernmental level. The existing Article 171 requires a member state 'to take the necessary measures to comply with the judgement of the Court of Justice', but provides the Court with no powers of sanction. This situation was partially addressed in the 1991 Maastricht Treaty (see Chapter 3). If it considers that the Court ruling has been ignored, the new Article 171.2 empowers the Commission to issue a further reasoned opinion specifying a deadline for compliance. If this is also ignored the Commission may take the offending state to court: '[I]n doing so it shall specify the amount of the lump sum or penalty payment to be paid by the Member State concerned which it considers appropriate in the circumstances.' The Court is then able to determine whether to impose the suggested sanction. This innovation potentially strengthens the supranational authority of the Commission and the Court of Justice significantly.

As the Community's development in the post-SEA period illustrates, the involvement of the Commission is indispensable to the creation of a supranational-based Union. Delors has done much to reclaim the Commission's rightful inheritance as the institutional catalyst for integration. However, as the challenge to both the Commission's natural role and the unicity of the Community that occurred in the early phase of the IGCs indicates, the future definition of the Commission's role within the new Union remains open. For Monnet and the Treaty framers, the Commission epitomized the central principle around which the Community idea was developed – supranationalism. The expectation that the Commission would progressively evolve into the kernel of a federal executive authority within a Union remains Utopian and at the mercy of future IGC reforms.

European Parliament

The original title of 'Assembly' found in the Treaty of Rome provides a clue to the confused personality of the European Parliament. Since 1957, this institution has undergone metamorphosis; its bugetary powers have grown; it has become popularly elected; its legislative contribution has been enhanced through the co-operation and co-decision procedures; and its right to consultation on appointments and certain aspects of external relations (such as enlargement and association agreements) formally recognized. These developments have not been without setbacks; the Luxembourg Compromise of 1966 stalled the extension of parliamentary powers, and despite reform concessions in both the SEA and the 1991 IGCs, many of the Parliament's more assertive and democratic aspirations have been thwarted. Increasingly, however, the Commission has come to view its supranational partner as instrumental to the wider process of Community integration. The call for a Union that is democratically accountable has placed the role and function of the European Parliament at centre stage in the reform process.

The original powers that the Assembly or Parliament could exercise were purely 'advisory and supervisory' (Article 137). The seeming absence of an autonomous legislative competence led many commentators to question the extent to which the European Parliament could legitimately be described as a parliament. This legislative incapacity was compounded by the apparent lack of other typical characteristics: executive supervision and budgetary control was fragmented, and 'its ability to perform information, education, communication, legitimation and representative functions was circumscribed' (Lodge, 1989, p. 64). However, the Parliament has very successfully exploited the limited original formal role assigned to it constitutionally since first becoming a directly elected chamber in 1979. Where the Treaty of Rome was silent, or provided for a possible parliamentary contribution, the Parliament has been eager to seize these opportunities and enhance its authority via convention and practice. This incrementalism was recognized and legally incorporated in the SEA and further clarified by the IGCs.

The Parliament's supervisory powers provide it with an ineffective mechanism for overseeing two of the Community's executive branches, the Commission and the Council of Ministers, and with no control whatsoever over the body at the apex of the Community structure, the European Council. As noted in the previous section, the Maastricht reforms empowered the Parliament with the right to approve the nomination of the Commission President (this innovation reflected what had been an informal practice during the Delors era). This complemented the Treaty of Rome Article 144, under which the Parliament may remove the Commission *en bloc*, but lacks the surgical precision to target a particular Commissioner. Furthermore, even where the Parliament dismisses the Commission (something it has occasionally contemplated but never done) it has no authority whatsoever to influence the appointment of the new Commission. If they so wished, the European Council acting intergovernmentally could reinstate the same Commission as a direct affront and challenge to Parliament's authority. Under Article 140 the Commission is required to reply either orally or in writing to questions raised by the European Parliament, and the annual programme of the Commission is subject to parliamentary debate. While such public scrutiny is an essential requirement for a democratic Community, the powers conferred on the Parliament in the Treaty of Rome are far from sufficient. During the 1980s the Parliament evolved a number of additional procedural mechanisms for examining executive power: for example, Parliament adopted a form of question time based upon the practice of the British House of Commons, and it gave its various committees a second-reading role and implied power to delay Council legislation. As the *Isoglucose* case ruling confirmed, the Parliament's opinion must be obtained before any Community legislation can be enacted (p. 64).

The major criticism of the European Parliament concentrates on its limited legislative function. While this has evolved considerably since 1979, both in practice and constitutionally through reforms, the legislative role for the Parliament remains generally a negative one: there is no balance of power between it and the dominant legislative body, the Council of Ministers. The European Parliament has no formal mechanisms for initiating legislation, this right residing, according to the treaties, exclusively with the Commission. A number of informal practices have accrued that give the Parliament an opportunity to indirectly contribute to the shape of the Community's legislative programme. For example, the force of quasi-convention is attributable to debates and reports that call on the Commission to investigate specific policies. Similarly, the investigative role of the Parliament's committee system can be instrumental in encouraging the Commission to consider drafting a proposal. However, all these procedures can only ever have the force of encouragement not of obligation. This inability to have a formal role in policy initiation must not be confused with the established right of Parliament to be consulted once the legislative process has begun. The Parliament may react, influence and under certain circumstances even prohibit legislation, but it cannot direct the legislative agenda.

The Parliament began to flex its fledgling muscles through two reforms introduced in the SEA: the assent and the co-operation procedures. The assent procedure stipulates that the European Parliament has to give its approval for treaties of accession or association to be valid. Thus future enlargements will need to meet the Parliament's conditions as well as those of the Council and Commission. Already this new authority has been exercised with the parliament refusing to renew an association agreement with Israel. The co-operation procedure empowers Parliament with a constitutional role for most of the legislation required to realize the Single Market of '1992'. Again, however, this involvement was limited to responding to proposals developed by the Commission and is not without qualifications. Ultimate authority remains largely with the Council and, as Pinder argues, '[W]hile the cooperation procedure gives the Parliament more influence over much Community legislation, it does not satisfy the principle of representative government, namely that legislative authority should be held by an assembly of the people's representatives' (1991, p. 206). The reality of Community legislation does not easily correspond to the concept of parliamentary sovereignty, either within the Community's own institutional structure, or between the European Parliament and the national parliaments. One mechanism advocated by the Parliament during the 1991 IGCs for redressing this imbalance was to establish a co-decision procedure providing for parity between the Council and the European Parliament. Such a radical proposal was floated in the Dutch Presidency's ill-fated IGC proposals; the widespread opposition to this supranationalism underlined the substantial intergovernmental constraints on democratizing the Community's decision-making procedures.

One area where the European Parliament has exercised a conspicuous degree of power is in financial control. When the Community was allocated its own financial autonomy, a degree of democratic control was introduced. The Parliament was given two specific powers: the ability to alter the shape of the budget as submitted by the Council and Commission; and the right to reject the budget in total. The Community's budgetary process distinguishes between compulsory and non-compulsory expenditure and provides the Parliament with considerable powers to amend proposals on the latter submitted by the Council. Compulsory expenditure predominantly covers spending related to the Common Agricultural Policy which, historically, has taken the bulk of the Community's funds: consequently, this parliamentary power was more latent than effective. However, the trend since the direct election of the Parliament in 1979 has been for the non-compulsory sector of the budget (such items as Social and Regional policy) to expand considerably. In 1991, for example, non-compulsory expenditure accounted for more than one third of the budget. For compulsory expenditure, the Parliament can attempt to alter specific items, but cannot challenge the total expenditure involved in this sector. This tinkering within a firm boundary stands in contrast to the Parliament's financial control over non-compulsory expenditure where it possesses a greater degree of discretion: its power even here, however, is not absolute. Parliament's ability is constrained by Article 203.9 of the EEC Treaty which sets a maximum rate for annual budgetary increase.

Since 1979, the European Parliament has used its power to approve the budget to great effect. Using Article 203.8, a two-thirds majority of the Parliament can reject the Community draft budget. The reasons for taking this drastic financial action are varied, but typically it has been used as a ploy to coerce the Council into budgetary revision. For example, this tactic was used by the new parliament in its first year after direct election; and yet on this and subsequent occasions, the real ability of the Parliament to force budgetary restraint on an unwilling Council is constrained. In the event of no budget being discharged, the Community operates under Article 204 which states that 'a sum equivalent to not more than one-twelfth of the budget appropriations for the preceding financial year may be spent each month'. Normally, this has the opposite effect of Parliament's intentions which is to expand the budget in the non-agricultural sectors; given inflation and the obligatory nature of CAP funding, maintaining the budget at the previous year's level fails to achieve the Parliament's objective. What has tended to happen is that the revised version submitted by the Commission and Council only differs in minor respects from the original budget that was rejected. However, given the chaos that tends to ensue under such conditions and the wasted time and energy that detracts from effective policy-making across all sectors, the Council has become more attentive to Parliament's concerns and sought to avoid such direct institutional confrontation.

The most obvious expression of the Parliament's supranational character is in its composition and behaviour. Originally the Rome Treaty paralleled the ECSC Paris Treaty and provided for national delegates to be appointed (until such time when direct elections could be introduced). Prior to 1979 there were 198 Members of the European Parliament (MEPs) appointed through the intergovernmental process of the dual mandate. This involved each of these MEPs being national as well as European representatives resulting, arguably, in neither responsibility being executed adequately. With the first direct elections in 1979 the Parliament can claim to be a supranational body, even if its membership is comprised from national quotas, not on the basis of the European electorate as a whole. The 1979 Parliament was comprised of 410 MEPs; successive enlargements saw this number rise to 518 for the third direct elections in 1989.

The allocation of MEPs to each member state is on a rough population basis. The minimum number of MEPs was set at six (to offer some degree of representation to Luxembourg which would only be eligible for a single representative on a strict proportionality rule) and the four largest member states are treated equally (France, Germany, Italy and the UK), each being allocated 81 seats. On its accession, Spain was deemed to be an intermediate case and given 60 MEPs; The Netherlands have 25 MEPs; Belgium, Greece and Portugal all 24 each; Denmark 16 and Ireland 15. During the process of reunification in Germany the question of increasing the total number of German MEPs was rejected; however, less than a year after the 3 October 1990 unification date the question of malapportionment was firmly on the Community agenda. One suggestion argued for German representation to be increased to 102, Italy's to 87 and France and the UK's to 86 MEPs to reflect population shifts. Given the expected significant enlargement of the Community before the end of the century, increasing the overall number of MEPs is a less attractive option to reapportioning individual country quotas within a maximum ceiling. The Parliament has consequently moved that the German allocation be set at 99 for the 1994 elections, with the total number of MEPs not to exceed 599 irrespective of the size of the future Community. This debate touches on a sensitive supranational and democratic issue: what is the logic behind having national quotas and national-based elections for the European Parliament; a federal integrated Community ought to adopt electoral characteristics that reflect the unicity of the European electorate, not reinforce the image of intergovernment-alism through national quotas and electoral laws (see Chapter 6 for an extended development of this theme).

The internal organization of the Parliament's business and the behaviour of MEPs emphasizes supranational over intergovernmental concerns: national political parties or national cross-party groupings are not recognized. The Parliament is organized through Political Groups which must be composed of more than one nationality or national political party. Political Groups are allocated speaking rights, chairs of committees and other parliamentary duties and resources. Thus while the basic allocation of seats is according to national quotas, once elected, MEPs do not sit in national blocks, but according to these transnational groupings. Thus for example, there were eleven Political Groups after the 1989 election: the two largest, the Socialist Group (180 MEPs) and the European People's Party (121) drew MEPs from all twelve Community states; to the other extreme, two Groups were only represented in three member states (the European Democratic Alliance with 20 MEPs; and, the European Right with 17), and one Group, the European Democrats, were composed of only British and Danish representatives in their total of 34 MEPs (Nicoll and Salmon, 1990, p. 67). This organizational requirement has had a very positive effect on developing supranational behaviour within the Parliament's deliberations: while the defence of nationalistic positions does still occur, the experience of the Parliament since its direct election predominantly has been towards addressing Community issues at the European not member state level. Although still rudimentary in many respects, a European party system is developing with several transnational Party Groups organizing manifestos, policies and programmes at the federal level.

Despite its many defects, the Parliament is an important supranational ally and a consistent intergovernmental opponent. As the 1991 IGC debates reflected, often it is left to the Parliament to remind the Community of its democratic shortcomings and the need for a pluralistic approach to legislative policy-making. The IGC reforms notwithstanding, the question can still legitimately be asked whether the European Parliament has become a parliament in a generally accepted sense. First, any such evaluation suffers from a difficulty in comparative methodology. There is no single list of parliamentary functions that can be used to make a valid comparison; functions differ in federal parliamentary systems, in unitary systems and in those systems that combined presidential with parliamentary features such as the Fifth Republic in France. To compound the confusion, the Community's vocation (federal, confederal or intergovernmental) has yet to be conclusively defined; consequently the nature of the Parliament and its appropriate functions are still difficult to prescribe. It may even be foolish to try to compare the European Parliament with its domestic counterparts; these various institutions may only share a similarity in nomenclature. The European Parliament does not perform a comparable legislative role or a governmental supporting function. Should we even wish to condemn it to the declining authority of so many national parliaments? To criticize its impotence (even in relation to national parliaments) may suggest a misunderstanding of the Community system and the unique role played by the European Parliament within it currently. The traditional function of the European Parliament has been as a representative, scrutinizing and consultative body, not a legislative parliament. However, while this could be defended in the original intergovernmental Community that expressed minimal transnational powers, such a limited role is no longer acceptable in the post-1992 Community of the Single Market. With the fundamental extension of the Community's competences into monetary union and domestic economies, Community development necessitates greater democratic control. The European Parliament has to be incorporated into the Community's legislative structure in a positive sense that will facilitate policy innovation as well as guarantee legislative scrutiny. However, as Pinder remarks, this 'reluctance to come to terms with the implications of Community legislation for parliamentary sovereignty may reflect a deeper concern about state sovereignty' (1991, p. 209). In this context, the 1991 reforms have been disappointing and have only succeeeded in shifting the issue of the European Parliament's role onto a future IGC agenda before the turn of the century.

The Court of Justice

The debate concerning the federal or intergovernmental nature of the Community does not rely exclusively on political interpretation: the Treaty of Rome provided the EC with a legal framework through which specific supranational authority is legitimated and exercised. Effective decision-making within the EC is dependent, to a large degree, on this legal code and on the Court of Justice's supervision and rulings. As Nugent argues, only through the uniform application of common laws can common policies be guaranteed; without this discipline, decisions risk becoming intergovernmental agreements often facilitating inconsistent application between the member states (1989, p. 143). The original and limited power conferred on the Community by the Treaty has been extended through both practice and constitutional reform, and increasingly this law-based Community authority has constrained the legal sovereignty of the member states. By signing treaties of accession, each member state accepts that in those areas where the Community has explicit treaty competences, Community law takes precedence over all forms of national legislation. This legal expression of supranationalism indicates that the Community is 'endowed with independent authority, with its own sovereign rights and a legal order independent of the Member States to which both the Member States and their citizens are subject in matters for which the Community is competent' (European Documentation, 1991, p. 9).

As a legal system, the Community draws on a precise set of constitutional rules. The most important of these are the founding treaties, although these are supplemented by legal instruments, values and custom to form a comprehensive constitutional framework. Thus the Community's legal character reflects its commitment to democracy, the maintenance of peace, unity, equality, fundamental rights and freedom, solidarity and security (pp. 10–14). It is the application of Community law that gives these constitutional provisions a meaningful substance. Wherever the Community acts, the rule of law applies to legitimate or to limit behaviour. The scope of the Community's competences distinguish it from the national states that make up its composition. It does not possess universal jurisdiction: only where there is an explicit treaty-based competence can the Community legitimately act. Nor do the Community institutions possess the power to increase their competences through their own decisions; this can only be achieved through an intergovernmental conference where the principle of unanimity governs.

Before examining the composition and functions of the Court of Justice, the Community's legal system needs to be outlined. There are two basic sources of Community law. Primary Community legislation is derived from the founding treaties and their later revisions which lay down the basic framework for Community objectives; secondary legislation is derived from law enacted by the Community institutions in the exercise of their powers as conferred by these treaties (pp. 24–5). The Community possesses a range of legal instruments to exercise its authority. Although the ECSC Treaty differs in its use of terms from both the EEC and Euratom Treaties, broadly speaking, the Community can act through five different legislative avenues: through regulations; directives; decisions; recommendations; and opinions. (A Commission proposal to the 1991 IGCs to introduce new categories of Community law was rejected by the Twelve in favour of the status quo.) These categories of legislation can be adopted by either the Council of Ministers or by the Commission and the precise operational differences between these types of Community legislation are set out in the Treaties. Thus,

> A regulation shall have general application. It shall be binding in its entirety and directly applicable in all Member States.
> A directive shall be binding, as to the result to be achieved, upon each Member

State to which it is addressed, but shall leave to the national authorities the choice of form and methods.

A decision shall be binding in its entirety upon those to whom it is addressed.

Recommendations and opinions shall have no binding force. (Article 189)

Regulations are by far the most important acts at the Community's disposal and they confer on the Community its most effective legal supranational tool. Their three characteristics of 'general application', 'binding in its entirety' and 'directly binding' mean that regulations constitute identical legislation across all member states, that they apply in full, and that legislation does not have to be transposed into national domestic legislation prior to implementation, but takes direct and immediate effect in each member state superseding any existing national provisions (Hartley, 1988, p. 99). Member states and their legal systems are thus bound directly by Community law and are required to comply fully with its provisions.

Community directives are also 'binding', but not in the uniform sense as required by regulations. Rather, directives are binding on those to whom they are addressed as to the results to be achieved, but leave the exact means to the discretion of each national government to interpret in a way consistent with their own legislative tradition. In essence, they specify objectives, but do not dictate precise details for implementation. Experience has shown that often common policies (particularly controversial ones) are only acceptable where these are enacted via the comparatively liberal regime of directives, not through the more disciplined regulations, betraying an intergovernmental preference on the part of some member states – and one that has occasionally led to a breach of good faith in the application of Community policy. In a more positive sense, it is often sensible to allow legislation to be enacted via directives where special national circumstances would make a uniform law inappropriate: directives can 'achieve the necessary measure of unity while preserving the multiplicity of national characteristics' (European Documentation, 1991, p. 27). As such, directives are the most common legislative form for achieving legislative harmonization (for example, in realizing the Single Market project of 1992), and where states neglect to comply with their requirements, directives, like regulations, have the right of redress through the Court of Justice. Consequently, while a less rigid option and open to possible circumvention, with adequate supervision and through the Court's authority, directives can be an effective supranational legislative instrument.

Decisions can be as effective as regulations or directives, but in general this legislative option is used where a specific state, institution or individual is addressed. Recommendations and opinions are simply that: they carry no obligations and as such, there is some debate as to whether they constitute a Community legislative instrument. However, in its rulings the Court has referred to these alternatives and provision is made for them in the treaties. In particular, the European Parliament's opinion and recommendations are sought across a range of topics and as the *Isoglucose* ruling of 1979 established, where the Community ignores the requirement to obtain Parliament's opinion, such legislation is in breach of the Community's constitution and can be struck down by the Court.

As a general principle, Community and national law work in tandem; without the various national legal frameworks, the Treaty of Rome would not in itself be sufficient to enact the Community's objectives. The governmental and legal system in each member state is required to implement, monitor and give effect to EC law (particularly directives). There exists, therefore, a natural symbiosis. However, as is obvious, where two systems of law are brought together there will be, on occasions, conflicts and incompatibilities that will require clear principles for ascertaining which law is superior. It is in this situation that two aspects of Community law, and the role of the Court in upholding them, present the greatest challenge to the authority of the nation-state within the Community: the direct applicability of Community law; and the primacy of Community law over conflicting national legislation (pp. 39–43).

The Court through its case history has established beyond doubt the legality of the directly applicable characteristic of Community regulations, not just over states and institutions, but for individuals as well. This has led to the establishment of a range of individual rights (such as the freedom of movement, of establishment and to provide services) that run counter to existing national rules. Where such a conflict exists, the second characteristic, the primacy of Community law comes into play. Surprisingly, none of the original Community treaties provide a clear statement pertaining to the superiority of EC legislation where conflict exists with pre-existing national legislation. Logically, for the Community to realize the objectives as expressed in the Treaty of Rome, EC law has to take precedence. Again, it is Court of Justice case law that has resolved this dilemma by providing two constitutional clarifications. First, through signing treaties of accession, member states have transferred sovereign rights to the Community which cannot unilaterally be revoked. And secondly, a basic Treaty principle is that no member state can question the status of Community law as a uniformly applicable system throughout the Community. Thus, EC law 'has priority over any conflicting law of the member states. Not only is it stronger than earlier national law, but it also has a limiting effect on laws adopted subsequently' (p. 43). Further case law has even extended this principle to give primacy to Community law over national constitutional law. Critics of the Community's democratic deficit complain that this 'superior' legislation lacks a democratic component as the European Parliament is not, necessarily, involved. Quite properly from a Community constitutional perspective, the appointed Commission can through its delegated powers impose regulations, say in the field of agriculture, that override the decisions of democratically elected national parliaments.

The Court of Justice forms part of the EC's institutional framework; however, its dominant characteristic is its independence and it is responsible for the supervision of the application of the treaties and the various Community laws created. The need for such a supreme arbitor was common to the ECSC structure as well as the Rome Treaty. The Court's role is not simply confined to the administration of the Community's legal system; it has also been a significant actor in defining supranational authority through its shaping, interpretation and extension of Community law. In general, it has 'defined the principles on which the Community legal order rests, thereby providing the process of European integration with a firm foundation' (p. 21). For example, through its activities, the Court of Justice has created case law that honours the spirit of the founding treaties. This pragmatic development corresponds to its constitutional functions as expressed in Article 164 of the Treaty of Rome which requires that the Court 'ensure that in the interpretation and application of this Treaty the law is observed'. This creation of judicial law is also of particular benefit to a supranational Community; rather than having to rely on a comprehensive and detailed legislative authority, key court rulings have established principles that can then be applied in a general sense for that category of Community activity. Thus a principle function of the Court is to interpret Community law and to ensure its consistent and uniform application (Nugent, 1989, p. 154).

The independence of the Court's thirteen judges and six Advocates-General is beyond doubt; they are appointed by common accord by the governments of the member states for terms of six years and they sit in six chambers. There are various types of proceedings that the Court can hear and its competences have been extended by the Single European Act. These can be summarized under the following headings:

actions for failure to fulfil obligations under the Treaties (normally brought by the Commission against member states);

actions by one member state against another;

actions on grounds of failure to act (usually taken against either the Council or the Commission);

actions for annulment of binding legal acts (can be brought by the Council, Commission, member state or in certain instances by individuals);

references from national courts for preliminary rulings to clarify the meaning and scope of Community law; and,

claims for damages against the Community. (European Documentation, 1991, p. 22; Nicoll and Salmon, 1990, pp. 73–5).

From a federalist perspective, the greatest potential weakness in the Community's legal system has been the lack of any direct punitive sanctions available to the Court. Where a transgression of Community law or the spirit of the treaties is proven, the Court's only option is to instruct the guilty state or institution to comply with the Community law: the Court has no direct powers to guarantee compliance. It is argued that a fundamental component of the *acquis communautaire* is the acceptance by all member states of the authority of the Court and that compliance must be forthcoming. Following from this, traditionally it has been suggested that were the Court to be given the power to sanction member states to comply against their will, such an imposed judicial form of integration would undermine the collective solidarity of the Community and actually be detrimental to the integration process as a whole. This interpretation was challenged during the 1991 IGCs. Experience had shown that while there were no examples of any member state refusing to comply with a Court ruling, many states were excessively tardy in applying a ruling made against them – delays of over two years were not unknown. Such delays, particularly in relation to establishing the Single Market, led to the introduction of sanctions available to the Court (see discussion above).

It should hardly be surprising given the Community's legal structure and formal constitutional provisions that the Court of Justice has an extremely high work-load. From 1953–85 the Court heard 3,727 direct actions, received 1,444 preliminary questions referred by national courts and made 2,094 judgements (Nicoll and Salmon, 1990, p. 76). There has been a noticeable explosion in the number of cases heard and judgements given since the 1980s: a normal load became between 300–400 compared with an average of 50 per year in the 1960s (Nugent, 1989, p. 162). This enormous case-load that the Court has traditionally had to cope with, and the substantial increase during the 1980s, led to the introduction via the Single European Act of a Court of First Instance (provided the Council was in unanimous agreement to do so). This court was limited to hearing 'points of law only . . . certain classes of action or proceeding brought by natural or legal persons' (Article 32d.1): it was not competent to hear actions brought by member states or other Community institutions. The Council finally agreed to create a Court of First Instance composed of twelve judges in a decision dated 24 October 1988 and its jurisdiction covers the ECSC Treaty, competition law, anti-dumping law and staffing regulations for Community employees (European Documentation, 1991, p. 23). The Court's role was confirmed in the 1992 Maastricht Treaty (Article 168a).

The contribution of the Court has been instrumental in defining and enhancing the supranational scope of the Community. Through its case law and Treaty interpretations it has proven to be an impeccable adversary of intergovernmentalism. The importance of having an impeccable legal basis on which to construct and develop an *acquis communautaire* cannot be undervalued. While member states may challenge the unwritten political philosophy underpinning the Community ideal, they are unable to refute the clear legal supranational authority of the Community institutions and system of law. This force of legal recognition and compliance touched a particularly sensitive intergovernmental nerve when it was suggested that reform of the Treaties included specifying a 'federal vocation'. As the Community's reluctant integrationist states knew through experience, any such formal commitment once incorporated into the Community's constitution will have the full force of law and be used to great effect by the Court in its future rulings.

The Intergovernmental Institutions

The Council of Ministers

The Council of Ministers represents the Janus face of the Community looking, simultaneously, towards both a federal and an intergovernmental future.

The commonly recognizable face of the Council is its representation of the strong intergovernmentalist strand entwined within the Treaty of Rome. Countless examples of member states using the Council to defend their particular national interests can be cited as evidence of this proclivity; but the alternative image cannot be ignored. It must be acknowledged that within the Community's institutional structure the Council remains the main forum through which supranational developments can be advanced. The Commission can propose, the Parliament cajole and the Court reprimand, but the necessary prerequisites for the Community to realize the integrative union envisaged by Monnet remain the Council's acquiescence, its support and goodwill. These antagonistic roles, although seemingly mutually exclusive, exist in tandem, and have been the dynamic behind Community integration since the signing of the treaties.

As already discussed, the introduction of a Council of Ministers within the institutional structure of the ECSC and the EEC was the necessary compromise that Monnet and his colleagues had to accept to gain a commitment from the original Six to establish the Community system based on supranational authority (represented by the High Authority and the Commission). This 'balance' has been a precarious one, too dependent on domestic political influence than on exclusively Community interests. As the historical review outlined in Chapter 2 suggested, the responsibility for the Community's chequered development, oscillating between periods of dynamic change and those of stagnation and regression, rests primarily with the Council. Despite the significant progress achieved since the mid-1980s, the Council remains an unpredictable body and the most stubborn proponent of an intergovernmental alternative to a Europe of a 'federal vocation'.

The Council performs both an executive and a legislative function within the Community. For most matters it is the Community's exclusive decision-making centre; while the Commission can enact a number of technical measures, for any substantive decision the Council's approval is required. As already noted, the title of legislature rests more comfortably with the Council than with the European Parliament. There is not, of course, a single Council of Ministers that determines all Community business; the Council is convened according to the topic under discussion. Thus, for example, if transport is under discussion the twelve national Ministers for Transport or their substitutes constitute the Council; if the topic is the monetary convergence and the Exchange Rate Mechanism, then the respective Finance Ministers or Chancellors of the Exchequer convene as the relevant Council. Thus there is a variable geometry in personnel, though never in number: all member states are represented on all Councils, cementing institutionally the principle of intergovernmental representation. There is also a marked variation in the frequency with which each Council meets; normally, the three most important Councils, the Agricultural Council, the Economic and Financial Council (ECOFIN) and the Foreign (General) Affairs Council meet monthly. Obviously the urgency or inherent importance of specific topics will determine the schedule for each Council. For example, those Councils directly concerned with the realization of the

Single Market of '1992' have been particularly active since the signing of the Single European Act. The required work-load can be almost excessive given that all members of the Council are also expected to perform simultaneously their domestic ministerial functions. It is interesting to note that the outcry about MEPs who hold a double mandate (serving as domestic as well as European parliamentarians), has never been extended to the obligatory double mandate for all members of the Council of Ministers. To combat this work-load, Ministers may be replaced by a lower-ranking member of their government.

The mutable nature of representation within the Council is both logical and a practical necessity; none the less, it can lead to political dilemmas. Where a less senior official is sent to substitute for a particular Minister, decision-making can be impeded as 'a reduction in the status and political weight of a delegation may make it difficult for binding decisions to be agreed' (Nugent, 1989, p. 91). In contrast, on occasions, Ministers have made agreements in the spirit of collegiality that go beyond their permissible brief, leading to either a rebuke by their national parliament or a retraction by their Prime Minister, or President, as in the case of France. However, this organizational principle of creating separate but linked Councils can assist a Community-based focus for integration. An *espirit communautaire* can develop between individual Ministers and often the rate of progress within each Council portfolio reflects the personal relationships between the respective Ministers. It is often easier for lower-ranking Ministers to concede issues during a Council meeting than it would be for John Major, Helmut Kohl or François Mitterrand to do so in the full glare of media attention. Thus an unexpected consequence of the organization of the Council of Ministers has been to facilitate compromise: it is rare for any country or Minister to achieve their objectives through consistent confrontation and isolation; as various Community policy-making studies have confirmed, the Community works on the basis of reciprocity and bargaining package deals. This contribution to the integration process is incremental and *ad hoc* certainly, but as such it is compatible with the strategy advocated by Monnet.

For each Council to operate effectively the preparatory work for the various individual meetings needs to be efficient and thorough. To assist the Council's political élite, topics for discussion are examined by the Committee of Permanent Representatives (COREPER), the Council's General Secretariat and the various working groups. COREPER is in fact divided into two sections and constitutes a particularly important body of national ambassadors who have the delegated authority to agree on behalf of their national governments to issues that are not controversial. A significant number of Council decisions are taken at this level, with the Council simply ratifying this diplomatic recommendation by conferring its approval collectively at a full Council of Ministers meeting. For more controversial issues, COREPER clarifies the points of contention in order to focus the political debate in the relevant Council of Ministers. COREPER is supported in this preparatory work by teams of member state officials organized hierarchically into working groups totalling some 150, and by the Council's General Secretariat.

No matter at what level, the policy-making process is dependent on negotiation and a common commitment to Community objectives. This Community style is of a different nature to traditional bilateral relations, and it is this difference that empitomized the uniqueness of the Community system for Monnet: he believed that the 'Council's task is to arrive at a common view, not to seek a compromise between national interests' (Monnet, 1978, p. 381). This expectation has become an increasing reality for the Community: however, inventing mechanisms for divining a 'common view' has seen the Community resort to voting procedures. The original treaties foreshadowed a move away from unanimity to majority voting within a short number of years. The Luxembourg Compromise forestalled this supranational tendency for two decades. The reforms enacted by the Single European Act have seen qualified majority voting extended both formally (for those areas specified in the Act) and informally as the practice has become the accepted normal procedure for a range of Community affairs. The definition of a qualified majority required by the Council is not a minimal one. Each country is allocated a notional number of votes which collectively amount to 76; 54 votes are needed to secure a qualified majority decision. The four largest states are each allocated ten votes, reducing proportionately down to two votes for Luxembourg. The practical effect of this distribution is that the four largest states cannot force through a majority decision that is opposed by the other eight member states; nor is it possible for two of these larger states to block a decision; a minimum of three states are required. By these rules, the interests of the Community's smaller states are protected at least procedurally, and the tendency for intergovernmental vetoes being constructed diminished somewhat. The preference is still to avoid formal voting where possible, but the removal of the implied veto suggested by the Luxembourg Compromise has encouraged states not to impede a decision where a clear majority exists. While the Community's decision-making process has yet to be perfected, since the mid-1980s it has become a streamlined and more efficient procedure.

The final area where the Janus face of the Council is evident is in the role of the presidency. Here, depending on the political objectives of each member state when holding the presidency, Community integration can be advanced or retarded. The presidency is responsible for setting the tone as well as the agenda for the Community on the basis of a six-monthly alphabetical rotation; the current size of the Community means that each state can only hold the presidency once every six years, a limitation that can frustrate some of the Community's more established international actors. However, it would be misleading to overstate the leadership role of the presidency: each country exercising this authority can only do so within the boundaries of what is commonly accepted. As Helen Wallace has correctly observed, 'while the presidency cannot substitute for political agreement, it can help to provide the conditions which foster consensus' (1985, p. 10). Persuasion and organizational skill are the presidency's most useful instruments; the presidency has no additional or even implied powers of veto, or additional voting strength in the Council. The political limitations of the presidency's ability to shape the Community's agenda were starkly highlighted during the 1991 Dutch Presidency's handling of the IGCs. The Dutch inherited the Draft Treaty as devised by the previous Luxembourg Presidency; however, they sought to instil a greater 'federal vocation' into their new version of the treaty. This direct use of the presidency to control the debate was comprehensively thwarted by a majority of member states who viewed the Dutch proposals as going too far beyond what had been agreed in common, confirming Wallace's dictum that 'the presidency cannot substitute for political agreement'. The Dutch were obliged to take the humiliating precedent of rescinding their proposal and readopting the Luxembourg draft as the basis for the conclusion of the IGC process in Maastricht in December 1991.

The Council remains the focus for criticism because of its inherently intergovernmental characteristics. While these have been modified through practice and by procedural reforms introduced by the Single European Act, the Council remains the most important barrier to a federal European Community, through its representation of explicit national interests. The Council does attempt to devise 'common views', but unlike the Commission it is under no constitutional commitment to promote *communautaire* solutions. If the Council collectively wishes to develop exclusively intergovernmental forms of integration, then there is very little any of the other Community institutions can do to counteract this. For those integrationists depressed by this reality, it should be acknowledged that the political objectives of the Council, in so far as there is a collective view on this, are constantly adapting to domestic changes in government. General elections, resignations of governments or of prime ministers are no longer purely domestic political events; there are significant repercussions for the Community and the political balance within the Council, as the removal of Mrs Thatcher, as British Prime Minister, bears witness. Consequently, an anti-supranational Council may be a transitory phenomenon, not a permanent feature. While the Community idea remains an 'experiment' and no outcome is as yet assured, the experience of collegiality and collective decision-making has had a clear impact upon the general behaviour of the Council, and the Community of the 1990s appears to have regained some of the earlier vision and commitment associated with both Monnet and Schuman in the 1950s.

The European Council

The other institution where the role of the presidency is replicated is in the European Council. Again, each presidency is responsible for organizing European Council business during its tenure and can have an important role in setting the agenda for the meetings. With the signing of the SEA the status of the European Council was transformed from its extra-Treaty origins to being fully incorporated and recognized in the Community's constitutional arrangements. Prior to this legal recognition, the European Council technically had acted outside the Treaties and was not empowered to make Community-based decisions, a situation more reminiscent of *Alice in Wonderland*, than *realpolitik*. The European Council brings together the Heads of State or of Government of the member states at least twice a year in order to discuss broad Community objectives and politically important policies and issues. The *raison d'être* behind formalizing these meetings in 1975 under the rubric of the European Council was to provide a clear focus for leadership in the wake of the Community's first enlargement. Its role can easily be differentiated from that played by the Council of Ministers: the European Council was not intended to be a forum where policy technicalities were to be discussed, or where majority voting was to be active. These were the legitimate domains of the Council of Ministers. Rather, the European Council was charged with seeking to establish a common European perspective at the macro-level: matters of principle, the Community's vision and future role were to be its concerns. In order to facilitate these general goals, European Council meetings combine the necessary structured meeting of experts and advisers with the more informal 'Gymnich' style gatherings where the involvement of officials is kept to a minimum, allowing the twelve national leaders to discuss Community matters frankly and at a personal level.

The European Council's record as the Community's potential supranational conclave is mixed. An early criticism of the meetings was that their agendas were too expansive and ambitious to facilitate significant policy development; often, the resultant declarations added little new in the way of substance to the Community's pre-existing positions. A further problem became evident between 1979 and 1984 when successive European Council meetings became subsumed by the intra-Community budgetary disputes, the so-called 'British problem', at the expense of less parochial European and international issues. The four European Council meetings between June 1979 and June 1980 were all dominated by this issue, as were many of the Council's subsequent meetings until the resolution of this issue at the 1984 Fontainebleau meeting. With the SEA relaunch the European Council has regained much of its lost prestige and reclaimed its instrumental role within the Community. It has become particularly involved in five categories of activity: the Community's economic and social situation; global economic and monetary issues; global political issues; specific Community issues; and the Community's constitutional reform and institutional relations (Bulmer and Wessels, 1987).

It is easy to criticize the European Council for its cautious achievements; but no matter how modest these may have been, the European Council is the only venue where they can be realized without incurring the reflex of an intergovernmental response. Agreements at this level can transcend the technical and parochial obstacles that lie in the path towards Community integration. Consequently, the European Council is the most powerful of the Community institutions for relaunching the Community on a new level of integration. The two decisions to establish intergovernmental conferences in 1985 and 1991 both sprang from European Council meetings.

Indeed, without this highest-level support, treaty reform and fuller integration would be in practice, difficult to achieve. The European Council's deliberations set the tone and the boundaries for the member state discussions in the Council of Ministers. As such, the European Council is essential to the development of a supranational Community; paradoxically, it can simultaneously be the primary intergovernmental barrier to further integration. Its role is subject to the political complexion of its twelve national members, and fraught with all the dangers and compromises that such a situation implies.

The evolving nature of the Community system makes a definitive conclusion as to its nature precarious and contextually specific. Indeed the pace of change since the mid-1980s has been remarkable: the Community of 1984 and the Community of 1992 and beyond differ in important ways. By way of illustration, academic writings prior to the relaunch of the SEA were dominated by the idea of a 'two-speed' Europe and of an ingrained intergovernmental authority; the federalist thrust of the Tindemans Report had been well and truly countered. Unexpectedly, the *communautaire* breakthrough of the SEA, the Single Market and the 1991 IGCs transformed this stultifying inertia into a new integrative dynamic. The catch-phrase of 'deepening and widening' emphasizing a supranational commitment replaced the fragmented nation-state orientations of the early 1980s. The key principle that facilitated this metamorphosis was the rediscovery of subsidiarity as a mechanism for achieving a decentralized form of federalism (see Chapter 8 for a fuller discussion).

The introductory theme of this chapter questioned whether the Community system was responsible for undermining the sovereignty of the nation-state, or whether it was simply a reflection of the global decline in independent nation-state authority. The symbiotic relationship between the member states and the Community is undergoing a significant transformation; the transition is from a nation-state dominated association to one that is becoming increasingly Community focused. Ascertaining cause and effect in this process is far more difficult than providing a descriptive account, particularly given the seeming paradox of pan-European developments since the fall of the Berlin Wall in November 1989. It is valid to question whether the Community's overt desire to create a Union is historically and politically incompatible with the wave of national sovereignty that has swept those countries formerly identified with Eastern Europe. Despite the apparent resurgence of national identity and the rejection of federations in the Soviet Union and Yugoslavia, the Community system cannot be legitimately compared to the federal marriages of convenience or coersion that until recently described the eastern half of the continent. The underlying principle that structures the Community is that there is a transferring and pooling of sovereignty through a legally binding treaty entered into voluntarily. This new Community system, despite the fears of intergovernmentalists, does not inevitably lead to a centralized federal organization. Even under the 1991 Treaty revisions, the member states remain the dominant actors: the pooling of sovereignty does not diminsh national sovereignty but enhances it.

Despite the historic events of the 1990s, the longer term trend in Western Europe has been towards co-operation, as in the case of EFTA, or integration, as in the Community. The agreement to create a European Economic Area (EEA), comprising of the member states of EFTA and the EC, has confirmed this tendency, particularly as two of the seven EFTA countries have already applied for full Community membership and at least two others are expected to apply during 1992. To coincide with the EC's own Single Market timetable, there is scheduled to be the free movement of goods produced in the EEA, of services, capital and of people within this new grouping of 19 countries. The contrast between the creation of the EEA and the dissolution of former East European federal organizations is misleading in its simplicity. There is nothing necessarily incompatible with the reassertion of nationhood in Europe and the simultaneous linking of a wider range of European countries through economic association. Such developments do not stand in conflict with the earlier aspirations behind the creation of the European Community; rather, the Community's inclusive nature was a characteristic strongly advocated by Monnet and his colleagues. As his *Memoirs* reveal, his vision of the Community was never limited to the original Six or constrained by existing political and constitutional realities:

> . . . the countries of Western Europe must turn their national efforts into a truly European effort. This will be possible only through a *federation* of the West . . .
> We can never sufficiently emphasize that the six Community countries are the forerunners of a broader united Europe, whose bounds are set only by those who have not yet joined. Our Community is not a coal and steel producers' association: it is the beginning of Europe. (1978, pp. 272–3; 392)

References

Bulmer, S. and Wessels, W., 1987, *The European Council*, Macmillan, London.

Commission of the European Communities, 1991, *Political Union: the structure of the Draft Treaty. Contribution by the European Commission to the Intergovernmental Conference*, 21 May, Commission of the EC, Brussels (reproduced in *Agence Europe: Europe Documents* No. 1715, 31 May 1991).

EIU (Economist Intelligence Unit), 1991, *European Trends*, No. 1.

European Documentation, 1991, *The ABC of Community law*, Office for the Official Publications of the European Communities, Luxembourg.

George, S., 1985, *Politics and policy in the European Community*, Clarendon Press, Oxford.

Hartley, T. C., 1988, *The foundations of European Community law* (2nd edn.), Clarendon Press, Oxford.

Lodge, J. (ed.), 1989, *The European Community and the challenge of the future*, Pinter, London.

Monnet, J., 1978, *Memoirs* (trans. R. Mayne), Doubleday and Company, New York.

Nicoll, W. and Salmon, T. C., 1990, *Understanding the European Communities*, Barnes and Noble, Savage, Maryland.

Nugent, N., 1989, *The government and politics of the European Community*, Macmillan, London.

Pinder, J., 1991, 'The European Community, the rule of law and representative government: the significance of the intergovernmental conferences', *Government and Opposition*, 26–2, pp. 199–214.
Wallace, H., 1985, 'The Presidency: tasks and evolution' in O'Nuallain, C. (ed.), *The Presidency of the European Council of Ministers*, Croom Helm, London.

5 Creating a common foreign policy

The control of foreign policy is central to the intergovernmental–federal debate on European Union. To the one extreme the creation of a common European foreign policy is equated with a federal Community: to the other, the Community appears tantamount to a purely intergovernmental association while the conduct of external foreign relations remains a national concern. Like all such dichotomies, although appealing in their simplicity, reality is more complex: the combination of both national and supranational authority has existed in the Community in the past, and it is this hybrid that is likely to persist at least through the 1990s.

This chapter is divided into two sections. First, the various attempts to develop a collective Community foreign policy are traced, beginning with the failed initiatives of the 1950s, the experience of European Political Cooperation (EPC) in the 1970s and 1980s and the contemporary expression of joint action, the Community's Common Foreign and Security Policy (CFSP) as proposed in the 1992 Treaty on European Union. The procedures, mechanisms and instruments available to the Community are investigated. Secondly, alternative theoretical frameworks for understanding the EC's foreign policy behaviour are presented. Against this theoretical discussion a series of case-studies drawn from international events of the 1990s are examined to illustrate the capabilities and limitations of Community foreign policy: the Gulf war; the Yugoslavian conflict; the aborted Soviet coup; and the Community's response to the abolition of apartheid in South Africa. These different foreign policy and external relations activities are used to highlight the instruments and options available to the Community. Based on this overall Community record in international affairs, the question is posed whether the Community constitutes an international actor in its own right, and can be regarded as comparable and equal to other state actors in the international system.

The origin and development of European Political Cooperation

As we have already seen; for Monnet, Europe could 'not be built all at once, or as a single whole', but rather by 'concrete achievements' encouraging a real sense of European solidarity (1978, p. 300). Consequently, the initial emphasis on creating institutions that could provide a basis for European consolidation precluded the incorporation of 'high politics' (international relations) into the functional 'low politics' (economic integration) described in the Treaty of Rome. The ultimate aim of Monnet was for a full federation which included political union and a single foreign policy for the Community; in 1957, however, such supranationalism was tempered by the experience of the putative European Political Community and European Defence Community (see Chapter 2).

Despite the seeming 'economic' exclusiveness of the original Community, within the Treaty of Rome there were at least the seeds, all be they scattered and poorly cultivated, of an international political role for the Community. The Treaty stipulated five areas in which the Community had an external role:

i)   the provision for a Common Trade Policy (Article 113);
ii) the association with Overseas Territories (Article 132);
iii) the association agreements with third countries (Article 238);
iv) the power to conclude international treaties (Article 228); and
v)   the ability of the EC to receive and establish diplomatic missions (Rhein, 1989, p. 1).

With the decision for the first enlargement of the Community, the 'political' content of these roles became pronounced as the Community of the then Nine sought to add a new impetus to the scope and depth of the integration process. According to Tsakaloyannis, the emergence of EPC was also facilitated by the superpower crises of the late 1960s (the Soviet invasion of Czechoslovakia, the American Tet offensive in Vietnam); the view that the fortunes of EPC 'have been inextricably linked with the vagaries of the international environment, in particular the twists and turns in relations between the superpowers', has been a consistent theme throughout the development of Community foreign policy (1991, p. 36). It was in this context that The Hague Heads of State and Government meeting of 1969 first launched European Political Cooperation as a prospective EC collective foreign policy, although the critics of EPC would probably argue that it was a pleasant substitute for the harsher realities of a common foreign policy. Whatever its purpose, the early 1970s witnessed the transformation of the EC's external relations from those technical issues supervised by the Commission, into a real political content tantamount to a recognizable foreign policy.

It is essential to acknowledge that the origin and much of the history of EPC has been versed in intergovernmentalism outside the formal provision of the Treaty of Rome. It is generally agreed that EPC as originally an extra-treaty activity 'has evolved through practice, shared experiences and a consistent, if limited series of successes' (Holland, 1988, p. 1). As de Schoutheete, an EPC practitioner, has pointed out EPC was not intended as a 'legalistic exercise, but as 'a pragmatic enterprise to establish common positions and common actions in foreign policy' which lacked an institutional structure and the formal obligations normally associated with Community policies (Regelsberger, et al., 1985, p. 41). This situation was transformed, at least formally, with the signing of the SEA which finally provided EPC with a treaty-basis. By the end of the 1980s EPC had become the normal diplomatic response for the member states, not necessarily replacing existing bilateral international relations, but complementing them. Familiarity and practice over two decades had produced an extensive and indispensable

communauté d'information, Communauté de vues and *communauté d'action.*
Consequently, '[C]ommon positions on all major international events
were refined and, more frequently than before, the Ten/Twelve were able
to agree to and to undertake concrete actions on a collective basis' (Pijpers,
et al., 1988, p. 37). This concertation in foreign affairs had both external and
internal merits; externally, a collective Community position assisted global
stability *vis-à-vis* superpower interdependence; and internally within the
Community EPC contributed to the impetus towards European Union.
The relative success of both of these external and internal dynamics
resulted in the convening of the 1991 IGC on Political Union which
debated extending the scope of EPC to include security and possibly
defence within a more structured Community CFSP (see below for further
discussion).

It is hardly original to note that the Community is a unique experience,
with *sui generis* institutional relationships. However, it is worth repeating
this uniqueness with respect to foreign policy co-ordination. How does
one create the basis of a collective foreign policy from scratch? Imitating
the *modus operandi* of Monnet, the Community approach was a pragmatic
one. Certain broad objectives and procedural guidelines were established,
but no definitive list of common policies, or policy areas, was ever stipulated. Collective foreign policy emerged in an organic way, often through
the necessity of an external crisis, incrementally constructing what was to
become a recognizable body of EC foreign policy positions. The scope was
neither comprehensive nor necessarily logically linked. The process was
essentially reactive, cautious and externally driven. Above all, EPC was a
procedure totally dependent on consensus which regarded the *communautaire*
method of majority voting as an anathema to national sovereignty. Thus while
facilitating intra-Community diplomatic co-operation, EPC boundaries
were dictated by an intergovernmental rather than by a supranational perspective.

The aspirations of the 1969 Hague Heads of State and Government
meeting were ambitious calling for 'a united Europe capable of assuming
its responsibilities in the world ... of making a contribution
commensurate with its tradition and its mission . . .' (Hague, 1969, p. 11).
In the subsequent Luxembourg Report the practical implementation of this
was expressed more conservatively: the objectives of EPC were: '[T]o
ensure greater mutual understanding with respect to major issues of international politics, by exchanging information and consulting regularly; to
increase their solidarity by working for a harmonization of views,
concertation of attitudes and joint action when it appears feasible and
desirable'. (1970, p. 11).

The importance of the Luxembourg Report was symbolic rather than
practical in nature: it signified the birth of EPC. As one distinguished
observer of EPC concluded 'as a procedure, it promised everything and
nothing. There was no commitment to agree, but simply to "consult on all
important questions of foreign policy" ' (Wallace, 1983a, p. 377). A formal
schedule for ministerial meetings to discuss foreign affairs was established
and bureaucratic support (in the form of a Political Committee and *ad hoc*

working groups) created. This intergovernmental procedure kept both the European Parliament and the Commission on the fringes of foreign policy. And yet, a new and untried diplomatic procedure had been created and the practice of working co-operatively was to have a strong socializing effect within the Community: over the following decades EPC consultation increasingly came to be seen as a normal and appropriate foreign policy reflex for member states (Holland, 1988, p. 3).

Throughout the 1970s and into the 1980s procedural reform (as opposed to an overall review of content) of EPC was attempted on a number of occasions. Although still difficult, engineering consensus on the mechanisms for developing political co-operation was significantly easier than addressing the more politically important question of the substance of the EC's joint foreign policy positions. Thus, the 1973 Copenhagen Report updated and codified procedural developments. These included recognition of the role of the Correspondents Group; a greater frequency of meetings; the establishment of the COREU telex network between the then nine Foreign Ministries; and greater co-ordination between member state embassies in third countries (p. 4). Although perhaps not fulfilling its own rhetoric (that 'Europe is becoming a real force in international relations'), the Report clarified the integrationist objective supporting EPC:

> Governments will consult each other on all important foreign policy questions and will work out priorities, observing the following criteria:
> (i) the purpose of the consultation is to seek common policies on practical problems;
> (ii) the subjects dealt with must concern European interests whether in Europe itself or elsewhere where the adoption of a common position is necessary or desirable.
> On these questions each state undertakes as a general rule not to take up final positions without prior consultation with its partners within the framework of the political cooperation machinery. (Copenhagen Report, 1973, pp. 17–18)

EPC was clearly intergovernmental, but the underlying principles were undeniably *communautaire* in their implications.

The first radical attempt to reform EPC was in the 1975 Tindemans Report which proposed what was to prove to be a too federalist vision of EPC development. The Report called for a single decision-making centre; the merging of EC and EPC business which, at that time, was kept separate at the ministerial level; and that involvement in EPC be extended to all the Community's institutions. Its most ambitious recommendation was that the basis of EPC should be revised from its existing voluntary concertation to a legally binding *obligation* on the member states to comply with common foreign policy decisions – aspirations that the 1991 IGC delegates were still unwilling to propose. Only in this way did Tindemans believe that Europe could present a consistent and 'united front' in its foreign relations (Tindemans, 1976, pp. 14–15).

Once again, it took a series of international crises to confront the then existing inadequate and pragmatic nature of EPC. The Community's response to the events of 1979–80 – the Soviet invasion of Afghanistan, the taking of American hostages by Iran and the Polish domestic crisis – highlighted the slowness of the EPC apparatus to respond and the debilitating dichotomy that still existed between EC and EPC competences. The Community responded in the 1981 London Report which began the process of codifying EPC practices. The important role of the European Council was recognized, the Troika arrangement was extended (whereby the current, preceding and succeeding presidencies operate collectively), and a 48-hour emergency procedure was introduced. However, the persistent distinction between the Community's economic and political affairs was maintained. EPC at this time remained an intergovernmental exercise outside the formal provisions set down in the Treaty of Rome. EC procedures and competences remained distinct from those of the looser EPC structure: a 'communautarization' of EPC – its incorporation within the EC's treaty framework – was not advocated. Echoing Monnet's words, intergovernmentalism 'embodied as much as possible at that time and that stage in men's (sic.) thinking' (1978, p. 423).

Despite repeated attempts to improve EPC during the early 1980s (with initiatives such as the Genscher-Colombo Plan, the Solemn Declaration on European Union and the Draft Treaty Establishing a European Union), the next *saut qualitif* was not achieved until the 1986 SEA. Again, the ambitions of the Act's preamble owed more to integrationist wishful-thinking than political realities. It calls for the member states to create a European Union which, in relation to foreign policy, will have the 'necessary means of action' with the purpose of 'speaking ever increasingly with one voice and to act with consistency and solidarity'. The more moderate proposals of the Act did, however, succeed in blurring the intergovernmental distinction between EC and EPC activities by linking EPC directly to the EC treaties. The Common Provisions of Title I state that '[T]he European Communities and European Political Cooperation shall have as their objective to contribute together to making concrete progress towards European unity.' More precisely, Title III of the SEA envisages the replacement of national foreign policy autonomy by the progressive development of EPC. The innovations introduced by the SEA appeared initially modest, but their cumulative effect has had a considerable impact upon the behaviour of the member states and their respective expectations of EPC.

Although the SEA provided EPC with a legal basis, a distinction between the EC's and EPC's judicial base was maintained (Nicoll and Salmon, 1990, p. 117). Article 3 specifies that Community activities are governed by the provisions of the original treaties and by the amendments of the SEA, whereas EPC could only draw on those competences explicitly delineated in Title III of the SEA. Consequently, EC and EPC business were distinguished by their decision-making structures (majority voting versus unanimity) and by the role of other Community institutions (EPC operating outside the normal structure that gave the Commission the exclusive right of initiative and redress through the Court of Justice). Whether the new status of EPC under Title III could actually be given any meaningful legal effect was a point of contention among the member states, the Community institutions and academics. The predominant view was that despite the 'legalization' of the procedure, the SEA failed to make any substantive transformation to the functioning of EPC. A competing interpretation regarded this transition from 'soft to hard law' as legally significant: the Act's seemingly modest proposals belie the fact that it is an international agreement and as such it can only strengthen the underlying legal effect of EPC and therefore enhance collective foreign policy-making (Dehousse and Weiler, 1991, pp. 121–42).

Title III introduced a series of procedural refinements and a number of innovations. First, the role of the Commission was clarified and extended. Article 30.3(a) provides for the Council of Foreign Ministers and a Commissioner to 'meet at least four times a year within the framework of European Political Cooperation' and Article 30.3(b) recognizes the Commission as 'fully associated with the proceedings of Political Cooperation'. Second, in contrast, the European Parliament was to be 'closely associated', with the presidency regularly informing the assembly on EPC matters in order to 'ensure that the views of the European Parliament are duly taken into consideration' (Article 30.4). Third, EPC was 'crowned' with its own secretariat (modest in size and limited in its function to assisting the presidency), and the interlocking roles of the Political Directors, Correspondents Groups and working groups were codified (Article 30.10(c–g)). Fourth, for the first time EPC was endowed with the responsibility 'to coordinate (their) positions more closely on the political and economic aspects of security' (Article 30.6(a)). Finally, Article 30 was resplendent in the optimistic, but fragile, rhetoric common to the previous statements on the future of EPC. Thus the member states:

> . . . shall endeavour jointly to formulate and implement a European foreign policy;
> . . . shall ensure that common principles and objectives are gradually developed and defined;
> . . . shall endeavour to avoid any action or position which impairs their effectiveness as a cohesive force in international relations;
> . . .shall, as far as possible, refrain from impeding the formation of a consensus and the joint action which this could produce. (Article 30.1–3)

Such good intentions, though commendable, are not sufficient guarantees for common action. While member states were instructed to do all they could to avoid prohibiting consensus positions to develop, the requirement of an obligatory common foreign policy as outlined by Tindemans a decade earlier, was once again absent. The opportunity to 'communautarize' EPC was wasted in favour of, admittedly improved, but essentially the same form of intergovernmentalism that inherently limited the development of an integrated Community common foreign policy.

By the end of the 1980s, the intergovernmental structure and mechanisms of EPC had become clearly defined: the presidency represented the Community in all international relations; in this task the Presidency was assisted by the EPC Secretariat; the Commission was the 'thirteenth' participant in EPC decision-making which continued to be governed by the principle of consensus; the European Parliament was 'informed', but with the exception of the power to ratify association agreements remained peripheral to the conduct of EPC; and lastly, the Community began to enhance its choice of foreign policy instruments by exercising its treaty-based competences more aggressively. Originally, the provisions relating to EPC in the SEA were due to be reviewed in 1992, however, the separate though parallel developments in progress towards Economic and Monetary Union accelerated this timetable. At the May 1990 Dublin Summit it was agreed that a second IGC on Political Union (with a major component being EPC) should be convened to coincide with the IGC timetable for EMU commencing in December 1990. This linkage was more than a calendar convenience; the success of each IGC was mutually dependent. As the history of the Community illustrates *ad nauseam*, 'package' bargains are fundamental to institutional progress.

The first two decades of EPC, though remarkably cohesive and successful in many respects, had highlighted a number of flaws that jeopardized the development of a more integrated Community. Reform of EPC was a necessity, for both domestic and international reasons. First, the debilitating constraints of the consensus principle imposed upon EPC had become increasingly apparent, be that in EC policy towards South Africa, Eastern Europe or the Gulf war. 'To speak with one voice' had proven to be somewhat of a charade and the euphoric ambitions of the London Report 'to shape and not merely react to international events' seemed particularly inappropriate a decade later. As two leading EPC commentators concluded, 'EPC turned out to be strong on points of secondary importance but proved to be of minor importance towards issues of real crucial nature' (Regelsberger and Wessels, 1990, p. 4). Incrementalism along the path of intergovernmentalism was no longer sufficient: the elusive *saut qualitif* became the prescribed remedy. Second, in 1990 the Community faced a potentially precarious disequilibrium between the modest accomplishments of EPC and the greater 'machismo' of EMU and the emergent European internal market. A balance between political and economic union seemed paramount, at least from the perspective of Germany and a majority of key Community partners. Thirdly, and in many respects imitating the Community's earlier history, external imperatives forced the Twelve to reassess their role in the international community. The tumultuous events in Eastern Europe since 1989, and the impact of German reunification, combined to force the Community to assume a more forceful role in Europe. Monnet's belief that peace in Europe could only be achieved through the Community acting as the avenue for the reconciliation of the East and West proved, at last, to be an intuitive and perceptive prophecy.

Other factors that contributed to the necessity for reform included the anticipated enlargement of the Community; the inadequacy of traditional diplomacy; and the crises posed by the Gulf war. Just as for EMU, a catalyst for Political Union was the anticipated consequences of Community enlargement during the 1990s. Clearly, any increase in member states to include existing applicant states (Austria, Cyprus, Finland, Malta, Sweden, Turkey) and potential applicants (Switzerland, Eastern and Central European countries), would necessitate the reform of the consensus principle in EPC. The numbers involved (17 or more) would be difficult enough to accommodate; but this coupled with the 'difficult' foreign policy positions of Austria, Sweden and Turkey, for example, determined that a consensus-only rule for EPC could not realistically work in an enlarged Community. Additionally, as an international actor, the EC increasingly had to use economic instruments to promote its policy (be this as trade sanctions, aid or development). Traditional nation-state diplomatic activity has declined in importance. However, within the existing EPC formula, such 'economic' activities fall, largely, under the auspices of the Commission, not the Council of Foreign Ministers or European Council, who still remain confined to 'political' or 'diplomatic' activity in the execution of foreign policy decisions. Clearly, some unity of instruments and competences between different actors in the EC was needed, particularly given the SEA's requirement that the 'external policies of the European Community and the policies agreed in European Political Cooperation must be consistent' (Article 30.5). Lastly, and almost *ex post facto* of the IGC, was the experience of the Gulf crisis. Whether one supported the British criticism of EC action as indicative of the immaturity of EPC, or concurred with the majority line that the crisis exemplified the absolute need for a common foreign policy, clearly the SEA procedures and lack of rigour could not be condoned as an appropriate or adequate mechanism. As Commission President Delors commented, the 'Gulf war has provided an abject lesson – if one were needed – on the limitations of the European Community', although he chose to 'interpret this as yet another argument for moving towards a form of political union embracing a common foreign and security policy' (1991, pp. 1–2). Either the pantomime of EPC had to end, or a more competent understudy introduced into the arena.

A Common Foreign and Security Policy (CFSP) for the Community goes far beyond the inherent characteristics associated with EPC. The March 1991 joint Franco-German communiqué detailed the objectives of those states committed to an integrated Community: the IGC was 'to precisely define the principles and procedures of a common foreign and security policy leading in time to a common defence policy . . . [to] obtain the best content and institutional formulas for the implementation of a common foreign and security policy that will allow Europe to act effectively in the world's important affairs.' (*Agence Europe*, 23 March, 1991)

The rejection of the Dutch Presidency draft and the deep divisions over the modest Luxembourg Draft Treaty that dominated the Political Union conference throughout 1991, clearly illustrated the incompatible intergovernmental and federal options for a future Community foreign policy structure. The debate focused on the following issues: the scope of CFSP; majority voting; the meaning of security; and the implications for a future defence policy.

In terms of the scope of a CFSP, the broad alternatives were whether such a policy should be guided by principle or by incrementalism. The debate that was waged throughout the 1991 IGC was between those who advocated establishing general principles that would define a Community foreign policy, and between those who sought to continue the existing incremental approach. The first option is expansive in its implications, the latter restrictive: it is easier to expand competences based on principle than on a case-by-case basis. It was argued that the general idea of subsidiarity mooted in the Draft Treaty could be used to define CFSP principles: those areas not specifically assigned to the EC level should remain in the domain of the member states. The conclusion of the Maastricht summit saw the intergovernmentalists remain in ascendancy, although significant concessions were made and an intensification of foreign policy co-ordination achieved. Without eradicating its intergovernmental basis, Community foreign policy became more *communautaire* and a *saut qualitif* beyond the SEA was established which promised a continuing development of CFSP throughout the 1990s.

Maastricht was limited to developing a 'common' foreign policy: the idea of a 'single' foreign policy for the Community was not on the agenda. This distinction is of paramount importance. Thus, member states could where there were justifiable reasons concerning essential interests, either historical or geographical, adopt a national policy provided that it did not contradict the aims of any common policy. Such an interpretation allows for the progressive evolution in the scope and implementation of collective Community foreign policy while providing for the possibility within the Community's legal framework for states to be excluded from a common policy because of specific obligations. While federalists and advocates of a CFSP based on principles and not pragmatism may be critical of this compromise, an expanding 'common' foreign policy can clearly be seen to be a necessary prerequisite to a 'single' European foreign, security and ultimately defence policy. For the foreseeable future, irrespective of the specific nomenclature (EPC or CFSP) and the implicit contradiction with a purist interpretation of Political Union, bilateral foreign policies in some circumstances will continue to exist in tandem with a Community policy.

While the scope and content of Community foreign policy would seem the more substantive issue, procedural reform can also be a significant catalyst. It has been argued at length by numerous EPC scholars that the consensus principle – the defining characteristic of the first two decades of EPC – has promoted policy sclerosis and typically led to decisions based on the lowest common denominator (see for example, Nicoll and Salmon, 1990; Wallace, 1990; Hill, 1988; Holland, 1991; Pijpers, 1988; Ifestos, 1987; and Regelsberger and Wessels, 1990). The abandonment of this principle was a divisive issue at the IGCs, with the UK, and to a lesser extent Denmark and Portugal, being resistant to this apparent concession to supranational authority and detrimental to sovereignty and national control of foreign policy. Advocates of majority decision-making argued that the existing consensus rule would be maintained for defining the scope or content of Community foreign policy; but once an issue had been unanimously accepted as an area of Community competence, majority voting would be used for the implementation of that policy. In this way a more effective use of Community instruments could be achieved without imposing a collective decision on a member state without its prior approval. The Community's policy towards South Africa can be used to illustrate this distinction (see below for further discussion of this case study). The principle of adopting sanctions against South Africa would remain a unanimous decision, but the timing and implementation of these sanctions could be made by qualified majority.

The related question of what constitutes a majority decision is neither new nor unique to the Maastricht reforms. Monnet, commenting on the Schuman Treaty signatories of 1952, noted that the member states were entering 'an unknown world where the veto would be the exception and the rule of the majority would be law. *But what majority?*' (1978, p. 353) (emphasis added). There was support for adopting a revised form of Article 103 which gave each state equal representation rather than the normal qualified majority procedure under Article 148. After considerable debate weighted majorities were adopted (see below): a simple majority principle was not appropriate. This move towards majority decision-making will enhance the *communautaire* nature of EPC/CFSP: however, as noted above, there needs to be an intergovernmental concession in the form of an exception clause which provides for 'vital national interests'. This would not, however, be the Luxembourg Compromise revisited, as there would be no implied veto of the majority position, but rather a procedure whereby an individual state can be excluded from the Community policy without jeopardizing collective action.

The SEA breached new ground by legitimating the discussion of 'economic aspects of security' within the EPC framework; the IGC explored options for extending this tentative beginning. Attention was largely focused on utilizing the existing Western European Union (WEU), either by incorporating it within the existing Community structure or reorienting it as a parallel but separate security regime for certain, not all, Community states. The additional problem of creating a European pillar within NATO compounded the question of an appropriate security 'architecture' for the Community within the post-cold war European context. In the Maastricht Treaty of 1992, the limited 'economic' constraint of the SEA was replaced by an open-ended commitment: the Community's common foreign policy would 'include all questions related to the security of the Union' (Article J.4.1). The structure for any future defence role was more complex: the Treaty stated that security matters which have defence implications may be wholly or partly implemented through the framework of the Western European Union (Article J.4.2). However, any such co-operation did not preclude the development of other forms of bilateral defence co-operation, or affect any existing defence obligations on member states in either the WEU or NATO frameworks.

If not the anticipated *saut qualitif*, the Treaty revisions produced at the Maastricht conclusion of the IGC in December 1991 moved the Community beyond the limitations of EPC and laid the foundations for the progressive refinement of a common foreign policy. Article J.1 states that the main treaty revisions were designed to 'define and implement a common foreign and security policy . . . covering all areas of foreign and security policy': as previously noted in chapter 3, specifically, the objectives of such a common policy were:

- to safeguard the common values, fundamental interests and independence of the Union;
- to strengthen the security of the Union and its Member States in all ways;
- to preserve peace and strengthen international security, in accordance with the principles of the United Nations Charter as well as the principles of the Helsinki Act and the objectives of the Paris Charter;
- to promote international co-operation;
- to develop and consolidate democracy and the rule of law, and respect for human rights and fundamental freedoms. (Article J.1.2)

These objectives were to be realized through enhanced and systematic co-operation between the member states leading to, eventually, 'joint action' where there are 'essential interests in common' (J.1.3). Mimicking earlier EPC protocol, in conducting the new CFSP, member states are to 'refrain from any action which is contrary to the interests of the Union or likely to impair its effectiveness as a cohesive force in international relations' (J.1.4). Such declarations were far from revolutionary, replicating broadly the existing EPC procedural behaviour. Similarly, the new CFSP provisions called for states to consult within the Council on any topic of general interest 'in order to ensure that their combined influence is exerted as effectively as possible by means of concerted and convergent action' (J.2.1); required national foreign policies to conform to EC common positions (J.2.2); and instructed the member states to co-ordinate their actions and to promote common positions in international organizations (J.2.3).

The most notable shift from a purely intergovernmental form of improved political co-operation to an approach commensurate with an embryonic 'communautarized' common foreign policy, was in the procedure for attaining and executing common action. The procedure for achieving common positions was to be orchestrated through the Council of Ministers (in accordance with the guidelines set-down by the European Council). Under Article C.1 the Council has the authority to determine which foreign policy topics are to be subject to joint action, this decision being by unanimity (Article J.3.1); once agreed to, the Community's 'general and specific objectives in carrying out such action, if necessary its duration, and the means, procedures and conditions for its implementation' are outlined for each joint policy. Importantly, as a general rule the specific details for implementing joint action 'are to be taken by qualified majority', with votes weighted as set out in Article 148.2 of the Treaty of Rome (currently 54 votes out of 76) with the supplementary proviso that a minimum of eight states support the measure (Article J.3.2). Once adopted by these conditions, any joint action becomes binding on the member states 'in the positions they adopt and in the conduct of their activity' (Article J.3.4). To balance this significant step towards Community sovereignty in foreign policy, Article J.3.7 provides for the possibility, with the Council's approval, of individual states excluding themselves from joint action provided that any such decision 'shall not run counter to the objectives of the joint action nor impair its effectiveness'.

The remaining aspects of the CFSP text clarified and only modestly enhanced the existing codification of EPC provisions in the SEA. Thus

Article J.5 confirms the role of the presidency and the 'fully associated' status of the Commission (replicating Article 30.3(b) and 30.10(b) of the SEA), whereas the formal recognition of the Troika procedure finally gave legal recognition to existing practice that predated the SEA. Article J.6 reformulated the content of Article 30.8 and 30.9 of the SEA and calls for closer diplomatic co-operation and consultation between member state missions in third countries and international organizations, and Article J.8 modifies the 48-hour emergency procedure as stipulated in Article 30.10(d) in the SEA. The powers of the European Parliament remain unchanged; it has to be 'kept regularly informed' and consulted, with its views 'duly taken into consideration', as was the case in Article 30.4 of the SEA. While formally requiring the Council to involve the Parliament, these Treaty reforms do not provide the Parliament with the ability to shape Community foreign policy. Its role remains that of a pressure group, albeit with a limited legal competence.

An area conspicuous by its absence during the 1991 IGCs was any discussion of foreign policy instruments available to the new CFSP. This, however, was hardly surprising: throughout the history of EPC, no document specifying Community-level foreign policy tools was ever issued. All such instruments were adopted on an *ad hoc* basis and drew on individual treaty articles for their authority. Despite this incremental and intergovernmental tendency, experience has shown that the Community possesses a wide range of options when implementing its foreign policy decisions, and the trend in the 1980s and into the 1990s has been for the 'more effective use of available instruments' (Pijpers, *et al.*, 1988, p. 267). What, then, are the foreign policy instruments at the Community's disposal? There is little consensus on this seemingly straightforward question. According to Weiler, given the necessary political will, all foreign policy instruments available to individual member states are, by logical extension, available to the Community in its conduct of foreign policy. While correct, this view of Community competences is too federal in its consequences to be acceptable to the current status of foreign policy co-ordination. In practice, the modesty of Community foreign policy instruments and the reliance on declarations rather than action have been the focus of criticism (Rummel, 1988, pp. 125–8). Irrespective of this experience, the Rome Treaty does provide an effective legal competence for adopting and implementing foreign policy instruments (Nuttall, 1988, p. 112). Typically, however, there has been a reluctance to use EC competences for past EPC activity.

To date, the Community has used quite a broad range on non-military policy instruments including financial aid, association or co-operation agreements and codes of practice (relating to terrorism or apartheid, for example). Sanctions, however, remain the most effective, public and commonly used Community foreign policy instrument. Drawing on the legal basis of the Treaty of Rome, Article 113 was utilized to invoke sanctions against Iran and the USSR in the early 1980s; if interpreted expansively, this article (which relates to the common commercial policy) could be used to much greater effect. Article 224 was invoked under the crisis conditions relating to the Falklands war, whereas Article 223 was employed for the 1980 arms embargo against Iran. If further legal basis is needed, Article 235 provides a very flexible and generous authority whereby the Council acting unanimously can take 'appropriate measures' to realize any treaty objective (Holland, 1991, p. 184).

The legal basis under which sanctions are invoked is fundamental to their success and credibility as an effective foreign policy instrument. Only sanctions that are based on Community regulations (which are both directly binding and directly effective) are guaranteed to achieve their objectives. Where less rigorous Community-level legislation is adopted, such as a directive, the uniform and comprehensive application of a sanction can be jeopardized through differing national interpretations of the Community legislation. Intergovernmentalism favours such Community-level competences that do not explicitly undermine national sovereignty; a federal-based common foreign policy would demand the greater use of regulations. The creation of the 1992 Single Market has undermined, albeit indirectly, the viability of bilateral action with respect to the imposition of sanctions. Within the Single Market it would be impossible, and probably illegal, for one state to implement a bilateral sanction on the imports from a target state. Once products are imported from a third country quite properly into another Community member state, they will then enjoy the free movement of goods explicit in the Single Market. After 1992, to work as an effective Community foreign policy instrument, sanctions will need to be comprehensive, multilateral and adopted through regulations rather than directives (p. 195).

Theories and case-studies

Turning from this empirical discussion of instruments and competences, how are EPC and CFSP to be understood theoretically? Like the debate over a common Community foreign policy itself, there is no agreement among academics on the most useful theoretical approach for comprehending this activity. The intergovernmental–federal dichotomy used throughout this book provides a basic starting-point from which more elaborate theories can be developed. In this regard, it is even useful to return to the traditional neofunctional perspective in a post-SEA context.

As outlined in Chapter 1, Keohane and Hoffmann have offered a reformulation of neofunctionalism that removes the *automatic* effect of spillover and sets successful intergovernmental bargaining as the prerequisite for integration. The question for Community foreign policy is the extent to which the 1991 IGC bargaining produced political spillover, and if so how far the effect will spread. From Keohane and Hoffmann's perspective, the fact that the process commenced at the intergovernmental level is a positive rather than anti-integrative omen. While spillover into Political Union cannot be guaranteed, at least at the theoretical level the possibility exists. History suggests that it is wise to be cautionary with regard to the development of foreign policy and a less than 'common' outcome should not be taken as indicative of failure or the absence of spillover. The process is evolutionary rather than revolutionary in nature. But for the first time since the heady days of Euro-optimism of the mid-1970s, key qualitative issues central to the integration of foreign policy were on the Community agenda – majority voting, agreement on 'common' policy areas, collective security and defence, and the EC's emerging role within the changing contexts of NATO and the WEU. The case for the re-evaluation of neofunctionalism with respect to foreign policy is strong: after an absence of some two decades the reality of Community politics is once again beginning to resemble the predictive elements of neofunctional theory.

In addition to neofunctionalism, the range of theoretical approaches that have been used to understand the contemporary expression of EPC is diverse: for example, international relations (realist, political economy and world systems approaches); comparative politics; and public policy analysis have all been legitimately used and with a degree of success. The fundamental theoretical issue addresses whether Community foreign policy is *sui generis* and demands its own empirically inductive theory, or whether EPC/CFSP can adequately be understood by reference to the existing political science literature. Some EPC commentators at the beginning of the 1990s chose to interpret European foreign policy within these existing overarching conceptual approaches (Holland, 1991). The following three alternatives illustrate this tendency.

First, a realist perspective demands that any discussion of collective foreign policy has to first confront the basic assumptions and concepts of this traditional school of international relations. Thus an appropriate framework for EPC or CFSP has to account for the anarchical structure of international society; the role of the state as an international actor; the pre-eminence of security; the concept of the balance of power; and the limited impact of domestic politics (Pijpers, 1991). The changing European security and superpower relationships of the 1990s do not, necessarily, undermine these *realpolitik* assumptions. Indeed, the chaos and confusion within European international relations since the crumbling of the Berlin Wall on 9 November 1989 points to the continued validity of an anarchical interpretation of international society. US–Soviet relations and security structures may be evolving, but they remain fundamental influences within the Community's foreign policy environment.

Second, a world systems approach offers a similarly expansive interpretation within which to locate the Community's foreign policy. This holistic approach stresses the relationship between Community foreign policy and the broader actions of the EC as a global, capitalist economic and political actor in competition with the two other rival economic cores, the USA and Japan (George, 1991). From this perspective, EPC or CFSP is not treated in isolation as a discrete sub-category of Community activity; all such narrow definitions are rejected as are the artificial barriers that have been built between EPC, EC and other forms of external relations activity (such as development aid and the Lomé agreements). Such a theoretical base demands a very broad understanding of the interconnected nature of Community activity. It accurately reflects the practical experience of policy bargaining within the Community and corresponds at a very general level to the idea of spillover. Compromises struck in an EPC forum are not without consequences for other aspects of Community policy-making, as the linkage between the 1991 EMU and Political Union IGCs bears witness.

Thirdly, an equally broad canvas has been suggested by Allen and Smith (1991). They reject EPC as the preferred focus for conceptualizing Europe's foreign policy behaviour: rather, they locate the discussion within the wider context which takes Western Europe (broadly defined in economic, military and political terms) as the appropriate international actor. Consequently, they prefer the general idea of Western Europe's 'presence' in the international system, which values the Community's past experience of EPC for its impact upon behaviour above its actual content or procedural developments. Using this expansive definition Western Europe's 'presence' as an international actor is significant and EPC/CFSP is treated as just one element within this process.

More typically, however, the characteristics of Community foreign policy have led to a conclusion that it is a *sui generis* activity that can best be comprehended through the application of more specific and precise theoretical approaches. Three related and compatible approaches have been used explicitly in relation to EPC: domestic politics, symbolic politics and agenda management. The domestic politics approach asserts that each national domestic political context can have a crucial impact on the policy-making decisions of the EC. The key question relevant to foreign policy is 'why a member state sees the EC as the most appropriate level of action on some issues, whilst on other issues, the nation-state or other international organizations are seen as the most appropriate' (Bulmer, 1983, p. 356). Differing domestic environments impose limitations on common action, leading one commentator to conclude that EPC can serve 'an extremely useful function as an alibi for inaction, a means of deflecting external pressure, and a cover for shifts in national policy' (Wallace, 1983b, p. 10). This perspective helps to shed light on the seeming inconsistencies and modesty of many of the Community's past endeavours to promote a collective stance in international affairs.

Building on this domestic context, the symbolic politics approach focuses on the public 'façade' and the actual policy purposes of the élite decision-makers involved. This approach derived from the public policy literature argues that often policies are either not intended to be fully implemented or are characterized by the poor application of available knowledge for effective implementation. With respect to EPC, four policy rationales can be identified. Decisions based on available knowledge for their implementation can either be 'real' (where such decisions are meant to be implemented), or 'symbolic' (if no such intention exists); decisions not based on sufficient knowledge for implementation are either 'pseudo' decisions (where there is a genuine intention to implement policy), or 'nonsense' decisions (if no such intention prevails) (Holland, 1987, p. 308). The third related perspective concerns the management of the political agenda. Here, the focus changes from examining policy 'intention' to the definition of the policy problem: the way in which a policy is defined can determine what is the best policy to adopt for its solution. The utility of this

approach is that it facilitates the critical examination of policies that are formulated simply in order to exclude an issue from the political agenda, and
involve no real attempt to solve the particular problem. Thus, the decision
of how to define an international crisis, whether it is to be part of the Community's common policies or remain a national concern, will determine
the scope and effectiveness of any Community action. In the past, this
definitional procedure within EPC has often seemed to reflect internal
Community priorities rather than be the most appropriate and effective
policy for resolving an international dispute. When considered in conjunction
with the domestic politics characteristics described above, the symbolic
politics and agenda management approach can be put to good effect in
understanding the empirical nature of Community foreign policy decisions.
The following case-studies drawn from the Community's international
involvement during the early 1990s all benefit from the different insights
each of these particular approaches can provide and from the more general-
level theories outlined in the work of Allen and Smith, George and Pijpers.

SOUTH AFRICA

The Community's policy towards South Africa provides a particularly useful
case-study for examining the effectiveness of EPC. First, opposition to
apartheid constituted the Community's longest collective foreign policy
(originating in 1977); second, over the subsequent fifteen years the substance of EPC has changed significantly illustrating that policy adaptation
is possible; and thirdly, a varied range of foreign policy instruments have
been used (Holland, 1991, p. 185). In order to trace these developments,
four distinct phases of EPC towards South Africa can be identified: that of
consensus (1974–84), of conflict (1985–86), of compromise (1987–89) and
of reformulation (1990 onwards).

During this first period, the Community exhibited a common policy
through a unique foreign policy instrument: the 1977 Community-wide
Code of Conduct for EC firms operating in South Africa. This established
guidelines for employment practices designed to counter discrimination
within South Africa's apartheid labour system, and its provisions were uniformly applicable (on a voluntary basis) to all EC firms. The respective
national governments were then responsible for producing annual reports
on its application (Holland, 1988, pp. 74–80). The *Code* and normal diplomatic
démarches were the Community's only foreign policy instruments used; the
presumption during this period being that the most effective mechanism for
abolishing apartheid was through continued economic relations: sanctions
or embargoes were not advocated. The relatively immature and experimental
status of EPC also meant that the agreement on a collective policy was
based on the principle of the lowest common denominator and largely
imitated the existing British policy towards the Republic. This seeming
harmony suffered from a lack of credibility, however. At one level the *Code*
was a uniform EC measure; and yet in its actual application, there were
serious discrepancies between different member states which resulted in

uniformity existing only at a superficial level. This level of co-operation was all that was possible during this period under the consensus principle of EPC; no Community state argued for a more stringent or comprehensive South African policy.

This Community policy consensus was disturbed by the domestic South African political turmoil that began towards the end of 1984. The following two years were characterized by increasing civil unrest, the imposition of a state of emergency and the banning of opposition groups, all of which heightened South Africa's pariah status and led to renewed international condemnation of apartheid legislation. These events caused the Community to reassess the appropriateness of its policy and the effectiveness of its instruments and jeopardized the collective consensual nature of EPC. The division within the EC differentiated between the majority of states who wished to adopt sanctions as the Community's new foreign policy instrument, and the minority (Germany, Portugal and the UK) who opposed the use of economic sanctions. After considerable delay, a compromise 'lowest common denominator' package of sanctions was adopted under EPC. This new policy introduced four types of sanctions: economic, military, cultural and diplomatic. For example, the economic sanctions encompassed the cessation of EC oil and sensitive technology exports; nuclear collaboration and new commercial investment were banned; and South African exports of krugerrands, iron and steel were prohibited. At the military level, the exchange of military attachés stopped, as did bilateral military co-operation and trade in paramilitary equipment. Cultural sanctions froze or discouraged all direct contact (including sporting and scientific relations), whereas at the diplomatic level the Community withdrew in unison the respective member state ambassadors for consultation and collective *démarche* became the usual diplomatic form of contact.

While the Community had proven itself capable of foreign policy action, the scope and application of these sanctions did little to enhance the credibility of the EC as a cohesive and unified international actor. In order to placate the anti-sanctions countries and to reach a collective agreement, the sanctions that were adopted were intentionally marginal in their effect. For example, the embargo of certain South African goods only affected 3.5 per cent of the Republic's trade with the EC: more importantly, there was a reluctance to use Community regulations as the basis for these sanctions and a preference for the legally less binding directives and decisions (Holland, 1988, p. 108–16).

Dissatisfied with the difficulty of engineering a consensus on punitive sanctions, the Community sought to develop a new consensus based on the issue of positive measures to assist the disadvantaged peoples in South Africa. This change in policy emphasis dominated the 1987–8 period. The foreign policy instruments utilized included the setting up of programmes within South Africa to provide development and educational funds for the 'victims of apartheid'. To balance this initiative, a renewed emphasis on assisting the Southern African region through the existing SADCC (Southern African Development and Coordination Conference) structure was agreed to. Consequently, EPC progressed from the use of sanctions as its policy mechanism to a more inclusive positive and negative strategy that encompassed the region as a whole and established a policy framework that was complementary rather than contradictory in focus.

With the release of Nelson Mandela in February 1990 and the gradual dismantling of apartheid structures in South Africa, Community policy underwent a further metamorphosis that again challenged the consensus principle of EPC. Within days, Britain unilaterally withdrew from the collective EC embargo on new investments and other economic sanctions. After months of deliberation the Community collectively agreed to follow this lead; however, subsequently the Danish Parliament vetoed this relaxation and the common content of EPC became increasingly questionable. Pragmatic bilateral initiatives began to supersede collective EPC decisions. This fracturing of EPC, albeit of a relatively minor nature, encapsulated the principle requirement for the effective exercise of a collective Community foreign policy instrument – the adoption of instruments that have their legal base at the Community, not the national level (Holland, 1991, p. 188).

The South African example provides a good illustration of the strengths and weaknesses of EPC; policy has been adaptable, responsive and generally applied collectively; the instruments used have been varied, but too often ineffectual due to the necessity of unanimous decision-making. And yet a common approach was maintained for a fifteen-year period, not an inconsiderable achievement given the different political and trade relations between each of the member states and South Africa.

THE GULF WAR

Most commentaries have concluded that the Community's response to the Iraqi invasion of Kuwait epitomized the inherent contradictions and weaknesses within EPC, though as Jacques Delors countered, rather than emphasizing the impossibility of a common foreign policy, for many it stressed its absolute necessity. A Community perspective to the crisis appeared missing and a common European approach to security questions was demonstrated by default: national responses predominated. The Community's collective role took, at best, third place behind the American and bilateral European responses. As one commentary concluded, '[As] long as a united European foreign and security policy is absent, the tendency of European countries to adopt purely national attitudes and, therefore, to align themselves with the United States or to denounce it will be very tempting' (Moîsi , 1991, p. 11).

Despite this dependence on national militarism, a Community perspective was present at a diplomatic and trade level. Once again, the individual member state embassies acted in concert and during the initial invasion Community nationals trapped in Kuwait City could seek refuge in any member state embassy irrespective of nationality. Diplomatic protests and declarations were also issued collectively. Four distinct Community actions were taken: humanitarian aid for refugees was provided; support was given to 'victim' countries (Egypt, Jordan and Turkey); the Community acted as a collective body with respect to co-operation with Arab and Mediterranean states; and the Community proceeded with its own embargo on trade and implemented the UN sanctions on all forms of military co-operation, the import of petroleum and the sale of arms. All of these actions met with popular support across the Community and 61 per cent regarded membership of the EC to be an important aspect of each national response to the Gulf crisis. There was a significant difference in the levels of popular awareness of the Community's Gulf policy. In October 1990, two months prior to military action, only 40 per cent of Germans were aware that a Community role existed, whereas over 70 per cent of British, Belgian, Danish, Irish, Italian and Spanish citizens knew that there was a Community policy (*European Affairs*, 1990, p. 15). For the Community to develop a common foreign policy which will assist integration, its actions have to be recognized and supported by the Community population at large.

Despite these attempts to maintain and exert a collective position, the Gulf crisis underlined the inherent weaknesses of EPC. It took a month for the Community to react effectively to the 2 August invasion of Kuwait and the initiatives introduced bore all the hallmarks of compromise. National interests and kudos clearly took precedence over *l'esprit communautaire*. The UK and France, both permanent members of the UN Security Council, at times adopted different and incompatible bilateral positions, with each proposing its own formula for resolution through independent, not Community sponsored, UN resolutions. Perhaps surprisingly given their generally more pro-EC position, the French co-operated more closely with the other permanent members of the Security Council than it did with its Community partners. However, the most distinctive feature was the independence of French foreign policy (epitomized by their counter proposal of 14 January which breached the American engineered common UN line).

To compound this European diffusion, Germany faced criticism from within and outside the Twelve for refusing to commit its armed forces to the Allied efforts, the German constitution prohibiting military activity beyond the immediate NATO area. Germany, together with Belgium and Italy, did commit fighter planes to Turkey under the UN umbrella. Only three states sent troops and military equipment for fighting the Gulf war, and each contribution was a national, not Community, decision. The UK sent 32,000 troops, France 11,000 and Italy 270, with each country sending 72, 24 and 10 bomber planes, respectively. These three were also the major contributors to the naval blockade, although six other EC states did commit marines and/or ships (Belgium, Denmark, Spain, Greece, The Netherlands and Portugal) (Dury, 1991, pp. 42–4).

The disappointment of the Community response was one of the catalysts behind the inclusion of a CFSP within the 1991 IGC discussions. It became painfully obvious that a common foreign policy was worthless without a compatible common security policy and at least a basic agreement on military co-operation. Although the 1991 Treaty reform once again hedged this necessary step, the future of Community integration, at least in keeping with that outlined by Monnet, remains inexorably linked with a collective political, security and military response at the Community level.

YUGOSLAVIA

The origins of the contemporary Yugoslavian crisis were traceable to early 1991, with hostilities eventually breaking out at the end of June, coinciding with the European Council Luxembourg summit meeting. This provided the Community with the opportunity to react immediately – in stark contrast to its often delayed response to international crises in the 1970s and 1980s. Having seen its initial EPC statements calling for institutional reform, support for Yugoslavia's 'territorial unity and integrity' and diplomatic appeals for restraint fail, on 28 June the Community dispatched a ministerial Troika (consisting of the Luxembourg, Italian and Dutch Foreign Ministers) to Yugoslavia to assess the situation. Although the efficacy of Community involvement seemed to be modest given the continuation of violent conflict throughout 1991–92, an important principle of Community foreign policy was established by this crisis: the possibility of acting autonomously and of invoking external political intervention within Europe's immediate sphere was added to the Community's list of foreign policy instruments and options.

During 1991, Community policy fell into two broad approaches: initially, the Community sent a team of diplomats to monitor the situation and attempted to intervene as a mediator; when this process failed to achieve practical results, the Twelve resorted to imposing selective economic sanctions. Agreement to a cease-fire on 18 October gave the Community the opportunity to bring the warring republics within the Yugoslav federation to a peace conference in The Hague under the chairmanship of Lord Carrington. Successive breaches of the cease-fire, predominantly by the Serbian controlled federal armed forces, and rejection of EC proposals for a reformulated federation saw this process derailed. At the 5 November Hague Conference on Yugoslavia, the republics failed to reach a consensus and this attempt at Community brokerage gave way to calls for economic sanctions and the recognition of Croatia and Slovenia by the Community. A week later a last-ditch attempt to deploy either a Community or a UN peace-keeping force was raised; but this initiative, like the dozen or so cease-fires that preceded it, failed to be enacted. Consequently, the Community moved to adopt a policy of economic sanctions aimed principally against the Serbian republic and federal government.

In a 12 November EPC statement the Community outlined the measures it intended to adopt (and which became effective as of 25 November):

- immediate suspension of the application of the trade and cooperation Agreement with Yugoslavia and a decision to terminate the same Agreement;
- restoration of the quantitative limits for textiles;
- removal of Yugoslavia from the list of benefits under the PHARE programme;
- exclusion from the G24 forum;

- encourage the UN to enhance its arms embargo and to introduce an oil embargo. (*Agence Europe*, 12/13 November 1991, p. 5)

These punitive economic measures were significant. The third financial protocol between the EC and Yugoslavia (for 1991–95) involved loans totalling 807m ECU and the PHARE programme involved over 100m ECU: estimates suggested that the trade embargo would weaken the Yugoslavian economy by between $650m and $1.2bn. Humanitarian aid to the value of 14.6m ECU was provided between September and December 1991 for all Yugoslavian populations affected by the conflict, irrespective of republic.

This blanket approach to the imposition of sanctions was an inappropriately blunt instrument; it failed to discriminate between those republics regarded as the aggressors (Serbia) and those whose territory was being violated (Croatia and Slovenia). Consequently, on 2 December the Community adopted a series of positive compensatory measures for those republics who had been negotiating in good faith and had respected the previous cease-fire agreements. These countervailing positive measures were applied to four 'good' republics – Slovenia, Croatia, Macedonia and Bosnia-Hercegovina. This preferential treatment involved the four being reintegrated into the system of trade preferences, the PHARE programme and the EIB loans facility of the EC–Yugoslavian financial protocol (all suspended on 25 November). While Greece opposed the positive measures, it chose to abstain rather than vote against the measures, thereby allowing EPC consensus to be enacted, although this fragile consensus was again tested by a German initiative in mid-December 1991.

The lifting of these economic sanctions was not intended to imply that the Community would recognize these four republics as independent states, despite the prompting of Germany. However, one week after the Maastricht meeting, the Community's collective policy was jeopardized by Germany's decision to recognize Croatia independently and to end its bilateral ties with the Yugoslavian federation in preparation for new relationships with the constituent states. To avoid this disintegration of EPC, the Community adopted a dual strategy: a general policy on the recognition of new states was adopted; and within this context, on 18 December the Community agreed to adopt a set of conditions which had to be met before any individual Yugoslavian republic would be recognized. In response, Germany agreed to only make its decision to recognize Croatia effective as of 15 January 1992, the same date set by the Community conditions (although it announced its intention to recognize Croatia and Slovenia on 23 December 1991).

The general 'Guidelines on the Recognition of New States in Eastern Europe and the Soviet Union' combine the principles outlined in the Helsinki Act and the Charter of Paris emphasizing the rule of law, democracy and human rights, with the commitment to the protection of ethnic minorities and national self-determination stipulated within the CSCE framework. In addition, the borders of any such new state must be established by peaceful common agreement, regional stability and security cannot be undermined, and all succession and regional disputes must be resolved through arbitration. Only new states that satisfy these conditions can be considered for recognition by the Community, and any new states that are formed through aggression are automatically excluded from possible recognition. The additional criteria specific to the Yugoslavian situation demanded by the Community stipulated that all Yugoslavian republics had until 23 December to state whether they wished to be recognized as independent states (all but two did so – Serbia and Montenegro). These new states had to accept the conditions set out in the 'Guidelines' for the recognition of new states, as well as those laid out in the Draft Convention of the Community sponsored Conference on Yugoslavia, and were required to continue supporting this conference process and the role of the UN.

Prior to reunification, Germany had an impeccable EPC record; its unexpected break with the principle of consensus underlined the weakness of foreign policy co-ordination based on voluntary practice and unanimity: the CFSP, which had been strongly advocated by Germany at the IGCs, was designed to prevent such intra-Community divisions. Without this discipline, Germany and other Community states were free to behave in a traditional as well as a *communautaire* manner. As well as illustrating this flaw central to EPC, the Yugoslavian case highlights three distinct positive elements of Community foreign policy. Firstly, at least until the end of 1991, the Community remained united in its position on the Yugoslavian conflict, despite different interests of the member states. The extreme and conflicting positions of Greece, on the one hand, and of Germany and to a lesser degree France, on the other, were accommodated within a common EPC approach. This international crisis illustrated how the experience of working co-operatively within EPC for over two decades had helped to produce a new form of diplomatic behaviour. Individual states were prepared to set aside their individual foreign policy objectives for the sake and clarity of a common European foreign policy. This important psychological step was fundamental to the development of a more definitive and binding CFSP.

Secondly, the conflict also illustrated the efficacy and discriminate effect of sanctions. Despite the Community's lack of military capability, geographic proximity, trade relations and Community assistance programmes all combined to provide the EC with an effective foreign policy instrument.

Thirdly, and perhaps most importantly for the Community's future international role, the EC functioned as a legitimate and appropriate mediator for conflict resolution. The Community was the dominant international actor with respect to resolving the Yugoslavian conflict during 1991, outweighing on this occasion the role and influence of both the US and the UN. In response, critics of EPC and opponents of a future CFSP can point to the relative failure of Community policy; countless cease-fires were broken during 1991–92, the Community conference process achieved few breakthroughs and the question of Yugoslavia's integrity and the recognition of its component states was fudged. EPC was certainly imperfect, but none the less, it is preferable to a dislocated and unco-ordinated bilateral approach to conflicts, especially those in areas contiguous to the Community itself. The experience of co-operation within EPC has led, quite naturally, to a harmonization of views and of interests on an increasingly wide range of international issues: political spillover by stealth.

THE 1991 SOVIET COUP AND DISSOLUTION OF THE USSR

The aborted and short-lived Soviet coup of August 1991 illustrated the general basis for consensus that exists between the Twelve on major foreign policy issues; the ability of the Community to respond to a crisis; and, the options that the Community possesses in relation to economic sanctions.

The Community was among the first to condemn the *coup d'état*: meeting almost immediately under the emergency crisis provisions outlined in the SEA, they issued a declaration on 20 August in which they pronounced the removal of President Gorbachev from office and the seizure of power as a flagrant violation of international norms and an unconstitutional act. Economic assistance to the Soviet Union (both technical and food aid) was suspended; only humanitarian food aid was to be continued, though strictly monitored; and the Community warned that unless constitutional order was restored, they would boycott the September CSCE meeting in Moscow. In the same communiqué the Dutch Presidency reaffirmed the Community's intention to conclude association agreements with Poland, Hungary and Czechoslovakia and extend ties with other emerging East European democracies. The suspension of economic assistance revoked the December 1990 European Council decision: this programme was worth 400m ECU in technical assistance, 250m ECU in direct food aid and 500m ECU in credit guarantees for EC food exports to the Soviet Union. With the collapse of the coup, the Community lifted its suspension of aid on 22 August.

Clearly, the Community displayed the ability to respond effectively and rapidly as an international actor: serious reservations, however, can be raised over the longer term viability of EPC cohesion had the Soviet coup succeeded. Faced with a threat of an unstable superpower, the purpose and good sense of imposing economic sanctions can be questioned. A continued crisis may have exposed the limitations of the Community's prototype foreign policy; conversely, it may have forced on the Community the urgency of adopting a collective defence and security policy. The development of EPC has rarely had the benefit of an external catalyst to promote policy reform. Arguably, only through such crisis situations will immediate change occur. In the wake of the Soviet coup and the continued economic and political instability that lasted through 1991, the necessity to reconsider Europe's common defence and security found a more significant place on the IGC agenda, even if progress was, for some states, too incremental and Atlanticist.

Mikhail Gorbachev's resignation on 25 December 1991 and the transition from the former Soviet Union to the new Commonwealth of Independent States (CIS) was again dealt with by the Community collectively, not bilaterally. It was agreed that Russia would succeed the USSR and accept all its rights and obligations, and in a statement issued on the last day of 1991 the Community indicated its readiness to recognize the eight republics (Armenia, Azerbaijan, Belorussia, Kazakhstan, Moldavia, Turkmenistan, Ukraine and Uzbekistan) who by that date had met the conditions set out in the 'Guidelines on the Recognition of New States in Eastern Europe and the Soviet Union' (see previous section). Assurances were still outstanding for both Kirghizia and Tadjikistan, whereas the civil war in Georgia precluded its consideration for recognition. Thus, more effectively than in the case of Yugoslavia, the EC used its collective instrument, the Guidelines, to resolve what could have been a divisive foreign policy issue. Collective action remained paramount.

A clear, if imperfect, picture of the Community's experience in international affairs has developed over the past two decades of political co-operation. The Twelve no longer conduct their foreign relations in splendid bilateral isolation; increasingly, the member states meet and discuss all aspects of international affairs and actively search for a consensus position that can accommodate existing national policies. But EPC has not been simply an experiment in the lowest common denominator: there are a number of examples in the 1980s and 1990s that have demonstrated that national foreign policies can be changed because of the expectations associated with a collective Community response. For example, with respect to South Africa, Britain acceded to a policy of sanctions, albeit a modest one, when their existing bilateral response was to reject such a position. Similarly, Greece suspended its bilateral preference not to impose sanctions on Yugoslavia in order to achieve Community consensus. The foreign policy behaviour of member states has clearly been affected by EPC and will continue to be so under the more rigorous demands of the CFSP introduced at Maastricht in December 1991.

The case-studies chosen have provided a broad overview of the instruments available to the Community. Despite the absence of a military aspect, the use of sanctions, diplomatic statements and activity in international organizations all correspond to normal recognizable international actor behaviour. The Treaty of Rome and the 1992 revisions do provide the legal competences for the Community to act in international affairs; the political will to adopt regulations with respect to sanctions remains, however, controversial. With the tentative extension of the security and defence component of a CFSP, utilizing where appropriate the WEU and NATO structures, the Community has begun to move significantly towards a *communautarization* of foreign policy. The 1990s could well see the Community develop into a significant international political actor commensurate with its role as the leading global economic actor. For its own internal as well as external credibility, however, its chosen foreign policy actions must be seen to be effective. The Community is not a usual international actor; consequently, the standards by which it is judged may often be harsher than those applied to the USA or Russia. Reluctantly adopting sanctions that have a marginal economic impact does little for the Community's credibility as an international force; nor does convening peace conferences that are abandoned due to the Community's inability to mediate or resolve disputes.

A further aspect of the Community's international role that requires comment with regard to its claims for international recognition is the development of diplomatic relations with third countries. As the Community's global influence has grown so have the demands of third countries for direct EC diplomatic representation. This has taken two institutional forms. First, the Commission has established a series of world-wide delegations that provide Brussels with its own independent third country information and communication. Secondly, the member state embassies have adopted a series of procedural mechanisms that have led to increased co-operation between the Twelve in third countries. Thus, in South Africa or Kuwait, for example, British, French or Dutch Ambassadors do not operate independently but in concert with the level of political integration existing in the Council of Ministers. Common declarations, collective actions and consistent and continuous communication between member state embassies in third countries are now the diplomatic norm. This form of co-operation has not replaced traditional bilateral diplomacy, but rather stands parallel to it and represents the practical execution of common positions adopted in EPC by the member state governments (Regelsberger, 1991).

To conclude, it is appropriate to return to the question raised earlier: can the Community be considered as an international actor comparable and equal to other state actors in the international system? The literature on EPC has identified several examples of Community foreign policy action. However, whether these can be considered as tantamount to 'actor-behaviour' as normally defined in international relations remains controversial. According to Taylor, EPC action has not been the product of 'a unified foreign policy-making procedure' (1982, pp. 7–9), but was the product of a decentralized and intergovernmental system. EPC was concerned with harmonization; for a truly 'common' foreign policy to develop it is argued that there must exist *centralized* actor-behaviour where an *obligation* to consult and act becomes the normal and exclusive practice replacing the option of independent bilateral foreign policy action. The Community's institutions and procedures up until the 1992 revisions did not exhibit any such comprehensive or compulsory characteristic. Even the CFSP reforms do not meet this stringent criteria, at least formally: only the experience through the 1990s will test whether the informal and procedural expectations set in motion by the Maastricht Treaty will produced a *de facto* if not *de jure* obligation making the Community in every respect a competent international actor.

References

Allen, D. and Smith, M., 1991, 'Western Europe's presence in the contemporary international arena' in Holland, M. (ed.), *The future of European Political Cooperation: essays on theory and practice*, pp. 95–120.

Bulmer, S., 1983, 'Domestic politics and European Community policy-making', *Journal of Common Market Studies*, 21, pp. 349–63.

Bulmer, S., 1991, 'Analysing EPC: the case for a two-tier analysis' in Holland, M. (ed.), *The future of European Political Cooperation: essays on theory and practice*, pp. 70–94.

Copenhagen Report, 1973, 'Second report on European Political Cooperation and foreign policy', *Bulletin of the EC*, 9, pp. 14–21.

Dehousse, R. and Weiler, J.H.H., 1991, 'EPC and the Single Act: from soft law to hard law' in Holland, M. (ed.), *The future of European Political Cooperation: essays on theory and practice*, pp. 121–42.

Delors, J., 1991, 'European integration and security', Alastair Buchan Memorial Lecture, 7 March, International Institute for Strategic Studies.

Dury, R., 1991, *La communaute Europeenne et la Guerre du Golfe*, Centre Européen Fernand Dehousse, Socialist Group of the European Parliament, Brussels.

European Affairs, 1990, 'Eurobarometer: Europeans about the Gulf War', 4, pp. 15–20.

George, S., 1985, *Politics and policy in the European Community*, Clarendon Press, Oxford.

George, S., 1991, 'European political cooperation: a World system's perspective' in Holland, M. (ed.), *The future of European Political Cooperation: essays on theory and practice*, pp. 52–69.

Haas, E., 1964, *The uniting of Europe: political, economic and social forces 1950–57*, Stanford University Press, Stanford.

Hague Conference, 1969, 'Final communiqué of the conference', *Bulletin of the EC*, 6.

Hill, C., 1988, 'Research into EPC: tasks for the future' in Pijpers, A., Regelsberger, R., Wessels, W. and Edwards, G. (eds), 1988, *European Political Cooperation in the 1980s*, pp. 211–28.

Holland, M., 1987, 'Three approaches for understanding European Political Co-operation: a case-study of EC–South African policy', *Journal of Common Market Studies*, 25, pp. 295–314.

Holland, M., 1988, *The European Community and South Africa: European Political Co-operation under strain*, Pinter, London.

Holland, M. (ed.), 1991, *The future of European Political Cooperation: essays on theory and practice*, Macmillan, London.

Ifestos, P., 1987, *European Political Cooperation: towards a framework of supranational diplomacy*, Avebury, Aldershot.

Keohane, R.O. and Hoffmann, S., 1990, 'Conclusions: Community politics and institutional change' in Wallace, W., (ed.), *The dynamics of European integration*, Pinter/RIIA, London, pp. 276–300.

Luxembourg Report, 1970, 'Report by the Foreign Ministers of the Member States on the problems of Political Unification', *Bulletin of the EC*, 6–11.

Moïsi, D., 1991, 'The causes of war', *European Affairs*, 5–1, pp. 10–11.

Monnet, J., 1978, *Memoirs* (trans. R. Mayne), Doubleday and Company, New York.

Nicoll, W. and Salmon, T.C., 1990, *Understanding the European Communities*, Barnes and Noble, Savage, Maryland.

Nuttall, S., 1988, 'Where the Commission comes in' in Pijpers, A., Regelsberger, R., Wessels, W. and Edwards G. (eds), 1988, *European Political Cooperation in the 1980s: a common foreign policy for Western Europe?* pp. 104–17.

Nuttall, S., 1989, 'The scope and the adequacy of the institutional interaction of EC and EPC', conference paper, *Colloquium: the collaboration of EC and EPC*, Brussels, 16 February.

Pijpers, A., Regelsberger, R., Wessels, W. and Edwards, G. (eds), 1988, *European Political Cooperation in the 1980s: a common foreign policy for Western Europe?*, Martinus Nijhoff/TEPSA, Dordrecht.

Pijpers, A., 1991, 'EPC and the realist paradigm' in Holland, M. (ed.), *The future of European Political Cooperation: essays on theory and practice*, pp. 8–35.

Regelsberger, E., Schoutheete, P. de, Nuttall, S. and Edwards, G., 1985, *The external relations of European Political Cooperation and the future of EPC*, EUI, Florence, Working Paper no. 172.

Regelsberger, E., 1991, 'The Twelve's dialogue with Third countries: progress towards a *Communauté d'action*' in Holland, M. (ed.), 1991, *The future of European Political Cooperation: essays on theory and practice*, pp. 143–60.

Regelsberger, E. and Wessels, W., 1990, 'Towards a Common Foreign and security policy – options for the reform of European Political Cooperation', Institut für Europäische Politik draft working paper, November.

Rhein, E., 1989, 'European foreign policy as seen from the Community perspective' conference paper, *Colloquium: the collaboration of EC and EPC*, Brussels, 16 February.

Rummel, R., 1988, 'Speaking with one voice – and beyond' in Pijpers, A., Regelsberger, R., Wessels, W. and Edwards, G. (eds), 1988, *European Political Cooperation in the 1980s: a common foreign policy for Western Europe?* pp. 118–142.

Taylor, P., 1982, 'The European Communities as an actor in international society', *Journal of European Integration*, 6, pp. 7–41.

Tindemans, L., 1976, *European Union: report to the European Council,Bulletin of the EC*, 1/76, supplement.

Tsakaloyannis, P., 1991, 'The EC, EPC and the decline of Political Cooperation' in Holland, M. (ed.), *The future of European Political Cooperation: essays on theory and practice*, pp. 36–51.

Wallace, H., 1985, 'The Presidency: tasks and evolution' in O'Nuallain, C. (ed.), *The Presidency of the European Council of Ministers*, Croom Helm, London.

Wallace, W., 1983a, 'Political Cooperation: integration through intergovernmentalism' in Wallace, H., Wallace, W. and Webb, C. (eds), *Policy-making in the European Communities*, John Wiley, London, pp. 373–402.

Wallace, W., 1983b, 'Introduction: cooperation and convergence in European foreign policy' in Hill, C. (ed.), *National foreign policies and European Political Cooperation*, George Allen and Unwin/RIIA, London, pp. 1–18.

Wallace, W. (ed.), 1990, *The dynamics of European integration*, Pinter/RIIA, London.

6 A People's Europe: representation, attitudes, citizenship and the Social Charter

Words can have an important symbolic meaning. At the 1991 Maastricht meeting the outmoded name of European 'Economic' Community was replaced with the more appropriate terms of European Community and Union. While important psychologically, this change also represented a fundamental practical advance – the acceptance of the notion of European citizenship and the democratic essence of the future Community. However, this supranational development was not without its intergovernmental opponent and the Community for the first time in its history allowed a member state (the UK) to absent itself from a key common legislative area – social policy. This chapter focuses on the idea of a People's Europe at four interrelated levels – representation, attitudes, citizenship and the Social Charter. Once again, the federal and intergovernmental assumptions underpinning the Community's development provide the theoretical context.

Representation

The democratic deficit within the Community institutional structure has been of concern since the 1960s. Monnet's original ideas and Community constitution initially provided for a parliamentary role that was limited but appropriate to the Community's fledgling experience. Before effective democratization could be introduced the Community had to prove itself worthy of supranational authority: but the eventual democratization of the Community was always part of Monnet's original plan. The task was '. . . to ensure that in their limited field the new institutions were thoroughly democratic . . . the Assembly should be elected by universal suffrage within a federal system . . . In this way, the pragmatic method we had adopted would also lead to a federation validated by the people's vote.' (Monnet, 1978, p. 367).

Consequently, it is neither surprising nor necessarily a criticism, that the Treaty of Rome drew more heavily on bureaucratic and political élite authority than on direct democracy. Within the context of the 1950s it was simply appropriate and expedient. Monnet's incrementalist pragmatism did not preclude a directly elected chamber; the only question was when such an innovation would be timely. As the Community has established itself in new areas of competence, this reliance on centralized authority has come under increasing scrutiny and led to successive reforms, albeit ponderously and in a piecemeal fashion.

Different forms of representation are expressed in the Community structure. As outlined in Chapter 4, the Community's direct representative responsibility falls on the European Parliament, but also indirectly on the Council of Ministers and European Council. Members of the Councils are all elected politicians but their mandate is a national one first and only by delegation do they assume their European portfolios. This form of indirect representation was initially extended to the ECSC and Treaty of Rome's original Common Assembly. From 1953 until 1979 those individuals who sat in these European assemblies were not directly elected but were national delegates elected to their domestic parliaments. Thus, prior to 1979, representation within the Community's institutional structure was indirect and delegated. No one could claim to have a European mandate.

The most widely accepted and direct measure of representation relates to the election of the European Parliament. The issue of the direct election was raised during the relaunch of the 1969 Hague summit; however, British procrastination delayed the final date for the elections until 7 June 1979. Although for democratic purists the supranational aspect of these first elections were marred somewhat (the allocation of seats was determined by national quota; there was no uniform date for the election; and each country was allowed to adopt its own electoral system), from this date onwards the Community can claim to express a supranational democratic authority. But the execution of this representative function has come under increasing criticism for a variety of reasons.

First, as noted above, the unicity of the elections has been fundamentally compromised by the decision to allow each country to adopt its own electoral system for determining representation. The discrepancies between countries have been substantial. For example, while the majority of member states have adopted a list-based form of proportional representation (PR) that extends the control of candidates by parties, Ireland (and Northern Ireland) use the Single Transferable Vote system which emphasizes voter choice, and Great Britain has adopted its national non-proportional simple plurality single ballot system. Not all forms of representation are similar or produce comparable results. Britain's first-past-the-post system produces the greatest distortion in terms of representation: in all three direct elections only one seat has ever gone to a party (the SNP) that was not Conservative or Labour; Britain's leading third parties (the former SDP, the Democrats and the Greens) have never won a seat, despite taking more than a quarter of the vote collectively in 1989. Consequently, Britain's third party voters are effectively denied representation at Strasbourg, tarnishing the democratic credentials of the institution. Even among those countries that appear to have similar proportional systems there are some, but admittedly minor, differences. Thus the various list systems vary in how votes are allocated and transferred (d'Hondt and natural quotient formulas), the degree to which voters can substitute candidates within lists and whether voters can choose candidates across lists. However, these discrepancies remain technical and do only minor representative injustice in comparison with the British method.

The British rationale seems particularly flawed with respect to the European Parliament. While a simple majority system may well be suited to an adversary system, it is wholly inappropriate to the system of political groupings that constitute the European Parliament. The direct elections do not serve to select a government, but to provide the widest possible representation in the Parliament: consequently, only a proportional system that can reflect diversity is an appropriate and valid form of representation. Britain's reluctance, of course, has little to do with redressing the Community's democratic deficit, but simply reflects a strong intergovernmental determination to protect its national electoral system from change. To concede PR at the European level, it is argued, would lead inevitably to a change in the voting system for the House of Commons. While this may be possible, it is also true that France's decision to opt for a list PR system for Community elections has not led to the renunciation of their plurality based second ballot system. However, these domestic sensitivities have all conspired to thwart the perennial attempts to agree on a uniform system for direct elections.

Second and consequently, for the first three direct elections there was no uniform eligibility for voting rights: this responsibility resided with the member states. Some member states allowed any Community national to vote, others restricted this to their own citizens and the eligibility for proxy voting again varied enormously. In the first direct elections in 1979, for example, the Irish and the Dutch allowed any citizen of a member state who was resident in their country to vote, whereas the French only allowed French citizens to vote. The British, on the other hand, followed their domestic rule of extending the franchise to include Irish as well as British citizens.

Third, the whole principle of national quotas is an anathema to the notion of a supranational election. Why should the division of electorates be based on national boundaries and a very imprecise population ratio? Accepting these national lines only reinforces the perception that the European parliamentary elections are in some way national non-elections or referendums on governments rather than distinct supranational activities.

Fourth, as noted in Chapter 2, irrespective of electoral system, all three direct elections held since 1979 have had a disappointingly low and a declining level of turn-out. The claim to be the representative voice of the Community's population has looked increasingly dubious. A partial explanation of this trend has been the lack of a European focus to the elections. Rarely are EC issues the focus of debate (despite a function of the elections being to stimulate such an interest): rather domestic issues colour the campaigns. As Bogdanor has observed, the elections of 1979, 1984 and 1989 were primarily an arena for individual national contests, confirming the interpretation that direct elections were 'second order elections, according to which their outcome is dependent upon national party allegiances, modified by the unpopularity of the incumbent government' (1989, p. 208).

The 1994 elections will certainly provide a test-case for Community aware-ness coming relatively soon after the creation of Europe's frontier-free Single Market, the decision on EMU and 'an ever closer Union'. If the 1994 elec-tions fail to reverse this decline, the representative base of the Community will be fundamentally challenged.

Fifth, the parliamentary elections suffer from the problem that the electors are not voting for a government, but for a representative body that can only boast modest legislative competence. As Pinder has commented, a 'system of representative government locates legislative authority in an assembly of representatives chosen in regular free elections. This is not how laws are made in the Community' (1991a, p. 204). Demonstrating the significance and purpose of the elections can, in specific member states, be a difficult undertaking. In the pre-SEA elections it was questionable whether the European Parliament did provide meaningful representation without any legislative authority. Even the reforms since the SEA have failed to enhance the public image of what often appears to be a peripheral democratic institution. The introduction of the co-operation procedure increased parliamentary influence, but it did not really meet the require-ment of legislative authority central to the idea of representative govern-ment.

Lastly, in all but the British elections, the link between the individual Members of the European Parliament (MEPs) and their electorates is tenu-ous: for example, 81 MEPs for a German population of some 80 million cannot provide the individual with any personal link with an MEP; at best, all that can be achieved is a party loyalty. Even in the British system, one virtue of which is the direct MEP-constituent link, the size of the 78 British Euro-constituencies make any close relationship and affiliation difficult. The traditional domestic parliamentary role of delegated individual repre-sentation via elected members does not transfer easily to the European Parliament. Representation exists, but at a more general pan-European level and as such it has remained something of an unexplained relation-ship for many European voters.

All of these deficiencies reflected the dominant intergovernmental con-straints imposed upon the extension of parliamentary power at Strasbourg. Adequate representation was only compatible with a signifi-cant reform of the Community's legislative process. The reforms agreed to at Maastricht have only partially met this requirement: co-decision and the third reading procedures were expanded (Article 189b), but the process was left incomplete and will require further revision at a future intergovernmental forum. However, in the interim there are a series of supranational based initiatives that could be taken to remedy this intergovernmental influence in the Community's representative process. In summary, these are: a uniform list system; the abolition of national MEP quotas; compulsory multinational list systems; common franchise rules; an enhanced calibre of candidates; and different national and domestic polling days.

In compliance with Article 138.3 of the Treaty of Rome, it has become normal practice for each new session of the European Parliament to convene a committee to determine a common electoral system in time for the next quinquennial election. To date, none have been successful: internal divisions within the Parliament and the hurdle of unanimity in the Council (stipulated in Article 138.3) have proved insurmountable. A common electoral system is the most basic condition for establishing a representative Community, and the clear preference for a form of list PR among the member states make this the obvious choice. Without a common system equality of representation cannot be achieved.

The distribution of MEPs according to nation is incompatible with the idea of a supranational federal Community. Once a common system is in place the logic behind national quotas disappears. Party lists would become trans-European in the truest sense: voters in Spain, for example, would not be limited to selecting Spanish candidates but would choose from party lists that were multinational in composition. An at large election treating the Twelve as a single 518 seat constituency could be adopted. Thus the voters would be presented with a choice between political party lists, not between individuals on the basis of nationality. The 'rules of the game' would force the electorate to behave in a supranational way rather than in the intergovernmental domestic fashion as presently determined. To enhance turn-out and awareness, European candidates would need to be drawn from the existing high profile domestic political élites to a much greater degree than has been the case since 1979. To complement this, common criteria for franchise need to be agreed (based on the definition of Community citizenship discussed below). Residency, rather than nationality, would become the dominant criterion in this new trans-European election. Lastly, to establish the independence and unique character of the elections, national elections should be prohibited from being held on the same day as that for the European Parliament.

If provisions such as these are adopted, then a truly European electoral identity can be established that can offer a distinct and pertinent form of representation. The longer the idiosyncrasies of national electoral rules are allowed to persist, the more difficult it will be to persuade Europe's electorate that the Community is founded on the principles of representative democracy.

A subsidiary aspect of the Community's democratic deficit that touches on the issue of representation is the control the Parliament can exert over other Community institutions. This form of parliamentary accountability has been substantially extended by the 1991 reforms. First, there is now a double investiture procedure whereby the Parliament has assumed the power to approve the appointment of the Commission President and the new Commission, the election of which is to coincide with each five-year parliamentary term. To back this up the Parliament retains its original power to dismiss the Commission *en bloc* by a two-thirds vote. Secondly, the new co-decision procedure, while disappointing the Parliament which wanted full legislative authority, has, like the SEA before it, extended the Parliament's ability to amend Community legislation. Cumulatively, each incremental step taken by the Parliament has significantly altered its legislative competence since its first direct election in 1979. The original Community was characterized by delegated representation without effective accountability; the Community of the 1990s has established direct representation (albeit imperfect) and mechanisms for accountability which can be effectively applied. The Community has not removed its democratic deficit and representation remains unbalanced, but the impetus created by Maastricht has pushed the Community further along the path of a supranational representative democracy.

Attitudes

Echoing the original 1957 Treaty, the 1992 Treaty on European Union calls for 'a new stage in the process creating an ever closer Union among the peoples of Europe'. Any such Union presupposes an attitudinal change on the part of Europe's population supplanting national affiliations with a Community loyalty. This section examines how successful the Community experience has been in modifying the attitudes of Europe's citizens and developing a Community awareness and allegiance. The empirical evidence used draws heavily from the data supplied by the Community's own social survey programme, *Eurobarometre*, Deheneffe (1986) and the social psychological analysis of Hewstone (1986). The analysis of European public opinion is divided between the periods before and after the SEA. As will become apparent, the length of membership is a crucial determinant of European attitudes (for a full-length review of *Eurobarometre* public opinion trends, see Reif and Inglehart, 1991).

   In Chapter 1 the role that can be played by popular attitudes in promoting integration was outlined. Functional theory dictated that mass attitudes had to change, rejecting national loyalties for a new commitment to co-operation. For neofunctionalists, such attitudinal change was not a prerequisite, but a consequence of integration in economic sectors. In addition, the more important attitudinal change for writers such as Haas was not at the level of mass support, but within political élites. Attitudinal theories of integration fell into general disfavour until the 1980s when empirical evidence first began to suggest that among the youth of the Community's founding nations a parallel loyalty and awareness was emerging comparable to the existing national loyalties. It is this development that is discussed below.

Developing attitudes 1957–85

Two Europes can be identified during the first three decades of Community development. Whereas membership has never been a contentious issue among the original Six, the newer members from each successive enlargement have generally been more reluctant to commit themselves whole-heartedly to the Community ideal at the popular level. The following five categories for measuring different attitudinal elements towards European integration illustrate this broad dichotomy: affective sentiment for European integration; support for Community membership; attachment to the European ideal; saliency of the Community; and affiliation to the European Parliament (Hewstone, 1986, p. 23).

While European popular opinion is far from monolithic, during the first 30 years a measure of *affective support* for a united Europe only varied between 83 and 91 per cent approval (although the intensity of support varied considerably), and for the original Community during the 1957–70 period the variation was even narrower (Deheneffe, 1986, p. 28). While the *Eurobarometre* question measuring this attitude was couched in very general terms ('In general, are you for or against efforts being made to unify Western Europe?'), lower responses were evident for those states who joined in 1973, especially the UK. During Britain's first ten years of membership support for European unification waivered between 50 and 64 per cent with between one-quarter and one-fifth of respondents firmly opposed (Hewstone, 1986, p. 25). The figures for Denmark exposed a similar level of hostility, and since 1981 Greek membership has added to the percentage of sceptical integrationists among the Community population.

A similar, if more moderate, trend was evident in estimates of *support for Community membership*. When asked whether Community membership was advantageous or disadvantageous to their own country, between 1973 and 1985 the Community as a whole averaged a 61 per cent positive response and a 14 per cent negative (Deheneffe, 1986, p. 30). Closer examination of attitudes in the four largest member states again isolated the UK as being the least impressed with the benefits of membership. Thus in Germany and France negative responses were invariably below 10 per cent and in Italy the highest score was 6 per cent. In contrast, in the UK the lowest figure for dissatisfaction was 21 per cent (May 1975, the date of the British referendum on membership), ranging up to 49 per cent (in 1980, the beginning of Britain's budgetary dispute). Just prior to the commencement of the intergovernmental process that eventually led to the SEA, the British electorate was evenly divided between those who were positive, negative or indifferent about the effect of Community membership, indicating that in Britain a reliable reservoir of support for the Community had yet to be established despite 14 years membership (Hewstone, 1986, p. 29).

One measure of *attachment to the European ideal* used in the *Eurobarometre* focused on identity and how Europeans viewed themselves – as Community citizens or as nationals. Even in the otherwise pro-Community states, responses to this question were generally constrained and provided only minimal support for the functionalist thesis that a shift in mass loyalties from national to supranational institutions would occur. For example, asked in 1982 if they ever thought of themselves as a citizen of Europe, only 8 per cent UK respondents did, with 15 per cent in Germany, 18 per cent in Italy and 21 per cent in France. In contrast, individuals who never conceived of themselves in that way totalled 74 per cent, 26 per cent, 45 per cent and 40 per cent respectively (p. 33). This indifferent level of support was also reflected in attitudes towards the *saliency of the Community*: just how important was the Community in the everyday life of Europeans? Between 1974 and 1985 respondents were asked for their opinion if the EC were scrapped tomorrow. Taking the combined scores for the original Six,

for every year there was a majority who felt 'very sorry' (ranging from 49
–65 per cent), whereas only between 4 and 7 per cent felt 'relieved'. When
the average for the enlarged Community was taken support for the Community ideal declined significantly (10–18 per cent felt 'relieved', whereas
42–56 per cent felt 'very sorry' (Deheneffe, 1986, p. 33).

The final measure of attitudinal change concerns public perception of
and affiliation to the European Parliament. This indicator is particularly
important given the direct representative role bestowed on the Parliament
after 1979. Public awareness of the Parliament has fluctuated enormously
over the past two decades: in 1978, one year before the first elections, a
bare 50 per cent of all EC citizens could recall hearing a recent item about
the Parliament. Immediately after the first direct elections this rose to two-
thirds before plummeting to just 37 per cent in the spring of 1983. The
highest level of awareness (75%) was recorded just after the second direct
elections, but again this figure began to decline as the election became
more distant. Examining individual countries revealed an interesting
attitudinal link. The three countries that scored the highest in assessing the
benefits of Community membership were also those which had the highest
levels of public awareness of the European Parliament (Luxembourg, Italy
and The Netherlands): conversely, the two countries with the lowest perception of benefit and of awareness were also the same – the UK and
Greece. For all countries, however, expectations of the Parliament always
exceed its perceived effectiveness (pp. 46–8).

Strengthening loyalties 1986–91

In the post-SEA era, European public opinion has in general matured in
response to developments such as the Single Market and Monetary Union.
However, there are still significant variations within the member states,
with the UK and Denmark consistently being the more reluctant Europeans
(for detailed overview, see Pinder, 1991b). Thus the results of *Eurobarometre*
34 (1990) showed that 81 per cent of all EC citizens supported the efforts
being made to unify the Community, with the Italians and Spanish the
most enthusiastic (87 and 84 per cent respectively). 69 per cent indicated
that Community membership was a 'good thing', the highest percentage
ever recorded, while a mere 7 per cent said that it was a 'bad thing' (though
the figures for the UK and Denmark were significantly higher at 16 and 19
per cent respectively). Disappointingly, only 49 per cent of Europeans
would regret the dissolution of the EC although just 6 per cent professed
relief at the prospect. Although these figures did not indicate a comprehensive and loyal affiliation to the Community, these combined scores for
the four measures were the highest recorded since 1975. Clearly, a European idea is being transmitted and accepted by the member states, but
acculturation is an extremely slow process. The Italians proved to be the
greatest Europhiles while the Portuguese recorded significant increases in
support for integration. Conversely, the UK came last on three measures
and second to last on the fourth. Interestingly, Danish support for EC

membership rose to 58 per cent easily the highest percentage since Denmark joined the Community in 1973. British public opinion appeared to be isolated and out of step with the Community as a whole, a reality reflected in, or caused by, the antagonistic positions often adopted by the Conservative British Government.

Despite the holding of the third direct elections and the growing debate on the role of the Parliament and the Community's democratic deficit, awareness of the European Parliament remained low (49 per cent) and inconsistent, though once again the Danish (41 per cent) and British (39 per cent) public seemed the worst informed. Those countries who had the highest regard for the work of the Parliament (ranging from 70–56 per cent approval compared with the Community average of 52 per cent) were either the poorest Community areas or those from southern Europe (in descending order Italy, Greece, Ireland, Portugal and Spain). Again, the British (32 per cent) and the Danes (30 per cent) had the highest percentage of people with unfavourable impressions. On a range of other issues concerning the Parliament this pattern was broadly duplicated: thus while 53 per cent of Europeans on average wanted the Parliament to become more important with just 4 per cent wanting its powers curtailed, just 25 per cent of Danes and 42 per cent of Britons supported the extension of parliamentary authority whereas 20 and 19 per cent respectively actually wanted the powers of the Parliament reduced! Finally, when asked whether they supported the idea of a European government being answerable to the European Parliament, support was 33 and 23 per cent in Britain and Denmark, with 37 and 61 per cent opposed. In comparison the EC average was 55 per cent in favour and 19 per cent opposed.

Many of the *Eurobarometre* questions are phrased in a general and perhaps too esoteric way: commitment to ideals and possible future scenarios may not be the best attitudinal measures of European loyalties. The practical realities of 1992 and the Gulf War may provide a more concrete assessment of the real level of mass integration that existed in the Community at the start of the 1990s. One year prior to the Maastricht proposals support for a single currency averaged 52 per cent throughout the Community with 23 per cent opposed. Again, the Italians and Greeks were the most supportive (72 and 64 per cent approval ratings) and the British and Danish the most hostile (with 43 and 50 per cent opposed respectively). A similar pattern was revealed for attitudes towards the 1992 Single Market. It remains to be seen whether and in which direction public opinion will consolidate as the Community draws closer to the implementation of 1992 and Monetary Union. Foreign policy is often regarded as an inviolable national prerogative, almost by definition the determining criterion of the nation-state. Almost two-thirds of EC citizens were aware of the EC's role in the Gulf crisis as early as October 1990, more than two months before hostilities broke out. Significantly, in nine member states the EC was seen as more capable of resolving the crisis than the individuals' own country (the exceptions being the UK, France and Italy, the three Community countries that eventually became militarily involved in the war). Furthermore, an average of 61 per cent of Community citizens believed that membership of the Community had played an important role in determining their respective country's foreign policy position. The French (70 per cent) and Italians (68 per cent) recorded the highest levels of opinion on this topic and even among the UK population 57 per cent acknowledged the EC's role. Thus the reality of the Gulf crisis helped to focus public opinion on the practical and concrete role that the Community plays in international affairs. It is contentious, however, whether the Community's record during the Gulf War has helped or hindered the development of favourable Community attitudes at the level of public opinion. No doubt future *Eurobarometres* will provide a satisfactory answer.

Measuring mass attitudes is a precarious endeavour; however, the longitudinal evidence presented in the *Eurobarometres* does allow some tentative conclusions to be made and general trends to be highlighted. Overall, the commitment to the European ideal remains solid, particularly amongst those countries that have been members either the longest (the original Six) or the shortest (Spain and Portugal). It is only among the states who joined in 1973 that an ambivalence towards the Community persists, even if outright opposition to the EC is declining. However, that this should still be the case after two decades of membership is a sobering reflection on the generational constraint on European integration. While mass attitudinal loyalty may not be the necessary prerequisite for European Union, clearly any enduring level of integration must be based on popular support. In this respect the Community still has significant progress to make: the heart of integration depends on achieving popular loyalties to the Community that are as strong and durable as those that already exist for each individual state.

Citizenship

The basic principle underlying the idea of Community citizenship is that irrespective of nationality, all member state nationals should have the same rights and freedoms. Just as the logic of the Single Market demands the abolition of local distortions, so the concept of European citizenship stresses the equality of human rights throughout the Community. Consequently, at the June 1984 European Council a working group on the area of a People's Europe was initiated. The major aspects concerning citizenship were to address electoral issues (the franchise and voting system for the European Parliament); the rights of permanent residents living in another member state; the rights of the Community's border inhabitants (in relation to cross-border environmental issues); the equality of legal redress throughout the Community; and common diplomatic provisions in third countries. The 1991 Maastricht agreement helped to make many of these ideas a reality. The Maastricht Treaty on European Union provided for legal recognition of Community citizenship, whereby '[E]very person holding the nationality of a Member State shall be a citizen of the Union . . . (and) enjoy the rights conferred by this Treaty and shall be subject to the duties imposed thereby' (Article 8.1–2). Every citizen of the Union had the right to petition the European Parliament or seek redress for maladministration through the newly established office of Ombudsman (Article 8d). Union citizenship specified the right to 'move and reside freely within the territory of the Member States' (Article 8a.1), and introduced certain common electoral rights (Article 8b). Citizens of the Union who reside in a member state for which they are not a national will be eligible to stand as candidates and vote in both municipal elections and those for the European Parliament (though the implementation of the detailed arrangements and specific derogations may mean that these provisions may only be activated by 1994). Article 8c extends the concept of Union citizenship to cover EC nationals in third countries. Where there is no national diplomatic authority in a third country, Union citizenship means that an individual is 'entitled to protection by the diplomatic or consular authorities of any Member State, on the same conditions as the nationals of the State'. This diplomatic innovation reflected the growing EPC informal practice and the actual execution of Community policy in the Gulf War.

Establishing the legal identity of Union citizenship in the Maastricht Treaty was a significant supranational advance for the Community: the conditions and terms of citizenship may have been constrained and limited in scope, but an important federal precedent was established. If attitudinal change is to occur, then there has to be a legal recognition that the citizens of the member states do enjoy similar rights and obligations. The Maastricht reforms began the process of demonstrating the existence of common and shared rights, and the liberal principles of the Single Market were seen to be equally applicable to democratic rights. While the common rules for eligibility for the European Parliament elections are not sufficient in themselves to create a uniform election, they do provide a common basis on which a uniform set of electoral procedures can be established (in terms of Article 138.3 of the original Rome Treaty).

The Social Charter

The importance of a People's Europe has developed in parallel with the creation of the economic benefits of 1992. The Single Market has an important social dimension that stems from its economic liberalism. The free movement of individuals, the mutual recognition qualifications, the abolition of internal border checks, for example, are all social aspects of the Single Market that directly affect the human dimension of the Community. Freedoms, of course, require commensurate obligations and to protect the rights of Community residents there has to be greater Community-level co-operation on issues such as border controls, immigration policy, and drugs surveillance.

The greatest disappointment at Maastricht was the refusal of the UK to accept the idea of a Community Social Charter that was designed to create a uniform basis for the protection of individual and collective rights within the Community. The other eleven states went ahead and created such an agreement that was to operate and be governed through the existing Community institutions and competences, but this decision was separate and different from the other Maastricht treaties that were binding on the Twelve. The absence of this collective policy clearly weakens the idea of a People's Europe: potentially British workers could be treated differently to workers in the other eleven states, limiting, arguably, the free movement of individuals.

An Annex of the Treaty on European Union signed at Maastricht commits 'the members of the European Community with the exception of the United Kingdom . . . to implement the 1989 Social Charter on the basis of the *acquis communautaire*'. This establishes a unique arrangement within the Community framework. EC institutions and procedures are used to govern certain social aspects but these are not applicable to Britain; indeed, in the Treaty Protocol on Social Policy the UK is explicitly prohibited from participating in, or influencing any policy covered by the agreement. Extending the *communautaire* procedures further, there is provision for social policy legislation (directives) derived from the Protocol to be governed by qualified majority voting (44 votes constituting a majority decision in the absence of the UK).

Articles 1–7 cover the Social Policy Agreement relevant to the eleven member state signatories. Contrary to British complaints, the policy is not an inflexible pan-European approach to labour relations and social concerns: individual national conditions and circumstances are accommodated. Thus Article 1 states that measures shall only be implemented 'which take account of the diverse forms of national practices, in particular in the field of contractual relations, and the need to maintain the competitiveness of the Community economy'. Furthermore, the existing directives effecting social policy on labour relations remain in force; it is only in the new areas defined in the Social Charter that Community competence is extended. But perhaps most importantly, Article 2 significantly limits the scope of Community involvement in what the UK views as crucial areas of national labour relations autonomy: thus, the Social Policy Protocol does 'not apply to pay, the right of association, the right to strike or the right to impose lock-outs'. Despite these guarantees of national autonomy in labour relations, at least at Maastricht the British Government set the precedent of institutionalizing an à la carte approach to integration which, if maintained, will be the antithesis of the common Community envisaged by Monnet in the 1950s and Jacques Delors in the 1990s.

The objectives of social policy are 'the promotion of employment, improved living and working conditions, proper social protection, dialogue between management and labour, the development of human resources with a view to lasting high employment and the combating of exclusion' (Article 1). In practice, this committed the eleven to supporting and complementing the following existing national activities:

- improvement in particular of the working environment to protect workers' health and safety;
- working conditions;
- the information and consultation of workers;

- equality between men and women with regard to labour market opportunities and treatment at work;
- the integration of persons excluded from the labour market. (Article 2)

These areas are governed by majority decision-making (under Article 189c); however, for a number of important policy areas unanimity is still required: social security and social protection of workers; redundancy protection; representation and collective bargaining; the treatment of third country employees; and national financial support for employment programmes (Article 2.3).

Discrimination on the grounds of sex is also covered in the Social Policy Agreement which enshrines the principle of equal pay for men and women. Again, however, national autonomy is preserved as this minimal requirement does not preclude provision for any additional measures of positive discrimination: any of the eleven may maintain or adopt 'measures providing for specific advantages in order to make it easier for women to pursue a vocational activity or to prevent or compensate for disadvantages in their professional careers' (Article 6).

Lastly, in relation to the new Social Policy Protocol, the Commission's role is twofold. Firstly, it is responsible for encouraging the individual member states to co-operate and co-ordinate their social policies in order to achieve the objectives set out in Article 1. The second Commission role is to facilitate a dialogue between management and workers at the Community level and respond to their needs in drawing up legislative proposals. Both management and labour are drawn into the policy process in a corporatist fashion, which may if so desired, lead to Community-level contractual arrangements being formulated.

The exclusion of the UK from this important aspect of a People's Europe may prove a short-lived, if costly, decision. In practice, the Protocol adds very little that is new, but through its voluntary exclusion the UK can have no further say on the development of these topics. The eleven are free to develop a common *communautaire* social policy establishing similar labour relations and social conditions: the greater the disparity between social and working conditions, the greater are the chances of distortions within the internal market between the UK and the rest of the Community. Whatever the merits of the case, the British decision is of great historical and psychological importance: despite the series of disputes that have punctuated relations between the Community and the UK since the 1950s, since becoming a member in 1973 Britain has never chosen to opt-out of a Community obligation. In December in Maastricht it did so for the first time. If this decision was not an aberration, but a sign of future national action, the existing level of European integration may be jeopardized and any expectations for a meaningful European Union based on the Community, illusory.

References

Bogdanor, V., 1989, 'Direct elections, representative democracy and European integration', *Electoral Studies*, 8, pp. 205–16.

Eurobarometre, 1990, No. 34, EC Commission, Brussels.

Deheneffe, J-C., 1986, *Europe as seen by Europeans: European polling 1973–86* European Documentation Series, Office for Official Publications of the European Communities, Luxembourg.

Hewstone, M., 1986, *Understanding attitudes to the European Community*, Cambridge University Press, Cambridge.

Monnet, J., 1978, *Memoirs* (trans. R. Mayne), Doubleday and Company, New York.

Pinder, J., 1991a, 'The European Community, the rule of law and representative government: The significance of the Intergovernmental Conferences', *Government and Opposition*, 26–2, pp. 199–214.

Pinder, J., 1991b, 'Public opinion and European Union: Thatcher versus the people of Europe' in Reif, K. and Inglehart, R. (eds), *Eurobarometer: the dynamics of European public opinion*.

Reif, K. and Inglehart, R. (eds), 1991, *Eurobarometer: the dynamics of European public opinion. Essays in honour of Jacques-René Rabier*, Macmillan, London.

7 Future enlargement: challenges and opportunities

This chapter is divided into three sections: first, the issues central to the contemporary enlargement debate are discussed; second, the experience of past enlargements is evaluated; and thirdly, the cases of the current applicant states and the problems associated with probable future applicants are considered. Throughout, the implications for integration theory are considered.

Prior to the 1990s, discussion of enlargement primarily focused on applicant states either from the Community's southern periphery or northern EFTA countries: with the spread of democratization through Central and Eastern Europe, the demise of the Soviet Union and the disintegration of the Yugoslavian Republic, the form, speed, scope and desirability of enlargement has become the Community's most pressing problem. This chapter examines all of these contemporary questions. How quickly can the Community grow? What are the institutional prerequisites for change? What are the policy consequences? Just how large a Community is a particularly difficult conundrum. Once again, many of the issues and problems first discussed by Monnet and his colleagues are pertinent to the current Community agenda. In particular, the relationship of integration and enlargement remains central to the debate. Simply, will further enlargement advance or retard the momentum towards European Union? Integration theory is ambivalent and inconclusive on this point; practical and historical experience is of greater direct relevance. Consequently, to understand these issues of future enlargement, it is useful to place the discussion within the context of the Community's past experience of transformation from the Six, to the Nine, to the Twelve.

The contemporary issues

Enlargement has been a consistent Community priority. The Community was originally devised to be a dynamic organisation with flexible institutional relations: it was not the end-point in the process of European integration but the beginning. The inclusion of a wider family of European states was always envisaged. While the conditions of the 1990s and the characteristics of several possible new members are unique, the Community currently faces familiar questions of institutional and policy adaptations. The 1957 Treaty of Rome adequately accommodated the original Six, all of whom shared relatively similar economies and levels of development. The doubling in size within the next 30 years required revision of the Community's structure and decision-making procedures. Both the 1986 SEA and the 1991 Maastricht reforms introduced policy and institutional reforms to assist the Community with its increased membership of twelve and to prepare it for further enlargement. However, the conclusion of Edwards writing some 15 years earlier still remains valid, despite Maastricht: he argued that further enlargement 'should not take place without substantial improvements being introduced into the Community's decision-making processes and the institutions strengthened' (1977, p. 164), a position that reflected the 'deepening versus widening' debate amongst integrationists. The pragmatic developments agreed to at Maastricht fell far short of the radical measures needed to prepare the EC for the expected substantial enlargement over the next decade. As is demonstrated elsewhere in this chapter, further institutional and decision-making reform is necessary in a number of Community areas.

The legal and technical procedures for enlargement are relatively uncomplicated; the political barriers are far more difficult to overcome. The preamble to the Treaty of Rome calls on members of the Community to 'preserve and strengthen peace and liberty' and invites 'the other peoples of Europe who share their ideal to join in their efforts'. The two paragraphs of Article 237 state the original conditions that needed to be met:

> Any European State may apply to become a member of the Community. It shall address its application to the Council, which shall act unanimously after obtaining the opinion of the Commission.
>
> The conditions of admission and the adjustments of this Treaty necessitated thereby shall be the subject of an agreement between the Member States and the applicant State. This agreement shall be submitted for ratification by all the Contracting States in accordance with their respective constitutional requirements.

In practice, additional criteria were employed to evaluate candidates: applicants had to be democratic regimes and their respective economic infrastructures and levels of development had to be compatible with those in the existing Community. In the past, both these criteria have been used to exclude or at least delay membership to applicant states. Greece's application was suspended while military rule was in force, and currently question marks remain as to the democratic basis of Turkey; the Community's rejection of Britain's application in 1963 reflected, in part, the economic incompatibility between the UK and the then Six. However, as the Greek and British cases also illustrate, and the accession of Spain and Portugal too, political considerations can and do override these purely technical conditions for membership. During the 1990s a third informal criteria emerged: all applicant states were expected to accept the existing *acquis communautaire* with respect to foreign policy co-ordination, underlining the dominant political nature of the Community's rationale for enlargement.

These conditions for membership were modified by Article 8 of the SEA. The first paragraph of Article 237 was replaced by the requirement that the Council is unanimous and the application receives the assent of the European Parliament, thereby making the accession of a new member state conditional on a favourable vote in the European Parliament. Given the number of new applicants and the political issues involved, this new power of the Parliament gives it considerable authority and influence over determining the shape of the future Community. The Parliament could also conceivably use this implied power of veto as a further way of expressing its discontent with its continued limited legislative role in domestic Community affairs. The rejection by Parliament of an otherwise acceptable applicant state for purely inter-institutional reasons is a not too unrealistic, if disturbing, prospect.

A detailed consideration of further enlargement was not within the IGC brief at Maastricht; all that was undertaken was some tidying-up of the existing procedures. Articles 237 and 238 were formally deleted; however, these were incorporated in a new article in the Maastricht Treaty, which with minor revisions, duplicated the original wording. The change was necessary in order to maintain terminological consistency throughout the Treaty and involved replacing the use of 'Treaty' and 'Community' with the new term 'Union'. Thus, the revised criteria for enlargement are:

> Any European State may apply to become a Member of the Union. It shall address its application to the Council, which shall act unanimously after consulting the Commission and after receiving the assent of the European Parliament, which shall act by an absolute majority of its component members.
>
> The conditions of admission and the adjustments to the Treaties on which the Union is founded which such admission entails shall be the subject of an agreement between the Member States and the applicant State. This agreement shall be submitted for ratification by all the Contracting States in accordance with their respective constitutional requirements. (Article X)

The Community did signal its enthusiasm for further enlargement through the Maastricht European Council's Presidency conclusions. Without identifying specific countries, the Council called on the Commission to prepare a report on enlargement for the next European Council summit (in Lisbon, June 1992) on the implications for the Union's future development. Significantly, the declaration addressed those states who at that time had already applied (Austria, Cyprus, Malta, Sweden and Turkey) as well as those who had only announced an intention to seek membership of the Union. The only limitation was that negotiations had to wait until the Community had resolved its budgetary 'own resources' issues for 1992.

Clearly, the European Council was politically committed to significant and fairly speedy enlargement: but this commitment was not a *carte blanche* guarantee, of course. Certain states would be treated preferentially. In previous enlargements the negotiation and application process had taken a minimum of three years, and more than ten years in particularly difficult cases. For obvious political, economic and cultural reasons, the applications of Austria and Sweden are expected to be dealt with in the shortest time. Austria formally applied in 1989, whereas Sweden's application was only submitted to the Community six months before the Maastricht summit.

Although the Commission gave a favourable response to the Austrian application, a moratorium was placed on formal consideration of any new member states until after the 1992 Single Market programme had been completed. Most observers expect at least these two countries to become full Community member states by 1995–6.

Such a piecemeal approach to enlargement is politically sensitive for the Community. The smaller states of Malta and Cyprus could legitimately claim a degree of discrimination if their applications were set aside, while Turkey's goodwill could be sorely tested if the Commission recommended, as seems likely, a delay postponing accession until the next century. Turkey's application has been held in abeyance since 1987. The more advanced new democracies (Czechoslovakia, Hungary and Poland) have indicated that they expect to apply for Community membership between 2001 and 2010: depending on circumstances a similar time-scale could be envisaged for any number of the new European states that have been internationally recognized during the 1990s. Without the benefit of a crystal-ball, it is most likely that the pace of enlargement will be cautious where necessary, and expedient where appropriate.

Irrespective of the pace of enlargement, there seems to be no definitive position on the question of how large the Community could, or should, become. Intergovernmentalist governments like that of the UK have supported the concept of a Europe from the Atlantic to the Urals, whereas those committed to a federal Union are more sceptical as to the viability of such a broad-based Community. What countries are the most likely candidates and what will the possible size of the Community be by the turn of the century? The creation of the European Economic Area (EEA) (whose members comprise the former EFTA states) suggests that the most probable new member states will be drawn from the seven participating countries (with the exception of Iceland and Liechtenstein who have formally rejected possible membership). The EEA establishes economic harmonization and free trade between these countries with the Community (scheduled to take effect to coincide with the creation of the Single Market) making any transition to full Community membership less difficult economically. If Malta and Cyprus are added to these, a Community of 21 member states is conceivable. If Turkey, Czechoslovakia, Hungary and Poland are added, and possibly the Baltic states and new independent republics from the Yugoslav federation, the Community could well have swollen to nigh on 30 states within its first 50 years of existence.

It is the implications of such an expansion that make further institutional and policy reform of the existing Community structure a priority during the 1990s. In the opinion of Jacques Delors, substantial enlargement would demand considerable institutional change otherwise the Community 'would return to a simple free-trade area and . . . we would lose all the acquisitions gained from thirty years of political and economical integration'. His solution was to create a European Government with a Chief Executive elected for three-year terms by majority vote in the European Council. Accordingly, 'there will therefore be one person to represent Europe in the areas where this Community is competent and solely in these areas'

(*Agence Europe*, 1992, no. 5640, p. 3). If somewhat radical, this proposal highlighted those institutional prerequisites for change. The most important issues that remain to be addressed include majority voting and the streamlining of decision-making; institutional structures and democratization; and common external action.

In its transition from the Six to the Twelve, the Community strategy was simply to expand the numbers involved in the decision-making process: thus the various Councils grew to twelve, the Commission to seventeen and the Parliament to 518. The existing practice is already too cumbersome, but Maastricht failed to introduce fundamental institutional reform despite debating the necessity of reducing the size of the Commission and increasing that of the Parliament. The only change made was to extend the term of the Commission to five years in 1995. However, a declaration to review the basis of representation by the end of 1992 was appended to the Treaty:

> Member States will examine the questions relating to the number of members of the Commission and the number of members of the European Parliament no later than at the end of 1992, with the view to reaching agreement which will permit the establishment of the necessary legal basis for fixing the number of members of the European Parliament in good time for the 1994 elections. The decisions will be taken in the light, inter alia, of the need to establish the overall size of the European Parliament in an enlarged Community. (Declaration 15)

Thus, while there is a consensus in principle that enlargement will necessitate a fundamental revision of the distribution of national and Community representation within the EC's institutions, the precise execution of that principle will prove more contentious. The most sensitive areas will be the Commission (whose numbers will eventually have to be reduced to below the number of member states) and the European Parliament. The current number of MEPs is unlikely to be increased significantly; representation for any new member states will require the existing national allocations to be reduced accordingly. An indication of the difficulties that this may pose was shown by the question of representation for the unified Germany which remained unresolved at the end of 1991.

To further complicate the numerical difficulties of representation, majority voting and the streamlining of the decision-making process are required. The SEA and Maastricht began this process, but the limited areas gained in both these reform packages were insufficient for anything other than a minor enlargement of the Community. A comprehensive application of the majority rule (the new meaning of which also has to be established) seems necessary. The Community of the Six was cohesive and manageable; the Community of the Twelve began to demonstrate national obstinacies and conflict over objectives; a Community of Eighteen or more may well be too large to work collectively under the existing institutional rules and guarantees. A seeming paradox for the Community is its intention to democratize decision-making while trying to simultaneously make it more efficient. Extending joint legislative competence to the Parliament may not be compatible with effective government in an enlarged Community. Parliamentary accountability has increased significantly and the Maastricht reforms have provided for a degree of co-decision in specified areas as well as brought the Commission under more precise scrutiny. However, if the Community moves towards the centralized authority suggested by Delors (albeit within a federal structure) a fundamental institutional reorganization would be required. Any such enlarged federal Union would need to redefine the relationship between national parliaments and the Community and the intra-Community institutional relations. The challenge for the Community is to harness enlargement to the benefit of deeper integration and to minimize any dysfunctional impact that could develop.

The dilemmas posed by further enlargement are not confined to institutional relations, but include issues of the scope and competence of Community policies. The most controversial of these concerns the development of a Common Foreign and Security Policy (CFSP) and a European defence structure. The Maastricht reforms in foreign policy were comparatively modest and do not in themselves create any additional barriers to enlargement. Prior to the disintegration of the Warsaw Pact and end of the cold war, the constitutional neutrality of EFTA countries such as Austria and Sweden was thought to be a prohibition to membership. With the changing security structures and collapse of communism, security and foreign policy issues are no longer intractable; however, it is crucial for the Community to establish its own clear foreign policy identity prior to enlargement. As noted above, the existing *acquis communautaire* in foreign policy has become an important informal criteria for membership. Maastricht began the process of cementing the Community's defence and security identity and role by placing these issues within a broader European context. In particular, the Western European Union (WEU) was included as an integral part of the development of the European Union. In a Declaration annexed to the Treaty the nine Community states that were WEU members (all but Denmark, Greece and Ireland) outlined the sequential process for developing 'a genuine European security and defence identity and a greater European responsibility on defence matters' (Annex V.1). The WEU was to become the defence component of the European Union and constitute the European pillar within NATO. To facilitate this, new mechanisms linking the Community and the WEU institutionally and procedurally were established. Consequently, the choice was not between a Community or a NATO or WEU framework, but between different mechanisms for making these three structures mutually supporting and overlapping. WEU, NATO and the new EC defence and security structures were to be compatible and share common objectives. Reflecting the evolving nature of the European security environment and the probable need for further revisions in the light of enlargement, the Maastricht Treaty committed the member states to a possible review of these structures at the next intergovernmental conference scheduled for 1996.

There are, of course, a range of other policy areas where enlargement will have an impact, ranging from the traditional area of agriculture to the latest innovation of Monetary Union. In one sense enlargement is best understood as a spillover effect: no existing Community policies remain untouched and the future development of policy initiatives all have to adjust to the new decision-making environment. What the Maastricht Treaty tried to establish was a clear definition of the Community's objective (despite the failed attempt to specify its 'federal vocation') so that all applicant states would be under no illusion as to the kind of Community they were joining. This reluctance on the part of the Community to clarify these issues, as well as a self-inflicted myopia on the part of some new member states, has been the source of considerable disequilibrium and discontent during past enlargements. A historical examination of these difficulties can shed light on the prospects for less controversial further enlargement.

Past experiences of enlargement

The Community has a significant experience of both successful and unsuccessful attempts to increase its membership. Enlargement has successfully taken place on three successive occasions (1973, 1981 and 1986). Two additional but unsuccessful attempts were made in the 1960s, and between 1952 and 1957 the six members of the ECSC sought to expand the original composition of the emerging European Community. Despite the unique characteristics of each, themes common to all three successful enlargements can be identified: the level of commitment to the European ideal; economic and political compatibility; and the impact on existing policy frameworks. Although the themes were common, the different issues raised by each provided the Community with a new set of problems to overcome in relation to further integration.

The political content of Community membership, particularly in 1973, has been underemphasized in comparison with the economic aspects linked to enlargement. This is most strikingly illustrated by the UK's accession in 1973. The Treaty of Rome's commitment 'to an ever closer union' was not adequately debated by Britain's political parties: despite strong cross-party opposition, the leadership of all three main parties were in favour of membership (although the Labour Party disagreed with the terms of accession accepted by the Conservative Government). The arguments used, however, at times appeared somewhat disingenuous. It was argued that British sovereignty would not be significantly compromised by accession and the suggestion that the Community was a putative federal organization was rejected by even Edward Heath, the British Prime Minister responsible for opening negotiations. It was one thing to advocate British membership of the Community; it was quite a different matter to embrace the idea of integration. As the first two decades of UK membership have illustrated, ignoring the political content of the Community can be a successful short-term domestic political strategy, it is not however, a solution to the ever present federal question – as Maastricht again underlined. As the leading commentator on British membership has concluded, membership brought:

more far-reaching consequences for Britain than were anticipated when the applications were made . . . These consequences were the result of Britain participating in a process of European integration which went further than the somewhat limited objectives of British governments. Despite the efforts of successive governments to limit the effects of membership, there was little room to doubt that British sovereignty had been diminished by membership of the EC, and that it would be diminished further. (George, 1991, p. 103)

Given this political hesitation, it is hardly surprising that British popular opinion has been so lukewarm towards the Community, or that a significant percentage of the population still remain opposed to membership. Thatcher's decade of Community-bashing and the creation of the anti-Community Bruges Group in 1989 are both indicative of the late realization among Britain's politicians of the political issues central to Community membership. The debate that began in September 1989 with Thatcher's infamous Bruges speech and continued beyond the Maastricht conference was exactly the debate that Britain should have had between 1970 and 1973 but avoided, with the consequence of the UK being crowned with the dubious honour of being the Community's most reluctant European.

Denmark has displayed a similar level of ambivalence towards the political vocation of the Community. Originally an EFTA member, Denmark mirrored Britain's path to membership, even to the extent of applying for membership on the same day as the UK in 1963. Denmark also shared the UK's preference for a wider free-trade area in Europe (combining the EC and EFTA states) and resistance to anything other than economic integration. During the 1980s Denmark shared the concerns of the UK and Greece over the supranational developments that emanated from the SEA. Influencing this Danish reluctance to accept deeper integration is its role as the bridge between the EC and the Nordic Council states of which it is also a member: it has sought to enlarge the Community northwards with the expectation that an increased Nordic contribution to the Community debate would be of direct economic as well as political benefit to Denmark (Pedersen, 1991, p. 115). As in the UK (and Greece), there is a history of anti-EC political parties (principally the Social Democrats) in contemporary Danish politics and public opinion towards the Community, even before the Maastricht referendum decision, was amongst the least enthusiastic among the Twelve. Such was the scepticism, Denmark together with the UK were initially opposed to extending the supranational content of the Community by allowing for the direct election of the European Parliament in the 1970s. Not surprisingly, half of Denmark's first elected MEPs in 1979 were elected on an anti-Community platform (Lodge and Herman, 1982, p. 238).

Denmark and the UK share two further similarities in their relations with the Community. Both have external commitments to other groupings that provide an alternative to the EC. Affiliation and loyalty is not exclusively focused on the Community, as say for Germany, but shared between the Community and the Commonwealth for the UK, and between the Community and the Nordic Council for Denmark. These options have become the focal point for continued opposition to Community membership in both these states, although this tendency has decreased recently. The lesson for future enlargements is simple: preferably, the new applicant states should not have any pre-existing loyalties to other regional or political groupings that stand in conflict with the development of Community awareness. Where such historical ties exist, the transfer of allegiance may be drawn-out and become a source of medium-term disruption to the process of integration.

One characteristic that distinguishes Britain from Denmark and other new member states was the use of a referendum to determine the acceptance of Community membership. The Community's first enlargement in 1973 best illustrates this method of evaluating popular commitment to Europe. In Denmark, Ireland and Norway referendums were held prior to entering the Community but after the Treaty of Accession had been signed. This test of mass attitudes resulted in positive responses in Ireland and Denmark and a rejection of Community membership in Norway by a narrow margin. This subsequently led to the withdrawal of the Norwegian application. In contrast, the electorate were never explicitly consulted on the question of British membership; the topic formed part of the 1970 Conservative Party election manifesto, but Heath's unexpected and comparatively slim majority in that election was hardly tantamount to a binding plebiscite as held in the other three applicant countries. Nevertheless, Heath argued that this General Election victory fought principally on domestic political issues, provided his government with 'the full-hearted consent' of the British people. No referendum was held before formally entering the Community on 1 January 1973 and the European issue was left undebated and unresolved to smoulder for the following two decades.

In 1975 after the change of government, Harold Wilson attempted to partially repair this democratic injury by calling a referendum on the renegotiated terms of British membership. However, this *ex post facto* procedure was a poor substitute for popular discussion of the issue of membership. The status quo had been changed – the UK was now a member – and the focus of the referendum was on the adequacy of the new terms, not specifically on the principle of membership. To unbalance the debate further, the leaders of all three political parties (Heath, Wilson and Thorpe) canvassed for a 'yes' vote for continued membership, whereas those opposed were a strange collection of radical and fringe personalities who were normally bitter antagonists and whose only common link was a dislike of the Community. Given such a scenario, it was hardly surprising that the British voter supported the renegotiated terms by a margin of two to one.

The further enlargements in 1981 and 1986 also had to face up to, somewhat more successfully, this basic question of commitment to the Community ideal. By the 1980s, however, the existing *acquis communautaire* was more definitively expressed, and the issue of integration and the evolution of the Community was not an issue that Greece, Portugal or Spain could properly ignore. The vague consensus on objectives and an immature Community spirit in the 1970s were largely responsible for the ensuing difficulties the Community experienced, particularly with the UK and

Denmark. Creating a clarity of purpose was exactly what the majority of member states attempted to promote at Maastricht by inserting the phrase 'federal vocation' into the new Treaty. Although this attempt was ultimately thwarted by the implied British veto, no current or future applicant states can be under any illusion as to the general direction of further integration. The commitment to the Community is a commitment to political as well as economic Union.

The second theme common to all three enlargements is that of economic and political compatibility. For different reasons, all applications for membership have been delayed on the grounds of compatibility. Greek accession was delayed by the underdeveloped nature of their economy *vis-à-vis* the then Community of the Nine. An Association Agreement was signed as early as 1962 designed to accelerate Greek economic development with a view to full membership once Greece was capable of shouldering the economic consequences of the common market. This progression was interrupted by the period of military rule from 1967–74. Negotiations for accession began in 1976 and five years later Greece finally entered the Community, although still as the weakest economy. The case of Greece illustrated the importance of political as well as economic considerations in determining membership. The Commission had given a negative response to Greek accession on the basis of economic disparity: the political arguments – the support of democracy and the retention of Greece in the Western camp – outweighed these considerations.

A similar scenario describes both Spain and Portugal's path to Community membership. Their shared heritage of non-democratic government and comparative economic underdevelopment precluded them from pursuing full membership until the late 1970s, although preferential trading agreements operated. With their transitions to democracy both applied for membership in 1977: the negotiations were protracted and membership only achieved in 1986 (Nugent, 1989, pp. 47–8). Thus, like Greece, the economic reasons for including Spain and Portugal were weak, but political considerations were of overriding importance. Community membership was seen as a mechanism for maintaining and nurturing fledgling democratic regimes and this consideration took precedence over all others. As the Commission concluded in its opinion on the southern enlargement, the Community was 'making a commitment which is primarily a political one . . . reflecting the concern of these three new democracies for their own consolidation and protection against the return of dictatorship and constituting an act of faith in a united Europe' (*Bulletin*, 1978, p. 6). The objectives of democracy and peace explicitly set out first in the preamble to the ECSC Treaty and adopted implicitly in the Treaty of Rome, were given practical expression not mere lip-service.

In the failed enlargements of the 1960s, both economic and political arguments were used, in this case to exclude the UK and by guilt of association, Denmark, Ireland and Norway. As discussed in Chapter 2, de Gaulle's double veto (in 1963 and 1967) was based upon specifically British issues. Economically, Britain's then industrial base was seen as incompatible with the Community's agricultural priorities; politically, the UK's allegiance was characterized as being first to the Commonwealth, second to the USA and only third, and then grudgingly, to Europe. The necessary *esprit de corps* was just a shallow imitation of the required *communautaire* commitment. With the benefit of hindsight it is somewhat ironic that four of Europe's developed economies and securer democracies should be denied accession to the Community, while a generation later three of Europe's weaker economies and most fragile democracies were welcomed as members. The newly democratic regimes of Central and Eastern Europe should take heart from this historical evidence.

The third element common to the three phases of enlargement concerns the impact on the organization of both existing and future Community policies. Enlargement can advance and retard harmonization. If one examines the Community's most developed existing policy area, the Common Agricultural Policy (CAP), the consequences of expanding membership to both the south and to the west have been fundamental in their impact on the pace and shape of integration. It must be remembered that the CAP was designed to address the economic and social conditions pertinent to the agricultural sector of the original Six of the 1950s and 1960s. The founding Community was predominantly agricultural in composition, and farming, albeit on a small scale, was the major source of employment and contributor to GNP for a number of member states. European integration if it was to mean anything had to gain the support of the agricultural population. The numerous and justified criticisms of the excesses of the CAP that have been voiced over the years all agree that the problem with the CAP was not one of failure, but of excessive success. Its original objectives – security of supply, improved standards of living for agricultural workers and the protection of Europe's agricultural sector – have been achieved, but at considerable cost, both financial and in terms of unwanted production. It should hardly be surprising that a policy determined in the middle of the twentieth century to suit six broadly complementary agricultural economies, where technology had yet to remove the spectre of food shortages or poverty, has struggled to adapt to the demands of the 1990s with a Community of twelve competing agricultural producers all of whom produce more efficiently for an ever decreasing global agricultural market.

Agriculture was the key area for negotiation between the Six and the applicant states. The first enlargement saw the Irish and Danish dairy sectors integrated into the Community agricultural support system, together with Britain's mixed arable large-scale farming enterprises. As the CAP was then organized, both Ireland and Denmark stood to benefit, but not the UK or many of its traditional Commonwealth suppliers (Hill, 1984, p. 43). In addition, the CAP was already producing a butter surplus and the inclusion of all three new member states could only lead to one conclusion; the production of further surpluses in an increasing number of agricultural sectors. The immediate concern, however, was not of structural dislocation, but of Britain's financial contribution to the CAP. This issue dominated the British renegotiations of 1975 and was behind the various attempts to reduce the percentage of the Community budget spent on the CAP up until the late 1980s. Thus the impact of the first enlargement was to make the CAP almost inoperative financially: the discontent that resulted from the annual budgetary disputes threatened the integration of the Community more than any other factor.

The disequilibrium created by the financing of the CAP was compounded by the southern enlargement during the 1980s. As noted already, there was significant economic disparity between the Nine and the individual economies of Greece, Portugal and Spain, and this unfavourable background had a detrimental consequence for the effect of the CAP on the new member states. As for the first enlargement, transition phases (up to ten years for some products) were instituted to both protect existing Community suppliers as well as the new producers. The agricultural balance was disturbed: output grew by a quarter and the agricultural population by half. More significantly, the largely Mediterranean products of these new members (particularly those of Spain) competed directly with the existing markets created by France and Italy. Through price support this additional production simply resulted in greater and greater surpluses (wine and olive oil 'lakes', citrus 'mountains'); this further added to the financial burden of the CAP, exacerbating an increasingly disgruntled British Government who were still net contributors, not beneficiaries of the EC budget. The southern enlargement indirectly brought the Community to the brink of crisis which could only be resolved by a fundamental reform of the CAP. Ceilings were placed on production levels, quotas introduced and in particularly oversupplied areas (typically the northern agricultural products), farmers were given incentives to change production. Thus enlargement, albeit indirectly and in a piecemeal way, has fundamentally influenced the development of the Community's first, and to date still most developed, common policy. This influence has not always been to the immediate benefit of Community integration: the agricultural crises that seemed to punctuate EC business annually dissipated much of the Community dynamism up to the mid-1980s. Conversely, without these enlargement caused crises the Community may never have been forced to address the structural problems of the CAP. In that respect, enlargement has had an overall positive impact on the level of integration achieved by the Community in the 1990s.

The impact of enlargement to expand existing or generate new policy areas should not be underestimated. A contemporary policy domain illustrates this importance: the pressures for regional development and Social Cohesion to complement and balance the economic consequences of the Single Market and European Monetary Union. From the beginning of the Community experience, unequal economic development between member states was regarded as an impediment to integration: consequently specific redistribution policies have always been part of the Community framework. This objective is acknowledged in the preamble to the Treaty of Rome which calls on the member states 'to strengthen the unity of their economies and to ensure their harmonious development by reducing the differences existing between the various regions and the backwardness of the less favoured regions'. Despite these policy intentions, in practice the Community only made modest progress in redressing these economic imbalances during its first 15 years. It took the pressures of enlargement to give sufficient political commitment to the existing EC Social and Regional policies (Molle, 1990, p. 63). Four of the six states that became members during the 1970s and 1980s were comparatively poor by Community standards and in the EC of the Twelve regional disparities have markedly increased. Prior to the southern enlargement the per capita income disparity between the richest and poorest areas was at a ratio of 5:1; after the Iberian accession this leaped to a ratio of 10:1 (p. 75). A similar perspective is given in relation to GDP levels. In 1987, for example, in percentage terms, four member states were significantly below the EC average (Greece recorded a GDP per capita figure of just 53.7 per cent of the EC average, Portugal 53.8 per cent, Ireland 62.7 per cent and Spain 73.9 per cent) (Marques Mendes, 1990, p. 18). Consequently, the European Regional Development Fund (which had first been established in 1975 to accommodate the problems associated with the first enlargement) was given a significantly higher share of the Community budget from 1987 onwards, with approximately two-thirds of funding now going on the four Mediterranean states of Greece, Italy, Spain and Portugal.

At the Maastricht conference Spain, together with Greece, Ireland and Portugal lobbied for an even higher priority to be given to what was now called Social Cohesion. The contemporary developments of the internal Single Market and the future implications of Economic and Monetary Union posed considerable challenges and adjustments for the Community's poorer states. These problems had a certain *déjà vu* quality to them, recalling early Community 'fears that the opening up of markets might increase disparities between countries, either by making the poor poorer or by degenerating into very uneven distribution of the gains from the opening up of markets' (p. 17). Consensus and compliance with the grander macro-economic aspirations of the IGC was only reached after concessions made by the Community to increase regional, social and economic expenditure for these four countries as well as to reconsider the whole structure of economic and social support. In return, states were required to move towards the economic policy convergence as specified in the EMU Treaty. However, the binding political commitment wanted by the four poorer states was not forthcoming. The provisions relating to Social Cohesion were removed from the body of the main Treaty and included as a protocol, although a complete evaluation of the existing social funds with a view to their reorganization was promised. The Council also agreed to establish before the end of 1993 a 'Cohesion Fund' to finance 'projects in the fields of environment and trans-European networks in the area of transport infrastructure' (Article 130d). Funds will only be available to member states whose GNP is less than 90 per cent of the EC average. The actual amounts to be made available were left for determination at the June 1992 Lisbon summit.

Although the outcome of Maastricht was largely positive, the consequences for integration of policy dissensus were clear. A grouping of member states that can create a blocking majority can use the threat of impeding integration in other fields if the Community refuses to meet their specific demands. Consequently, in order to maintain the momentum of integration, the policy-making process often has to accept compromises and solutions that are far from optimal, and occasionally conflicting. This 'technique of issue linkage as a negotiating tool' is a well-documented Community procedure, and one that has been used to both promote and inhibit integration (Weber and Wiesmeth, 1991, p. 265). Expansion of the Community can only complicate this process further by changing the arithmetic required for majorities and by introducing new pressures for additional policy perspectives. In short, the practical reality of enlargement appears to coincide closely with the theoretical requirements of neofunctionalism and logic of spillover.

Further enlargement: from the Twelve to . . . ?

The current applicants

By the end of 1991 the Community had before it applications for membership from five countries: Austria, Cyprus, Malta, Sweden and Turkey. The deadline of the Single Market had been used by the Community to defer decisions on each of these applications until 1 January 1993, although a preliminary opinion was issued by the Commission during 1991. The case of Malta is relatively easy for the Community to accommodate provided that two conditions are met. First, adequate transition procedures need to be in place: here, the existing association agreement between Malta and the EC provides an obvious framework. Secondly, Malta's neutral status will have to be clarified to see whether it is compatible with the foreign-policy provisions of the SEA and the Maastricht Treaty (as is also the case for two other applicant states – see below) (Albioni, 1991, p. 164). The major difficulty relates to its level of representation. A proliferation of very small new members could impose severe institutional difficulties and further complicate the decision-making process. Within the Community, Malta is most comparable in size to Luxembourg; but as has been argued earlier in this chapter, an expansion in the number of MEPs, Commissioners, etc., cannot be continued. The precondition for Maltese accession (and possibly that for Cyprus) is a fundamental revision of these institutional issues. The accession of Cyprus, another applicant state with an existing association agreement, also faces a further problem: the continued territorial disputes between Greek and Turkish Cypriot authorities. Until these are resolved and internationally accepted, membership may be resisted on political grounds.

The Austrian and Swedish applications appear to be the most likely to succeed in the short term. Both countries were members of EFTA, boast advanced economies and have already significantly adapted their domestic economic policies to converge with the discipline of Community membership. While membership would not be without its transitional economic adjustments, the changes required would be comparatively modest. It is in the political realm that both these countries may experience greater difficulties, although this prospect has declined with the demise of the Soviet Union. Both countries conduct their foreign affairs on a similar basis of neutrality, but the origins and status of each policy is different. The 1955 Austrian State Treaty re-established the independence and democratic basis of the Austrian state and allowed the removal of Soviet forces; Article 1 committed Austria to 'perpetual neutrality', whereby 'in all future times Austria will not join any military alliances and will not permit the establishment of any foreign military bases on her territory' (Luif, 1991, p. 125). In contrast to this externally imposed condition, Swedish neutrality has its origins in domestic politics and has developed over the past 150 years without any legal basis. Traditionally it was believed that these different approaches to neutrality held by Sweden and Austria would preclude both these countries from membership: the Community had stipulated that the existing *acquis communautaire* for foreign policy had to be accepted as a condition of membership. The obligation, albeit not a binding one, to co-operate within EPC and latterly CFSP seems to be incompatible with a commitment to neutrality. The changed, and changing, European security situation has led to the rapid evolution of the definition of neutrality, and former Swedish anxiety and scepticism regarding the amelioration of East–West tensions evaporated by the end of 1991. As one commentator noted 'a completely new matrix of trade-offs between security considerations, new territorial systems and changing patterns of interaction is becoming apparent' (Stalvant and Hamilton, 1991, p. 213). This development, together with the Community's decision to work within the existing WEU and CSCE structures suggests that both Austria and Sweden will be able to whole-heartedly accept the new foreign policy *acquis politique* in much the same way that Ireland has managed to maintain her constitutional neutrality and yet participate fully in EPC.

Through its membership of EFTA, Austria had maintained close links with the Community while avoiding any formal association agreements. In 1972 a free trade agreement on industrial goods was signed with the Community and the ECSC. This was the extent of the relationship until the launching of the EC's internal Single Market plan in the mid-1980s. In response Austria proposed, unsuccessfully, closer economic, social and political integration with the Community without becoming full members, a position that was reversed when Austria eventually applied in July 1989 (Luif, 1991, pp. 126–33).

The two economic areas where convergence with Community practice is most needed is in the high level of subsidies for state-owned industries and agriculture. Austria subsidizes agriculture through an expensive price-support structure and will need to adjust to the Community's mixed price and quantity regime. But the economic adjustments will be modest: during the 1980s the Austrian economy shifted its emphasis from East to West European trade, and of the EFTA states Austria boasts the highest percentage of exports to the EC. Consequently, the benefits of membership, while positive, are not as dramatic as for applicant states with a less advanced and integrated economy. Projections suggest that during the first five years of membership the GDP growth rate would increase by an additional 1.6

per cent, inflation would decrease by 5.2 per cent, but unemployment would increase by 1.5 per cent and the budget deficit would rise by 1.1 per cent (as Austria would become a net contributor to the EC budget) (Luif, 1991, pp. 135–40). Austrian membership is far from a foregone conclusion, however: scepticism over the virtues of joining have grown from just 13 per cent in 1987 to 37 per cent in 1991 (*European Affairs*, 1991, p. 51). The low point was reached in early 1989 when there was a small majority actually opposed to membership. While this trend was reversed by the time of Austria's application and support has risen to around 50 per cent since then, a negative vote in a referendum on membership is not an impossibility. In August 1991 the Commission issued its positive response to Austria's application though it stated that negotiations on the conditions of membership should not commence before 1993. In its conclusions the Commission noted the qualitative difference in Austria's case compared with previous applicants:

> no previous applicant has started from a position where, by virtue of numerous agreements, it already had completely free trade in industrial products with the Community, or had already committed itself to apply a substantial part of the *acquis communautaire*, or where its degree of economic integration with the Community was so advanced.
>
> After accession there should not be any fundamental shift in the direction of Austria's economic policy . . . only agriculture and transit seem likely to give rise to a need for anything other than technical adjustments.
>
> The Community will on the whole benefit from the accession of Austria, which would widen the circle of countries whose economic, monetary and budgetary performance will speed Economic and Monetary Union on its way.
>
> On the basis of the economic considerations, therefore, the Commission considers that the Community should accept Austria's application for accession. (Europe Documents, 1991, pp. 2–3)

Sweden, a more recent applicant county, has long advocated a wider European grouping, and has encouraged the remaining EFTA states, particularly its Nordic neighbours, to apply for full membership. Sweden's accession will represent an additional stabilizing factor, both politically and economically in the Community. EC-Swedish economic relations are extremely close with around 70 bilateral agreements already existing. The dependence is understandably asymmetrical: for example, in 1985 the EC supplied 25 per cent of Sweden's domestic market for manufactures, whereas Swedish exports to the Community only captured 1 per cent of the much larger European home market (Stalvant and Hamilton, 1991, p. 195). Only 3 per cent of the work-force is engaged in agriculture and the principles underpinning agricultural policy in both the Community and Sweden are similar. Some adjustments are necessary: state subsidies need to be reduced to EC levels and high food import levies abolished. Swedish industry is among the most technologically sophisticated and successful in Europe and is well placed to benefit from the Community's Single Market.

Sweden has indicated that it favours membership in the near future, perhaps by 1995, although like Austria this will be conditional on the result of a referendum to be held in 1994. To facilitate an easy transition to full membership, Sweden, like Austria, through the EEA agreement has begun to align its economic policy and legislation to converge with the existing Community structure. At the monetary level, two months prior to lodging their application on 1 July 1991, the krona was linked to the ECU and the Swedish Government has given its commitment to EMU and a single European currency. The most difficult outstanding economic issue will be the progressive harmonization of Sweden's high indirect taxation regime to a lower level compatible with the Community's lower target figure for value added tax (VAT). A similarly difficult and sensitive political area is the incorporation of the Community's legislative *acquis communautaire*. Sweden needs to harmonize its existing legislation with past and current Community directives and regulations, a task that has been estimated at involving the revision of 1,400 legislative acts (p. 204).

Irrespective of the finer details and problems associated with membership, the accession of Austria and Sweden, and that of Malta and Cyprus, constitute a positive contribution to Community integration. In these cases widening and deepening are not mutually exclusive options, but compatible processes. Collectively they will add to the stability of the European economy; they have indicated clear support for the objectives of EMU and Political Union (acceptance of which is a pre-condition for entry); and for those countries where foreign policy issues constitute a constitutional problem, a redefinition of neutrality to suit the changed circumstances of the 1990s seems to be compatible with the Community's collective foreign policy behaviour. The prospects for an EC of the Sixteen seem, at this stage, encouraging for the supporters of a more integrated federal Community. The inclusion of the fifth applicant state, Turkey, however, is a dilemma that carries with it significant dangers for further integration.

Turkey first applied for membership of the EC in 1959 (as did Greece); although this was unsuccessful, in 1963 the Community did sign the Ankara Agreement, a three-stage association agreement designed to prepare Turkey for eventual accession by establishing conditions that would accelerate the commercial development of the Turkish economy to a level commensurate with that of the then Six. The second stage was commenced in 1970 with the signing of the Additional Protocol. This reduced industrial tariffs and eliminated other customs duties over an extended transitional period and committed Turkey to accepting and applying the Community's CAP legislation and measures. In compensation, within ten years, the free movement of workers was to be established (Bourguignon, 1990, p. 54). It was expected that Turkey would achieve membership by 1995 at the latest. While progress towards these objectives was made, the pace of convergence was slow and during the 1970s and 1980s EC–Turkish relations were characterized by disillusionment, incoherence and policy conflicts. Turkey's last application for membership in 1987 could not have come at a more inopportune moment: the Community was still acclimatizing to the accession of Spain and Portugal; the EC budget was approaching deficit; and the Community had become preoccupied with its internal dynamic (the Single Market). Further enlargement was not an immediate priority.

These factors, plus the obvious political and economic problems associated with Turkish membership, saw the application deferred until after the completion of the Single Market at the earliest.

The probability of Turkey gaining Community membership is not solely dependent on the normal economic policy and *acquis communautaire* issues used to evaluate other applicant states: they are also linked to geo-political factors, some of which are beyond its control (Cremasco, 1990). First, the resolution of the Cyprus question and a *rapprochement* between Ankara and Athens would facilitate an eastern Mediterranean solution to enlargement, grouping Turkey's accession with those of Cyprus and Malta. If neither of these conditions are met, then a uniform and negative approach to these three applicants is more likely (Aliboni, 1991, p. 165). Second, the enmity between Greece and Turkey provides the former with an implicit veto on the Turkish application. Greco-Turkish conflict transcends the question of Cyprus and includes disputes concerning rights over the Aegean (control of airspace, territorial waters exploration rights on the continental shelf and the militarization of contiguous islands) (Cremasco, 1990, p. 131). Thirdly, in the past Turkey's strongest political argument for membership was its pivotal role in NATO's southern flank; the altered security structures on the 1990s have considerably undermined this strategic rationale, although as contemporary history has shown it would be foolhardy to ignore the possible future threat of regional instability. Turkey borders not just on Iraq and Iran, but also the troubled former Soviet republic of Georgia. The relaxation of East–West tension may not necessarily indicate a less strategic role for Turkey in the short term.

In addition to these global geo-political factors, Turkey's application poses a number of additional problems for the Community, in particular agriculture and the free movement of labour. Turkey remains a highly agrarian society: it is estimated that 40–50 per cent of the workforce is employed in the agricultural sector, and in 1986 agricultural production contributed 22 per cent to the GDP, although this figure has steadily fallen as Turkey's industrial sector has developed. As noted above, the Additional Protocol committed Turkey to adjusting its agricultural policy in line with the CAP; in return, Turkish agricultural exports to the EC were given preferential or partial tariff rates. These were eliminated in 1987 when all Turkish agricultural products (with some exceptions for sensitive products) were freed of Community customs duties. Turkey's major exports to the Community are figs, raisins, hazelnuts, tobacco and raw cotton. (Hale, 1990, pp. 142–44).

The implications of Community membership for Turkish agriculture are mixed. Turkey would certainly benefit from the unimpeded opportunity to sell its products within the Community, but domestically there would be a real cost as domestic food prices would increase significantly to reflect VAT charges and CAP subsidies. For the Community the issue is clear-cut: how expensive would the CAP price support mechanisms become when applied to Turkish agriculture. The addition of another Mediterranean producer will further intensify the budgetary disputes over comparative support levels for northern and southern agricultural products. The combined influence of Portugal, Spain, Italy, Greece and Turkey could well see a switch in funding priorities away from the predominantly northern cereal and dairy products in favour of Mediterranean products. Without any such reform of the CAP, the agricultural aspects of membership could prove destabilizing. This, coupled with the certainty that Turkey will be a financial net beneficiary from the Community budget, may be sufficient to deny Turkey a future place within the Community (Hale, 1990, pp. 149–51).

The free movement of labour is one of the founding principles of the Community: the Single Market of 1992 is finally expected to make this prospect a reality. This important aspect of Community integration may prove, however, to be a further barrier to membership for Turkey. Turkish migrant workers have traditionally been employed in significant numbers in Germany (around 75 per cent of the total); in 1985 there were 1.6 million Turkish migrant workers resident in Germany and Berlin has the second largest urban Turkish population after Ankara (Ergün, 1990, p. 184). These workers were an essential addition to the German labour force during the expansion of the German economy from the 1960s onwards; recently, however, there has developed increasing opposition to the scale of the migration and a fear that the extension of the principle of the free movement of individuals would result in an immigration exodus from Turkey to Germany and possibly other industrial parts of the Community. The reunification of Germany and the migrant pressures on Germany from its Eastern neighbours, particularly Poland and Russia, have made the issue of immigration a new consideration in evaluating the enlargement of the Community. Despite the seeming progress in integrating the peoples of the European Community, xenophobia has yet to be eradicated at the popular level. The challenge for the Community is to dissipate this prejudice, and its more pernicious offshoot, racism, and prepare the Community economically, politically and socially for enlargement to both the south and to the east of Europe.

Prospective applicants

Predicting Europe's political cartography even in the relative short term has never been a more precarious occupation than in the 1990s. Old realities have disappeared and a phlethora of national identities have re-emerged. With this cautionary rider in mind, it is possible to classify potential future applicant states into two groups: the relatively 'easy' cases of the remaining EFTA/EEA countries; and, the 'harder' cases of the newly democratic countries of Eastern Europe. This classification is not meant to imply the inevitability of membership. The Community may well decide that for the survival of its own internal integration enlargement beyond 16 countries is undesirable. Conversely, a number of potential applicants may for domestic reasons shy away from membership in preference for a different form of association. Without attempting to predict this outcome, some of the conditions and issues that are raised by each country's possible application are discussed in this final section.

The efforts to create an EEA during 1991–2 were intended to provide a framework for the former EFTA states irrespective of which eventually chose to remain outside the Community. The EEA was designed to provide even closer links with the Community by encouraging economic harmonization and integration between the Twelve and the EEA countries (Austria, Finland, Iceland, Liechtenstein, Norway, Sweden and Switzerland). The four basic freedoms enshrined in the Community constitution – the freedom of persons, goods, services and capital – were to be implemented across this new grouping of 19 states creating an enlarged single economic market. Trade between these two groups was already significant (amounting to 65 per cent of EFTA's exports and 25 per cent of Community trade); the total value of EC-EFTA trade was greater than the combined value of EC trade with Japan and the USA. As one writer observed, 'all the EFTA countries are in a similar position and that therefore they have a common interest in acting together in order to improve their negotiating position' (Antola, 1991, p. 156).

The Agreement was concluded in October 1991 and is due to come into force on 1 January 1993 to coincide with the creation of the Single Market. However, this date was put in some jeopardy by a Court of Justice decision of January 1992 that found the system of judicial supervision established under the EEA to be incompatible with the Community's own legal provisions as expressed in the Treaty of Rome. For the EEA to be implemented on schedule either the Agreement has to be amended to make it compatible with existing Community procedures or the Community's constitution has to be revised again. If implemented, the EEA will make any future transition to full Community membership for the seven non-EC countries extremely simple economically and legislatively. And if this procedure proves successful, it could constitute a model for the accession of Eastern and Central European states at a later date.

The rationale behind creating the EEA was weakened by the applications of Austria and Sweden and the intention of three other EEA states (Finland, Norway and Switzerland) to consider the possibility of full Community membership in the near future. Throughout 1991 there was intense speculation that there would be a common Scandinavian application: while this failed to eventuate and Sweden went ahead unilaterally, the existing links through the Nordic Council as well as the new EEA agreement suggest that an enlarged Scandinavian aspect within the Community is extremely likely. In the light of the foreign policy agreements determined at Maastricht, in early 1992 a Finnish Government report concluded that Finland's policy of neutrality was compatible with Community membership. This decision signified a fundamental revision of Finland's European role. Prior to the changes in the former Soviet Union and Eastern Europe, Finland's sensitive geo-political position and its post-war status quo of neutrality prohibited the development of anything more than limited economic integration within the Nordic or EFTA spheres. The Community's political content and supranationalism was at that time politically unacceptable (Antola, 1991, pp. 146–9). The EEA was originally Finland's preferred relationship with the Community (roughly 45 per cent of Finnish exports already went to the EC (Stalvant, 1990, p. 136)); but the unbalanced conditions of the new relationship (in which the Community was dominant), combined with the legal difficulties and accelerating defection of EEA members, have conspired to encourage Finland that there is little alternative to eventual EC membership.

Norway has the most ambivalent history towards membership of the Community; it was part of the ill-fated applications of 1963 and 1967; reapplied in 1970 and signed the Treaty of Accession in 1972 only to revoke its membership prior to the date of entry after a 53 per cent 'No' vote in the September referendum held on Norwegian membership (Saeter and Knudsen, 1991, pp. 180–2). The 1973 EC-EFTA free trade agreement has seen the EC grow as Norway's most important market. By the late 1980s around 57 per cent of Norway's exports were with the Community and domestic political pressure grew correspondingly for Norway to re-evaluate its future *vis-à-vis* membership (Stalvant, 1990, p. 137). The definitive position on Norwegian accession is now expected towards the end of 1992. Norway, like Turkey and Iceland, is a member of NATO, so the neutrality difficulties that confront other EFTA–EEA countries are not an impediment to membership. The Maastricht decisions on defence make it even easier for Norway to accept the discipline of CFSP. However, the trauma of the 1972 debate and rejection of membership has had a lasting impact on Norwegian political parties and public opinion. The question of membership remains a crucial domestic issue and one where public opinion is divided. The consistent pattern that has emerged is that those in favour of membership have been in the minority (totalling no more than one-third of the electorate in the late 1980s) with between one-third and one-fifth falling into the volatile 'don't know' category. As Saeter and Knudsen conclude '[J]udging by these polls, even by the end of 1989 the Norwegian electorate was nowhere near giving its blessing to a pro-membership policy' (1991, p. 183). While international events since then have altered many of the perceived realities within European politics, the future shape of Norway's relations with the Community will undoubtedly be shaped through popular opinion and a subsequent referendum. However, as is the case for the other EFTA states, the gloomy scenario for the EEA seems effectively to remove this option: in the long term the alternatives are either full Community membership or an increasingly peripheral association in a weakened Nordic grouping.

Some 700 years of Confederation and independence has provided Switzerland with a high degree of self-reliance and international political autonomy. The original EFTA arrangement suited the Swiss mercantile priorities and the prospect of Community membership has only been seriously raised during the 1990s. The intermediate step of the EEA was only acceptable because Switzerland could retain control over immigration: the free movement of individuals, a fundamental principle of the Treaty of Rome, presents the Swiss with the greatest obstacle to membership. But despite the clear boundaries that divide the Community and Swiss experiences, Switzerland has become increasingly influenced by the strength of the Community's economic attraction. Around four-fifths of Swiss imports, and three-fifths of its exports were with the Community in 1988 (Senti, 1991, p. 217). Since 1988 there has been a voluntary attempt by the Swiss authorities to create parallel legal structures as a means of facilitating a smooth transition to closer integration, whatever precise form that might take. This, coupled with over 180 bilateral agreements with the EC and trans-Alpine transport co-operation have all contrived to entangle Switzerland increasingly within the Community's economic orbit.

Agriculture is one area that may prove contentious if Switzerland decides to apply for eventual membership. Although the actual numbers directly involved in agricultural production are comparatively low, the farm lobby, the food industry and rural communities are an influential voice in Swiss cantonal and federal politics, and in general these groups are critical of the costs of membership. At current levels Swiss agricultural prices are between one-third and two-thirds higher than the equivalent Community prices (p. 226). Membership would result in substantial subsidy reductions for Swiss farmers, with a commensurate compensating effect, presumably, on consumer prices. Conversely, as for the other EFTA countries, the question of neutrality is no longer the barrier to membership it once seemed. At the popular level, membership has not been an issue of any priority until recently: consequently, public opinion has really not solidified either for or against possible accession. The constitutional aspects of eventual Swiss accession seem the most likely to pose significant problems. The confederal institutions, respect for direct democracy and collegiate nature of the federal government (composed of seven members among whom the chairpersonship rotates annually) all lead to a prolonged policy-making process. The amateur and part-time status of Switzerland's legislators further complicates matters. Quite how all this will mesh with the Community's Council of Ministers, majority decisions and continued democratic deficit, has yet to be addressed. On an economic criterion, Switzerland may be one of the most suitable future members: politically and constitutionally it poses more complications than any other probable applicant state.

The demise of the Soviet and Yugoslavian federations has confronted the Community with a new set of dilemmas concerning further enlargement. While enlargement beyond the EFTA–EEA states to include the newly democratic countries of Eastern and Central Europe may be part of the Community agenda, the timing and precise arrangements for any new relationship has yet to be finalized. A new framework for accommodating these massive changes has to be constructed in order to protect the Community's own internal dynamic as well as provide suitable economic structures for these states. If full membership is contemplated, even the most optimistic time-scale for this possible development considers that practically this could not take place before 2010. Two decades or more of economic restructuring and development will be needed before these countries are sufficiently strong economically to integrate effectively with the Community. Czechoslovakia, Hungary and Poland have all registered membership as their long-term objective. The economic reforms being undertaken there place this group of Central European states as the next most likely new members.

The prospects for the other newly independent states in Europe are less clear-cut. For the foreseeable future association agreements between the Community and these Eastern and Central European states are likely to shape economic and political relationships. Eventual membership cannot be expected or presumed at this stage. This position was reflected in the Community's initial response to the creation of the Commonwealth of Independent States (CIS). The Community document on the recognition of new states (used in the case of Yugoslavia) was used as the criterion for establishing diplomatic and economic relations within Europe. However, close association agreements of the kind signed with Czechoslovakia, Hungary and Poland were impossible to implement at this stage: the CIS states were, by comparison, too economically and politically undeveloped. The most important distinction between these types of association agreements and the ones previously signed with other European states, was that they were not necessarily seen as a preparatory phase leading to eventual membership. Such restricted forms of association might constitute the full extent of the Community relationship. While the possibility existed, eventual full membership could not be presumed to be the ultimate policy objective.

The attraction of membership may not be as powerful as a Community-centric view suggests: for many of Europe's new states there are considerable disadvantages and disincentives in addition to the obvious ones of economic adjustment. The Baltic states of Estonia, Latvia and Lithuania have, understandably, been reluctant to trade their newly found independence immediately for the obligations of European federation. Similarly, it is still too soon for the now independent and internationally recognized Balkan republics to decide how they wish to arrange their future economic relations within Europe. Despite the Community's support for Slovenia and Croatia, and the historical links and geographical proximity of these two countries, rediscovered nationalism and sovereignty may well outweigh economic advantage. Clearly from the perspective of the early 1990s it is foolish to more than outline the possible shape of Community relations for the next generation. However, without specifying the kind of Community that may eventually emerge, the prescient words of Jean Monnet can still provide a guide to the chaos of contemporary international politics:

> The roots of the Community are strong now, and deep in the soil of Europe. They have survived some hard seasons, and can survive more. On the surface, appearances change. In a quarter-century, naturally, new generations arise, with new ambitions; images of the past disappear; the balance of the world is altered. Yet amid this changing scenery the European idea goes on; and no one seeing it, and seeing how stable the Community institutions are, can doubt that this is a deep and powerful movement on a historic scale. (1978, p. 523)

To conclude, enlargement represents the Community's most difficult topic. The momentum towards a larger Community seems almost unstoppable: all that can be influenced is the conditions under which further accession to the Community is allowed and the timing of each new addition. The prospect of an inner and outer Community, reflecting the EC–EEA approach although with different memberships, seems an appealing and practical solution to the possible explosion in candidate states seeking Community membership. Without any such safeguard, the Community could well face a doubling of its existing size (and a quadrupling of its original membership) sometime around the Community's fiftieth birthday. Under such a scenario substantial reform of the existing institutional structures will be a pre-condition of enlargement, as will a comprehensive revision of the scope and authority of Community policies. It is to this area of Community policy competence that the final chapter now turns.

References

Aliboni, R., 1991, 'The Mediterranean dimension' in Wallace, W. (ed.), *The dynamics of European integration*, Pinter/RIIA, London, pp. 155–70.

Antola, E., 1991, 'Finland' in Wallace, H. (ed.), *The wider Western Europe*, Pinter/RIIA, London, pp. 146–58.

Bourguignon, R., 1990, 'The history of the Association Agreement between Turkey and the European Community' in Evin, A. and Denton, G. (eds), *Turkey and the European Community*, Leske and Budrich/ Schriften des Deutschen Orient-Instituts, Opladen, pp. 51–64.

Bulletin of the European Communities, 1978, supplement 1/78 Commission of the EC, Brussels.

Cremasco, M., 1990, 'The strategic importance of relations between Turkey and the European Community' in Evin, A. and Denton, G. (eds), *Turkey and the European Community*, Leske and Budrich/ Schriften des Deutschen Orient-Instituts, Opladen, pp. 117–40.

Edwards, G., 1977, 'How large a Community?' in Burrows, B., Denton, G. and Edwards, G., *Federal solutions to European issues*, Macmillan/The Federal Trust, London, pp. 163–73.

Ergün, I., 1990, 'The problem of freedom of movement of Turkish workers in the European Community' in Evin, A. and Denton, G. (eds), *Turkey and the European Community*, Leske and Budrich/ Schriften des Deutschen Orient-Instituts, Opladen, pp. 183–94.

Europe Documents, 1991, *European Commission opinion on Austria's request for membership to the European Community*, Agence Europe No. 1730, 3 August, pp. 1–3.

European Affairs, 1991, 'Country report: Austria – successful sceptic', 5, pp. 50–5.

George, S., 1991, *Britain and European integration since 1945*, Blackwell, Oxford.

Hale, W., 1990, 'Turkish agriculture and the Common Agricultural Policy' in Evin, A. and Denton, G. (eds), *Turkey and the European Community*, Leske and Budrich/ Schriften des Deutschen Orient-Instituts, Opladen, pp. 141–52.

Hill, B., 1984, *The Common Agricultural Policy: past, present and future*, Methuen, London.

Lodge, J. and Herman, V., 1982, *Direct elections to the European Parliament: a Community perspective*, Macmillan, London.

Luif, P., 1991, 'Austria' in Wallace, H. (ed.), *The wider Western Europe*, Pinter/RIIA, London, pp. 124–45.

Marques Mendes, A.J., 1990, 'Economic cohesion in Europe: the impact of the Delors Plan', *Journal of Common Market Studies*, 29, pp. 17–36.

Molle, W., 1990, 'Regional policy' in Coffey, P. (ed.), *Main economic policy areas of the EEC–toward 1992*, Kluwer, Dordrecht.

Monnet, J., 1978, *Memoirs* (trans. R. Mayne), Doubleday and Company, New York.

Nugent, N., 1989, *The government and politics of the European Community*, Macmillan, London.

Pedersen, T., 1991, 'Community attitudes and interests' in Wallace, H. (ed.), *The wider Western Europe*, Pinter/RIIA, London, pp. 109–23.

Saeter, M. and Knudsen, O., 1991, 'Norway' in Wallace, H. (ed.), *The wider Western Europe*, Pinter/RIIA, London, pp. 179–93.

Senti, R., 1991, 'Switzerland' in Wallace, H. (ed.), *The wider Western Europe*, Pinter/RIIA, London, pp. 215–30.

Stalvant, C–E., 1990, 'Nordic cooperation' in Wallace, W. (ed.), *The dynamics of European integration*, Pinter/RIIA, London, pp. 125–40.

Stalvant, C-E., 1990, 'Nordic cooperation' in Wallace, W. (ed.), *The dynamics of European integration*, Pinter/RIIA, London, pp. 125–40.

Weber, S. and Wiesmeth, H., 1991, 'Issue linkage in the European Community', *Journal of Common Market Studies*, 29, pp. 255–68.

8 Common policies and subsidiarity

The Community is not omnipotent: the scope of its competences are clearly defined and in many respects comparatively modest. There are other sources of authority and decision-making for member states: indeed, for a vast range of legislation, national parliaments and governments remain sovereign, their powers unrestrained by the Consolidated Treaty on European Union. None the less, the pejorative use of the term 'Brussels', typically found in the English language popular press, conjures up a picture of a monolithic leviathan controlling all aspects of everyday life in Europe. Quite an achievement for a bureaucracy of less than 13,000 employees. Despite its fraudulent nature, it is this image of absolute Community authority, personified by the Commission, which has often been the cause of misinformed popular opinion and perceptions of the Community, particularly in those member states regarded as reluctant Europeans. This chapter outlines the boundaries of Community competences, particularly in relation to the principle of subsidiarity. Examples of the Community policies are examined (agriculture, Monetary Union, environment) and distinctions are made between those policies for which the Community has complete responsibility and those where its authority is shared and circumscribed by national authority. The most important feature to keep in mind when examining the Community's array of policies is that they are extremely varied and often incomplete in nature. There is no typical policy organization, each is shaped according to the circumstances and the level of autonomy the individual member states are willing to surrender to the Community.

The Maastricht debate concerning the federal scope of the Community was not confined to political rhetoric or institutional relations: it had a direct impact on the Community's policy competences. The problem was how to define where it was appropriate and desirable for the Community to take overall policy responsibility, and where it was preferable or more practical for the member states to retain their domestic authority. As the dispute over the Social Charter illustrated, this choice was not always clear-cut. The Community solution was to apply the notion of subsidiarity as a general principle to guide existing and future policy debates. Subsidiarity, it is hoped, will offer an appealingly simple mechanism for determining the contentious division of respective powers between the Community (or a future Union) and the member states. It is both a substitute for a fully federal constitution and the fundamental basis on which such a treaty revision could be based: it offers a possible solution to the question of which powers are to remain within the competence of the member states, and which are to become exclusively Community-based responsibilities.

Neunreither describes subsidiarity in the following terms: '[S]ubsidiarity means that a larger unit only assumes functions in so far as the smaller units of which it is composed are unable or less qualified to fulfil their role' (1991, p. 1). This underlying principle was incorporated in Article 3b of the Maastricht Treaty:

> The Community shall act within the limits of the powers conferred upon it by this Treaty and of the objectives assigned to it therein. In the areas which do not fall within its exclusive jurisdiction, the Community shall only take action, in accordance with the principle of subsidiarity, only if, and insofar as the objectives of the proposed action cannot be sufficiently achieved by the Member States and can therefore, by reason of the scale or effects of proposed action, be better achieved by the Community.
>
> Any action by the Community shall not go beyond what is necessary to achieve the objectives of this Treaty.

Both the supporters and critics of European Union have linked the idea of subsidiarity to the federal vocation of the Community. It suggests a procedure that will accommodate both the widening and deepening of the Community without a necessarily implied centralization of authority. As a federal principle, however, subsidiarity remains untested within the Community context and while seductive, it may prove less effective in practice. There is no absolute distinction between what can 'be better achieved' at the EC rather than the national level and there will invariably be areas of dispute. It is also contentious whether this new treaty article provides an appropriate and workable legal guideline. As with all treaty matters it will be the responsibility of the Court of Justice to interpret this new constitutional principle. The past record of the Court suggests that it might well be expansive and *communautaire* in its interpretation providing a very significant federal impetus to European Union. If the Community is confirmed as having a federal vocation, the case for retaining specific power and authority at the national or sub-national level may become increasingly difficult to sustain. Indeed, the existing logic of a Single Market and harmonization demands that subsidiarity be increasingly used to promote Community-wide solutions over national solutions. Monetary Union, economic policy, the environment as well as common citizenship rights, are all examples that indicate the potential scope for the Community's legislative supremacy. Such a centralized federal interpretation may exacerbate the democratic deficit that already exists within the Community; subsidiarity may be used to take decision-making further away from national parliaments and accountability without any necessary compensation through the extension of the powers of the European Parliament. In summary, there is the expectation, yet to be tested, that this principle will be capable of deliberating between rival intergovernmental and federal strands within the Community.

The principles underlying the Community's approach to common policies were redefined at Maastricht. Article 2 of the new Consolidated

Treaty on European Union (which is comprised of the various ECSC, EC, SEA and Maastricht treaties) defines these in the following terms.

> The Community shall have as its task, by establishing a common market, an economic and monetary union and by implementing the common policies or activities referred to in Article 3, the promotion, throughout the Community, of a harmonious and balanced development of economic activities, sustainable and non-inflationary growth respecting the environment, a high degree of convergence of economic performance, a high level of employment and of social protection, the raising of the standard and quality of living, and economic and social cohesion and solidarity among Member States.

The backbone of this approach is the creation of the Single Market abolishing customs duties, quantitative restrictions and any other measures of equivalent effect for trade between the member states. Article 3 lists specific areas where the EC has direct competence: included here are provisions for a common commercial policy, a common agricultural and fisheries policy, and a common transport policy. However, the existence of a treaty commitment to a common policy does not necessarily mean that such a policy has been successfully enacted by the Community: the example of a common transport policy bears witness to this (Nugent, 1989, p. 209). The introduction of a single currency and a single monetary and exchange rate policy is also foreshadowed, though specific conditions have to be met before this will be a common policy for all of the member states. In other areas such as energy, the environment, development co-operation, or a European Social Fund, for example, a common policy is not stipulated and complementary national measures exist in addition to any Community initiatives.

Since the creation of a European supranational authority in the 1950s, the Community has gradually brought specific economic areas under its ambit, coal, steel and agriculture being historically the most important, and the Single Market and EMU the most contemporary examples of this policy expansion. Despite the relatively slow progression and the long periods of seeming stagnation, the overall pattern is clear; neofunctional theorists have regarded the reforms and policy innovations agreed to in both the SEA and the Maastricht Treaty as evidence of the efficacy of spillover. Before examining the application of some of the Community's common policies it is important to understand the factors that work to limit the comprehensive extension of common EC policies.

First, while EMU implies a growing convergence across a range of policies, it is wrong to conclude that the scope of Community policy has made the role of the member states redundant. The member states still retain absolute control over their individual domestic policies and legal systems. Community decisions take priority over national law only for those areas specified as common policies. Membership of the Community does necessitate limitations being imposed on a state's former absolute sovereignty. But, whatever common policies exist are the result of unanimous decisions by the member states. Consequently, national interests have been a major barrier to the adoption or execution of several policies. No member state can claim that a common policy was imposed against its will. New states have to accept the full *acquis politique* as a pre-condition to membership, thereby giving their explicit acceptance of the existing common policies. In short, common policies exist where there is common (unanimous) consent. Even in those areas where majority decisions have been introduced (aspects of agriculture and policies covered by the SEA), the Community had unanimously to approve the application of majority voting in each instance.

A second aspect of the limitations imposed by individual member states concerns the funding of EC policies. The 1990 budget was 46.9 billion ECU and while this figure was twice that spent in 1983, in comparison with each national budget, the Community budget is extremely small. For example, in 1988 the EC budget only represented 1.15 per cent of the GDPs of the member states and 3.0 per cent of their combined total domestic budgets (Nugent, 1989, p. 259). Although the GDP ceiling for 'own resources' was to rise to 2 per cent by 1992, these financial constraints considerably inhibit the range and scope of common policies. This limitation is even more severe as up to two-thirds of expenditure goes to fund the CAP. Indeed, extending common policies beyond those initially stipulated in the Treaty of Rome was impossible until after the SEA inspired relaunch of the Community and implementation of the Single Market. The Community currently derives its funding from a combination of its 'own resources': customs duties on imports and agricultural levies collected by the member states; a low (1.6 per cent) percentage of VAT revenue; and a proportional share of each countries GNP (Nicoll and Salmon, 1990, p. 85).

A third consideration that concerns the implementation of Community policies is the political commitment to give effect to treaty provisions. Constitutionally the member states have always been required to co-operate and co-ordinate their macro-economic and financial policies; however, prior to the SEA this obligation was regularly dishonoured by some member states often for domestic political reasons. A constitutional commitment was a necessary but far from sufficient catalyst for 'an ever closer union'. The Maastricht division of the federal nature of the Community illustrated that the importance of political will has not diminished. Conversely, where a political commitment does exist within the Community, a lack of any direct legal competence has not been an impediment to the development of a Community-wide response. An example of this was the emergence of a Community environmental policy: no reference to such a policy was made in the original Treaty, none the less the Community began to formulate an environmental policy as early as 1970. The existence of this was only constitutionally recognized in the SEA (Nugent, 1989, p. 210). Because there was a political agreement to develop an environmental policy, the Community could use either Article 100 or 235 to provide a legal base for action. These two articles allow for Community action which will 'directly affect the establishment or functioning of the common market', or to take appropriate measures to attain a Community objective where 'the Treaty has not provided the necessary powers'. However, the Council has to approve unanimously any such policy initiatives making both these expansive Articles totally dependent on engineering a political consensus to expand the scope of Community policy.

The most striking characteristics of Community policies have been described as their range and diversity; the variable levels of Community involvement for each policy; and, the somewhat unco-ordinated nature of these policies (Nugent, 1989, pp. 225–9). These characteristics are not necessarily in harmony with one another, further blurring what is already a complex policy-making process linking the Community's internal institutional relations with those domestic policy-making structures in each member state. Despite the expansion of tasks under the SEA and Maastricht Treaty, the limited nature of the Community's centralized federal control, rather than incursions into domestic policy spheres, still characterizes the Community's policy-making in the 1990s. The following examination of certain key Community policies illustrates these characteristics, particularly the variation that exists between policies due to either constitutional limitations or political will.

The Common Agricultural Policy (CAP) is the Community's most developed policy. Its origins can be found in the Treaty of Rome and its effective implementation was one of the EC's first policy achievements. Of all the Community's policies the CAP is the most comprehensive and regulated and involves the Community institutions to a higher degree. It is also the Community policy that takes the greatest proportion of the EC budget and has historically been the focus for major policy disputes between member states. For those critics of the Brussels monolith, the CAP represents all that is wrong with a federal Europe. Despite its obvious shortcomings, all of which are readily acknowledged by those involved in the policy process, no member state has ever advocated that twelve national agricultural policies would be a preferable, more efficient or more economical framework for structuring Europe's agricultural sector. Using the principle of subsidiarity, the CAP's imperfection does not disqualify the Community from being the appropriate level for policy implementation. The experience of the CAP demonstrates that effective policy integration is both appropriate and possible at the Community level.

Agriculture was an obvious common policy area for the original Six. First, given that the Community was based on the four freedoms (of goods, workers, services and capital) it would have been illogical to have left the responsibility of this central area of economic activity with the member states. Second, the existing ECSC provisions addressed some of the industrial issues of the common market; to balance these an agricultural common market was needed. Third, agriculture was clearly the political price that had to be paid to satisfy French demands. The Community offered Germany the advantages of free access to the French industrial market: to compensate, France, the largest agricultural producer among the Six, required a free trade regime in agriculture to provide equal opportunities in the German and other member-state markets (Noort, 1990, pp. 30–1). Fourth, during the 1950s and 1960s, the social structure of the Six still contained an important agrarian sector that exercised both economic and political power: for example, in 1959, 24 per cent of the Community's population was employed in the agricultural sector. And lastly, the contribution of agriculture to GDP and employment was considerable.

Consequently, the rationale underlying the CAP was not exclusively economic, but combined a very strong social structural element in its mix of objectives. It is this human aspect of the CAP that is often overlooked in criticisms of the policy's implementation and unintended over-production. It should not be. In the immediate post-war years rural depopulation had already begun to manifest itself and agricultural incomes were invariably lower than industrial wages. While modernization was encouraged, no government could support technological changes in agriculture irrespective of the costs of social disruption – not if they wanted to be re-elected. The CAP was created to achieve a delicate balance: to preserve the social fabric of Europe's small agricultural communities while simultaneously stimulating the efficient utilization of farming resources.

As described in Chapter 2, Articles 38–47 of the Treaty of Rome set out the mechanisms for achieving a common market in agriculture. The objectives of the CAP are:

> to increase agricultural productivity by promoting technical progress and by ensuring the rational development of agricultural production and the optimum utilization of the factors of production, in particular labour;
> . . . thus, to ensure a fair standard of living for the agricultural community, in particular by increasing the individual earnings of persons engaged in agriculture;
> to stabilize markets;
> to assure the availability of supplies; and
> to ensure that supplies reach consumers at reasonable prices. (Article 39.1 a–e)

Whether these objectives are in practice compatible has been a matter of conjecture. The CAP sought to guarantee a constant and more productive food supply and provide a fair deal for both producers and consumers, at least in theory. To meet these objectives three fundamental principles were enacted: the concept of an agricultural single market and common prices; Community preference; and joint financial responsibility.

Although the Treaty of Rome provided the framework for the CAP, it took several conferences to work out the policy mechanisms involved, and it was only in 1962 that the CAP became operational. The agricultural sector provided the Community with its first attempt to produce a common market and acted as a model for the subsequent extension of the 1992 Single Market for all goods within the Twelve. The CAP did not set up an unrestrained liberal free trade market, however: it provided for specific support mechanisms and product prices were set by the Community (the Council and the Commission) and not by market forces (Nugent, 1989, p. 287). Within these constraints a common market for agriculture was established through the removal of internal customs duties, subsidies and other policy instruments that had the effect of distorting the free exchange of agricultural products between member states. Approximately 95 per cent of EC farm products are covered under the CAP, the two major exceptions being potatoes and agricultural alcohol which are both controlled by domestic legislation. In addition, the single agricultural market required a common administrative and legislative framework. This necessitated the harmonization of relevant domestic legislation and where necessary, the progressive introduction of EC regulations that were superior to national law. Cumulatively this has resulted in virtually all aspects of agricultural policy control being transferred from domestic parliaments to the Community. Only in limited sectors do national governments retain the ability to offer special assistance to its farmers.

Obviously, for a single market to operate effectively there has to be a minimal price variation between countries. In the absence of a single European currency the Community introduced a fixed-rate 'green' ECU and monetary compensation amounts (MCAs), a system of border levies and subsidies, to compensate for fluctuations between domestic currency values against the ECU. Consequently, agricultural policy is not an insulated common market within the Community, but is directly affected by general exchange rate policy (p. 289). These procedures provide national governments with some degree of manœuvre within the CAP and have been defended against frequent Commission proposals for their abolition. The planned EMU and single currency will undoubtedly make these compensating but distorting instruments irrelevant for those member states who surrender their currency in favour of the ECU. However, for those who prefer to retain their own national currencies and for new member states who require transitional procedures, the continuation of these existing agricultural instruments may well be necessary.

The CAP is financed through the European Agricultural Guidance and Guarantee Fund (EAGGF). The Fund helps to protect European farming either by imposing import levies on competing CAP products, or as is more common, by providing price support for Community producers. The support given varies according to agricultural products, but in general the following mechanisms apply. The bulk of products have traditionally benefited from price support, particularly through intervention levels which act to maintain agricultural prices at a predetermined level irrespective of the world price for a particular product. The system has three trigger mechanisms and works in the following way: an annual 'target' price is set for each EC product; 'threshold' prices are established below which imports into the Community cannot fall; when an agricultural price falls below the agreed minimum, the Community intervenes to buy production surpluses at guaranteed minimum 'intervention levels'. These are then stored until, or if, market prices recover. Intervention levels are one facet of the CAP's social component: the mechanism provides an insurance policy for farmers by protecting them from fluctuating market forces. The value of these support prices are revised annually and constitute one of the major sources of internal Community conflict.

Practices have altered considerably since the late-1980s after criticism of the profligate spending associated with intervention levels and the storage of 'lakes' and 'mountains' of agricultural products. Reforms designed to limit the cost of guaranteed prices and to reduce production levels were introduced in the form of quotas, co-responsibility levies and production ceilings. Co-responsibility levies involved the producers directly sharing the cost of over-production with the Community: future surpluses were no longer to be without financial penalty (Marsh, 1989, p. 152). Ceilings, in the form of 'stabilizers' were introduced which fixed the upper limit for guaranteed production for specific products (Nicoll and Salmon, 1990, p. 181). Cumulatively these reforms have begun the difficult and sensitive process of removing the *carte blanche* guarantees that European farmers had known for the previous 30 years. Further pressures, both internal from member states determined to reduce the cost of the EAGGF and external in the guise of the 1991–2 GATT Round negotiations, make further reform of the CAP a Community priority. However, any radical or rapid solutions cannot be expected: the pace of change and the margins for manœuvre are limited. Expenditure on agricultural support has already been extensively reduced and any structural changes in the organization of the CAP would be difficult to achieve politically. The agricultural lobby is still a vital sector in many member state economies and of significant electoral importance.

The principle of Community preference is a logical extension of the price support regime and again has an underlying social rationale. Community preference works by giving the EC market additional protection from cheaper imports and fluctuations in world market prices. It is, regardless of hyperbole and explanations, a protectionist policy to advantage Europe's farmers. The system operates a combination of customs duties and levies. Where the price of an imported agricultural product is lower than the Community price, an import levy is imposed to equalize prices. Conversely, if world prices are higher, an export levy can be imposed to dissuade Community producers from selling abroad, thereby guaranteeing supplies within the Community, a basic objective of the CAP. This second alternative has only occurred once, between 1974 and 1975: normally, Community prices exceed world prices for most products. The major exception to the Community preference regime is the system of generalized preferences which provides certain developing countries with specific preferential product access to the Community's agricultural market. This concession is particularly important for the 69 ACP states who are linked to the Community through the Lomé Conventions.

The third principle underpinning the CAP is that of joint financing. The bulk of agricultural financing is through the EAGGF which provides funds for the guaranteed price support policies and for structural policy. However, the demands placed upon the EAGGF by the intervention mechanism has meant that as much as 95 per cent of the Fund is devoted to price maintenance, leaving structural policy generally ignored. The Commission is responsible for the administration and financial accounting of the EAGGF and the annual price reviews begin with its estimates of the coming year's expenditure. Despite concerted efforts to balance expenditure and to introduce structural reforms, national interests in maintaining the agricultural status quo have so far prevailed. Additional agricultural financing is made from other Community sources, such as the Regional Fund, as well as from national budgets. The CAP does not prohibit individual countries from aiding their own farmers provided that any support given does not contradict the objectives of the CAP or of the Community's overall common market.

How 'common' is the CAP? Of all the EC's policies agricultural policy is the most developed and detailed drawing on a high proportion of the Community's resources. But the CAP is not a fully comprehensive policy. It could be extended in a number of ways: for example, a common currency would help to produce greater price comparability as would a narrow VAT band on consumer prices. Certain products are excluded and new member states are provided with lengthy transition periods (up to ten years) before having to adopt the CAP's conditions fully. The CAP does, however, demonstrate some important centralized characteristics such as the Commission's role in administering and overseeing funding. The most important attribute, and a prerequisite to a federal common policy structure, is the use of majority voting in the Council. The informal veto associated with the 1966 Luxembourg Compromise has fallen into disuse in the 1990s and national interests can, on occasions, be overruled.

In terms of its own criteria, has the CAP achieved its objectives (Hill, 1984, pp. 104–11)? Agricultural productivity has clearly developed at a phenomenal rate due largely to intensified farming practices, although some of these practices have been prey to recent criticism. But this increase has not been uniform and the CAP supports an awkward mix of large productive farms and smaller less-efficient farms in rural communities that would not otherwise be cost-effective. The objective of the 'optimum utilization' of labour has proved somewhat paradoxical: technological improvements have seen agricultural labour decline by over 50 per cent during the life of the CAP. However, in sensitive rural areas the CAP has helped to stem massive depopulation at a time when urban unemployment levels were at their peak. Despite annual fluctuations, on average, agricultural earnings have increased in line with other sectors of the economy. The greatest disparities are between the size of the farming operations and their products. Northern large-scale farmers producing dairy, cereals or beef have been the major beneficiaries (thanks to CAP price support mechanisms), whereas smaller farmers, particularly those producing Mediterranean products (fruits, olive oil, etc.,) have been less favoured. The stabilization of markets and the availability of supplies have both been realized. Agricultural prices have been comparatively unaffected by fluctuations in world prices and overall increases have been lower than the EC consumer price index. The fear of specific food shortages that was a real concern to the original Six is no longer a worry in the Community – in fact quite the reverse! The Community is effectively self-sufficient in all the agricultural products that can be grown climatically in Europe, with certain products being consistently in surplus. Quite what constitutes a 'reasonable' price for consumers is probably impossible to determine. Europeans often pay at levels above world prices, especially for dairy products, but this consumer price has to be balanced against security of supply and the maintenance of agricultural living standards. Furthermore, national governments, not the CAP, determine domestic levels of taxation, such as VAT rates, on foodstuffs and these have a greater influence on consumer prices than the global cost of the CAP.

Rather than failing in its objectives as set out in Article 39.1 of the Treaty, the CAP stands accused of being too successful. Efficiency, production technology, stable and secure markets that produce surpluses and not shortages are all symptoms of overachievement. It is valid to question whether the objectives of the 1950s are still appropriate for the 1990s. The 1980s saw fundamental reform in the CAP's pricing structures and guaranteed production levels, but left the overall policy intact. There are increasing pressures to rethink the philosophy of the CAP, particularly in relation to environmental issues. Chemical fertilization and intensive farming techniques have added to Europe's environmental pollution. Incentives to leave land fallow, or to introduce forestry are recent innovations designed to control environmental damage that could be caused by an unrestrained CAP. The effect, often detrimental, on world agricultural markets has also led to criticism of the CAP from both domestic and the Community's external competitors. Despite the obvious inadequacies and difficulties, the CAP is still relevant to the 1990s: European agriculture without a common policy is unthinkable. A real free market where prices are set by demand is not likely: central price setting and support where necessary are fundamental principles without which the CAP would be meaningless. Undoubtedly, the 1990s will witness continued policy reform to address the problems of adjustment, especially in an enlarged Community. However, the fundamental characteristics of the CAP are ingrained and have proved themselves an impressive model for common policies in other areas of Community involvement.

Agriculture was the Community's first comprehensive common policy, and in many ways it remains the only policy area where Community competences are of more importance than national legislation. In an integrated Community one would expect to find a wider range of common policies – commercial, social, fiscal, energy, environment, transport and so on. But in contrast with the CAP, the other common policy areas outlined in the Treaty of Rome have developed in a fragmented and rudimentary manner. The common transport policy provides an example of this. Transport, along with agriculture, was one of the few policy areas elevated to the status of a common policy. Although a comparative small percentage of the Six's work-force was employed in the transport sector, the constitution planners who met at Messina appreciated that transport was a key factor in establishing a common market. The experience of the ECSC had shown that differential transportation costs had a distorting effect on the Community's coal and steel policy. Free trade, particularly in agriculture, could only be promoted if there really were no national barriers to cross-border transportation and the movement of goods. This was not the situation for transport; rather 'it was well known that state intervention in this sector was very extensive; as a result, transport charges frequently discriminated between national and foreign users, the effect being to erect serious barriers to imports and to protect domestic producers against competition from abroad' (Nevin, 1990, p. 185).

Articles 74–84 of Title IV-2 outline the provisions for the common transport policy. Originally the common transport policy was thought to be confined to road, rail and inland waterways; this was extended in 1973 to cover air and sea transportation within the Community. This enhanced scope of the policy was not matched by any substantive application of a common set of provisions for European transport. The major difficulty was in the existing massive level of state involvement in various transportation sectors, with national railway systems presenting the greatest problems with respect to state subsidies. The indirect assistance that could be given to other key national industries through road, rail or canal tariffs further confused the political issues involved with a common approach to transport. This complexity resulted in a series of largely ineffectual attempts to design a common transport policy. The 1960s was a decade of virtual policy failure in this sector (pp. 187–92).

The geography of the Community's putative transport policy was radically altered by the first enlargement in 1973, introducing a sea and air component to the existing predominant land transport structures of the original Six. The new approach was the antithesis of the failed interventionism of the 1960s: it sought to establish general principles with which national legislation should conform rather than attempt to specify binding Community regulations. This retreat from a *communautaire* discipline has led to the conclusion that 'the Community can hardly be said to have sought, and certainly has not achieved, anything which could realistically be described as a distinctive transport policy' (p. 193). The European Parliament was in agreement with this assessment. In 1983 it took the Council of Ministers before the Court of Justice because of its failure to implement a common policy: the Court found the Council to be in breach of its obligations under the Rome Treaty.

Subsequently, some policy initiatives were accepted by the Community: common maximum weights and dimensions for lorries were established (with some derogations reflecting road limitations); road freight quotas between member states were to be raised and eventually abolished to coincide with the creation of the Single European Market in 1993; and the practice of cabotage was liberalized to allow sea and road carriers to collect and deliver freight irrespective of country of origin, something that had remained illegal despite the rhetoric of a common market and common transport policy (p. 193). The most ambitious intervention by the Commission has been its attempt to deregulate European air traffic: this sector became a priority under the second Delors Commission. Tellingly, however, the Commission has preferred to use the general provisions of Article 85 concerning competition policy as its legal basis (rather than Articles 74–84 which are specifically devoted to transport policy). Despite the removal of certain bilateral protectionist rules that existed within the Community these combined developments in all transport sectors are modest and cumulatively do not constitute even a basic framework for a common transport policy. Further road, rail, air and sea transport reforms are needed to facilitate the objectives of the 1992 Single Market.

One other area, environment, has taken an opposite path; despite not being mentioned in the original Treaty this policy developed significantly before being recognized as a legitimate area of EC competence in the SEA. Of all the areas in which the Community is involved, a common approach to environmental policy is logically the most defensible. Despite the cliché, environmental issues and pollution do not respect national borders or sovereignty: a common approach is the most effective policy mechanism. The Community has adopted five Action Programmes on the Environment between 1973 and 1992. These various initiatives covered topics such as water quality, atmospheric pollution, noise, toxic waste and wildlife protection (Nicoll and Salmon, 1990, p. 202). Unlike the case of the CAP, legally binding Community regulations were not used to implement policy; Council resolutions that were simply indicative and relied on political goodwill rather than legal compulsion or directives that allowed for national interpretation were the preferred policy instruments. This resulted in policy competence being shared between the member states and the Community and lacking the uniformity that can only be provided by regulations. Events have shown that for financial considerations member states are often tempted to shirk their environmental obligations (Lodge, 1989, p. 322).

The effectiveness of this approach was significantly hampered by the strong domestic industrial lobbies in each country and by the lack of any environmental component in the Treaty of Rome. Those opposed to specific environment initiatives could legitimately oppose EC action by arguing that there was no explicit treaty basis on which to act. Arguably certain environmental concerns could be considered to be incompatible with the EC's broader economic and agricultural objectives as specified in the Treaty. The SEA remedied this constitutional quirk by confirming the right of Community institutions to legislate on environmental issues, albeit within the constraints of unanimity in the Council or in certain circumstances the co-operation procedure with the Parliament. The objectives of environmental policy were: '(i) to preserve, protect and improve the quality of the environment; (ii) to contribute towards protecting human health; (iii) to ensure a prudent and rational utilization of natural resources' (Article 130R.1). Within this framework preventative action was a policy priority. Where environmental damage takes place the principle 'that the polluter should pay' takes precedence. Environmental policy was not compartmentalized but was to constitute 'a component of the Community's other policies' (Article 130R.2). Anticipating the subsidiarity language of the Maastricht Treaty, Community action was only permissible where the environment objectives specified in the SEA 'can be attained better at Community level than at the level of the individual Member States' (130R.4). Even where it was accepted that the Community constituted the appropriate level, the SEA only established minimal environmental standards: provided that there was no conflict with the general provisions of the SEA nothing prevented any member state 'from maintaining or introducing more stringent protective measures' (Article 130T). These conditional terms weaken the ability of the Community to set uniform standards.

The Maastricht Treaty reconsidered the Community's environmental policy, confirming its growing importance as a policy sector. A fourth policy objective was added committing the Community to 'promoting measures at the international level to deal with regional or worldwide environmental problems'. The decision-making procedures were modified somewhat allowing for majority voting for some types of decisions, although unanimity was retained for fiscal policy. However, in general, member states retained responsibility for both the financing and the implementation of environmental policy adopted within the Community framework. Although comparatively modest, the Maastricht Treaty confirms Lodge's prediction that environmental policy will become an increasingly important and difficult issue within the Community in the 1990s, not just for the obvious reason of the environmental catastrophe that exists both within and beyond the EC's borders, but because a more active environmental policy challenges many of the Community's other existing policies. The most immediate conflict is with the CAP, but areas such as the internal market, transport and energy all pose potential policy contradictions for the Community (Lodge, 1989, p. 325).

The establishment of comprehensive sectoral policies in the early 1950s by the ECSC provided an unrealistic model for the future Community. Only agriculture approximated the common provisions agreed for coal and steel. Consequently, while the Community has extended its activity across a range of other policy areas, the degree of involvement and the respective claims to be common policies varies between different economic areas. As already noted in relation to transport policy, the Commission has become active in establishing a competition policy under the direction of Leon Brittan. Both regional and social policy are long-standing Community concerns where common policies have been introduced to supplement, not replace, national approaches. They have both gained an increasing share of the EC budget at the expense of the CAP. Energy and industrial policies are only dealt with on an *ad hoc* basis, neither having any direct treaty competence for a common policy. In addition to these and other internal policies, the Community exercises a common external commercial policy through its joint relations with EFTA/EEA, neighbouring states with whom there are association or 'Europe' Agreements, and with 69 developing nations covered by the various Lomé Conventions.

Both the SEA and the Maastricht reforms were designed to address the past incremental nature of the Community's common policies. The Single European Market and Economic and Monetary Union agreed in 1985 and 1991 respectively, constitute the two most important common policy initiatives the Community has made since introducing the CAP. If both are successful, the spillover to other internal sectors will accelerate the extension of common policies across the Community and act as a catalyst for a more integrated federal Union.

Lodge has identified the creation of the Single Market as the dominant Community policy issue of the early 1990s (1989, p. 83). This policy constitutes a fundamental step towards establishing a common macro-economic framework for introducing other specific common economic policies. The Common Market concept was at the heart of the original Treaty; and yet the free trade expectations of the Treaty framers failed to materialize during the first 25 years of the Community's existence, largely because of political resistance. It took the SEA to renew Community commitment to this principle setting 1992 as the deadline for the establishment of a Single European Market. The 1985 Treaty reform committed the Community to 'adopt measures with the aim of progressively establishing the internal market over a period expiring on 31 December 1992 . . . The internal market shall comprise an area without internal frontiers in which the free movement of goods, persons, services and capital is ensured' (Article 8A). The most important *communautaire* concession was the agreement that decisions relating to establishing the Single Market would be taken on the basis of qualified majority in the Council and that the European Parliament would be given a greater legislative role (see Chapter 3). The major exception to this was that provisions for the harmonization of indirect taxation between member states required Council unanimity.

The 1985 Commission White Paper, *Completing the Internal Market*, written by Lord Cockfield, outlined 282 directives that had to be implemented in order to complete an EC internal market (an objective originally conceived in 1957). The Community's earlier experience of an open-ended timetable for realizing a common market showed that it was essential that a fixed deadline was established and abided by if the internal market was to be established. Thus the slogan of '1992' served as a decision-making catalyst and by Community standards consistent progress was made over the seven-year transition period. By July 1991, 73 per cent (201) of the necessary directives had been adopted as Community measures with 71 per cent of this total having been transposed into national legislation (Belmont, 1991, p. 18). Not surprisingly, the greatest difficulty has been in adopting VAT directives (which required Council unanimity). From a practical perspective, an internal single market requires standardized VAT and excise duties: only three out of eleven VAT directives were in place by mid-1991, although agreement was reached in 1991 on establishing a standard minimum 15 per cent VAT rate by the end of 1992.

An ideal-type internal market is not feasible under the SEA; member states will retain certain prerogatives and subsequent political decisions will determine the extent of economic integration. What is envisaged is the dismantling of various physical, technical and fiscal barriers that impede intra-EC trade combined with an approximation of national economic policy measures. Frontier controls on individuals and goods are the physical barriers; fiscal barriers constitute all obstacles or distortions between member states derived from the indirect taxation levels discussed above; whereas technical barriers cover such things as public procurement, and limitations on the free movement of labour, services and capital (Pelkmans and Winters, 1988, pp. 4–10). A particularly important change that the SEA exploited concerned differential product standards. In the past, differences in technical specifications were used to exclude competing products. The 1979 Court of Justice ruling on the Cassis de Dijon case, established the principle of 'mutual recognition' of similar product standards and not identical standards. Consequently, this ruling can be used as the general basis for intra-Community trade, avoiding the laborious and potentially acrimonious process of specification item by item (Pinder, 1989, p. 98). As Community history illustrates very clearly, such measures are not in themselves sufficient. The transposition of Community directives into national law requires a commonly agreed commitment on objectives. This has yet to be achieved: some Community states consider the internal market to be exclusively confined to economic liberalization, whereas others welcome it as a neofunctional prerequisite to federal integration.

Completing the internal market will have economic and political consequences. The Cecchini Report quantified the costs to the Community of the economic status quo and estimated the economic benefits of 1992. For example, the annual cost of maintaining frontier controls on goods and persons was put at 8–9 billion ECU (1988, p. 84). Domestic rules governing public procurement restricting a government's choice of product to their own national producers reduced the value of this trade to 0.14 per cent of GDP, less than one-fiftieth of the projected value in a free internal market (p. 16). Overall, Cecchini estimated that the Single European Market would increase the EC's combined GDP by approximately 5 per cent. The greatest savings would come from the removal of production barriers (public procurement preferences, different standards and restrictive national regulatory structures), followed by economies of scale, competitive efficiency, and in last place the abolition of frontier controls. Other predicted economic consequences for the Community included a consumer price drop of around 6 per cent, and an increase in the EC unemployment level by 1.8 million (pp. 83–98). Cumulatively, these measures ought to be anti-inflationary with consumers, at least those in employment, and taxpayers the beneficiaries of efficiency, economies and greater choice.

The political impact of the Single Market is of equal importance. For federalists, the implementation of the internal market outlined by the SEA demands that new common policies be created and that institutional control of these be enhanced (Pinder, 1989, p. 104). National freedom to set macro-economic policy, including indirect taxation rates, has been constrained and the range of barriers that are being removed all limit the individual economic autonomy for each member state. The physical removal of border checks and common rules for immigrants and the movement of EC citizens all pose sensitive political problems. The right to select who enters or resides in a country has shifted from an exclusive national prerogative to a joint Community authority. These and other extensions of the Community's common policy competence have already had wide-ranging political implications. As Pinder has concluded from a federalist vantage, the 'Single Market programme and the SEA have thus not only given the EC an impulse towards monetary union, social solidarity, foreign policy and security cooperation, budgetary and institutional reform, but also an impulse towards the European Union' (p. 109).

Undoubtedly, the pressure of the economic effects of the Single Market helped to persuade the Twelve to convene the 1991 IGC to discuss the prospects for complete Economic and Monetary Union, the EC's most contemporary and ambitious attempt to establish a common policy. EMU constitutes the next major macro-economic step towards a common policy, building on the existing European Monetary System (EMS) and Exchange Rate Mechanism (ERM) framework. The Maastricht Treaty commits the

Community, under certain conditions to Monetary Union this century. A common fiscal policy challenges the traditional idea of national sovereignty in a more powerful and more obvious way than any of the other existing common Community policies. If EMU is enacted according to the agreed timetable, by 1999 the balance of authority within the EC will have clearly shifted in favour of common policies and away from national autonomy.

Previous attempts to establish Monetary Union had been unsuccessful. The Snake, launched in 1971, disintegrated within two years when confronted with international monetary volatility and the final collapse of the Bretton Woods exchange rate system. However, the importance for the EC of exercising a degree of control over European currency values independent of the US dollar did not dissipate, but rather increased during the 1970s. Currency fluctuations distorted the Community's internal market, monetary stability became a priority and an essential prerequisite for further economic integration. In 1979 the first phase of the EMS was launched to achieve three objectives: a high degree of stability between the exchange rate of participating currencies; to encourage greater convergence in economic policies; and to introduce the ECU as an international currency (and the Community's prospective common currency) whose value comprised a basket of national currencies (Nevin, 1990, p. 278). The EMS was operated through the ERM, a procedure that confined national currency variations within a narrow band. Thus by common agreement in the Council, the value of the currencies of the then member states were fixed against the ECU, with the exception of the pound sterling which only joined the ERM in October 1990.

In terms of its own objectives the EMS's record is mixed. For the period 1979–89, the level of instability for the participating EMS currencies was significantly less than for the non-participating currencies. However, instability was not removed: during the decade there were twelve realignments in currency rates, the Deutschemark appreciated by 18 per cent, whereas the lira depreciated by 29 per cent. There was no evidence of macro-economic policy convergence, and the ECU did not have the impact as an international currency alternative to the US dollar as hoped. On balance, however, the EMS was a Community success and it paved the way for the more ambitious policy of Economic and Monetary Union initiated by Jacques Delors (pp. 278–81).

The SEA gave legal recognition to EMU. It provided for 'the convergence of economic and monetary policies which is necessary for the further development of the Community' (Article 102A.1). However, this general requirement lacked any specific mechanisms for implementation. This was partially rectified in the 1989 Delors Report that proposed a three-stage path to EMU. Only a date for the first phase was defined (1990), and it was left to the 1991 IGC discussions to outline the necessary structures and timetable for stages two and three leading to full Economic and Monetary Union. The magnitude of this development cannot be over-emphasized: as Nevin demonstrates, these proposals implied profound political changes. If implemented, national governments would not merely surrender the right to vary their own exchange rates; they would be transferring to central Community institutions all power over monetary policy and most of their power to determine budgetary policy. The Delors committee was proposing a version of monetary union which led inescapably to a federal European government presiding over national governments (1990, p. 284).

Despite these economic implications, and in contrast with the divisions over Political Union and the Community's 'federal vocation', a consensus on the shape of EMU was quick to emerge, although difficulties in implementing this did surface. Maastricht produced a broad commitment to the irreversible nature of EMU (including a common currency) and established a timetable and the conditions under which the Community could move to the second and final third stage of Union before the end of this century. The details of the EMU Treaty are summarized below.

Maastricht added a new principle to the Community *aquis*: Article 3A.2 confirms 'the irrevocable fixing of exchange rates leading to the introduction of a single currency, the ECU, the definition and conduct of a single monetary policy and exchange rate policy'. The Community and the member states were expected to comply with policies based on 'stable prices, sound public finances and monetary conditions and a sustainable balance of payments' (3A.3). Two new institutions were also established: the European System of Central Banks (ESCB) and the European Central Bank (ECB). The general thrust of Economic Union is that the member states should regard their economic policies 'as a matter of common concern', the broad guidelines for which are to be determined by a qualified majority in Council (Article 103.1–2). Member states are required to 'avoid excessive government deficits'; the Commission is charged with the responsibility of monitoring the ratio of debt to GDP for each member and where this fails to meet specific criteria the Commission is obliged to prepare a report for the Council which will then decide by qualified majority. The Council can instruct the member state concerned to adopt certain recommendations: if these are not followed the Community is empowered to take a range of punitive actions, including fines (Article 104B.1–14).

The objective of monetary policy is the maintenance of price stability through the operation of the ESCB (composed of the ECB and the central banks of the member states). Control of these bodies is through overlapping non-voting membership with the relevant EC Council meetings and through an annual ECB report to all of the Community's main institutions, including the European Parliament which can debate the report and invite the Executive Board of the ECB to participate in parliamentary committees (Article 109A). Membership of the ECB Executive Board is for eight-year non-renewable terms. The independence of the ECB is emphasized and it is prohibited from taking instructions from other Community institutions or the member states (Article 107). The ECB has to be consulted on any proposed EC legislation that falls within its field of competence.

During the second stage of EMU an advisory monetary committee is to be established to promote the co-ordination of member state policies relevant to the functioning of the internal market. This is to be replaced by an economic and financial committee from the start of the third and final stage of EMU. This committee will be composed of no more than two members from each of the member states, the Commission and the ECB. Its tasks will be to deliver opinions for consideration by the Community institutions and to review and report regularly on the financial situation of the Community and of the member states, including those who opt not to participate in the third stage of EMU.

The timetable for the second stage of EMU has been fixed for 1 January 1994: before this date all member states are required to implement measures to allow for the free movement of capital and adopt long-term programmes fostering the economic convergence necessary for the completion of EMU (particularly with respect to price stability and public finances). During this second stage a range of financial constraints are to be placed on the member states; the transition to a system of independent national central banks commenced; and, members states are to 'endeavour to avoid excessive government deficits' (Article 109C.3–5). Also at this stage a European Monetary Institute (EMI) will be created as the forerunner to the ECB, with the task to promote greater co-ordination of monetary policy and to prepare the instruments necessary for all aspects of a single monetary policy (Article 109D.1–9).

Article 109F is the most important for the development of a common economic and monetary policy. It specifies the conditions for the transition from the second to the third stage of EMU. This is dependent on favourable reports from the Commission and the EMI on the member states progress towards meeting the conditions set for EMU: namely, the development of the ECU; the compatibility of national legislation; price stability; the sustainability of national financial positions; currency stability; long-term interest rate levels; and, the experience of the ERM and the durability of the convergence process. On the basis of these reports the Council acting by qualified majority will assess which member states have met the conditions for EMU and a single currency and whether there is a majority of states in this position. After consultation between the Council of Ministers and the European Parliament, the European Council will consider a report on the viability of entering the final stage of EMU. The European Council, acting by qualified majority, will then have until 31 December 1996 to decide whether a simple majority of member states meet the conditions established for EMU and, if so, when it would be appropriate to commence the third stage of Union. If these conditions are not met, then the third stage of EMU will automatically begin as of 1 January 1999 (Article 109F.1–4) for those states who wish to participate. At this stage the Council acting unanimously will set 'irrevocably fixed' conversion rates for each participating national currency vis-à-vis the ECU which would then become the single currency for those states (Article 109H.4).

This seemingly conveyor belt to monetary union has one crucial escape clause. The British Government insisted on a derogation claiming that any such moves towards the irrevocable integration of the economies and currencies of the Community states had to gain the explicit approval of the British Parliament. This intergovernmental brake on EMU resulted in a protocol being attached to the Treaty which excluded the UK from the obligations and automaticity of the process: it also reduced the UK's ability to influence monetary developments or participate in setting up the transitional structures. Consequently, at Maastricht the Eleven committed themselves to a fuller Union and the creation of a common financial and economic structure for the Community, while the UK reserved judgement. Clearly, much can influence events between 1992 and 1999, the latest date established for EMU. A different British government may well have a more *communautaire* approach and convergence may proceed smoothly. Without disregarding the unforeseen, Maastricht took the irreversible step towards a single currency for the Community this century and for the progressive alignment of the member state economies. If fully realized, EMU will be the most important common policy operated by the Community and constitutes the basis for the development of EC competences across a range of other policy areas. The consequences are of historic magnitude.

In summary, any interpretation of the policy-making competence of the Community has to acknowledge that the process is characterized by the range and diversity of common policies; the differential level of Community involvement; and, at least prior to the SEA, incrementalism and the lack of an overarching co-ordinated structure (Nugent, 1989, pp. 225-9). The Single Market and EMU provide the key to transform this pragmatic and essential intergovernmental approach into a comprehensive framework for common Community policies. The common market of Monnet's Europe has been extremely slow to develop. If the Single Market and the commitments made at Maastricht continue to be given political as well as bureaucratic support, and provided that the decision-making structures are revised to accommodate future enlargements, there is every expectation that a more integrated Community will result. As with every aspect of Community development, the introduction of new common policy areas is directly affected by intergovernmental sensitivities. And it is this continuing debate between supranational and intergovernmental interests that will determine what kind of Europe will emerge at the beginning of the twenty-first century. As Monnet sagely advised, 'It is impossible to foresee today the decisions that could be taken in a new context tomorrow' (1978, p. 523).

References

Belmont European Policy Centre, 1991, *From Luxembourg to Maastricht: 100 critical days for Europe*, Belmont EPC, Brussels.

Cecchini, P., 1988, *The European challenge: 1992: the benefits of a Single Market*, Wildwood House, Aldershot.

Hill, B., 1984, *The Common Agricultural Policy: past, present and future*, Methuen, London.

Lodge, J. (ed.), 1989, *The European Community and the challenge of the future*, Pinter, London.

Marsh, J.,1989, 'The Common Agricultural Policy' in J. Lodge (ed.), *The European Community and the challenge of the future*, Pinter, London, pp. 148–66.

Monnet, J., 1978, *Memoirs* (trans. R. Mayne,), Doubleday and Company, New York.

Neunreither, K., 1991, 'Euphoria about subsidiarity? A constitutional debate in the European Community', *Political Science and European Unification*, newsletter of the IPSA research committee of European Unification, no. 2.

Nevin, E., 1990, *The economics of Europe*, St Martin's Press, New York.

Nicoll, W. and Salmon, T., 1990, *Understanding the European Communities*, Barnes and Noble, Savage.

Noort, P. van den, 1990, 'The contribution of agricultural protection to European integration' in Coffey, P. (ed.), *Main economic policy areas of the EEC – towards 1992*, third edn., Kluwer, Dordrecht, pp. 29–52.

Nugent, N., 1989, *The government and politics of the European Community*, Macmillan, London.

Pelkmans, J. and Winters, A., 1988, *Europe's domestic market*, Chatham House Paper No. 43, Routledge/RIIA, London.

Pinder, J., 1989, 'The Single Market:a step towards European Union' in Lodge, J. (ed.), *The European Community and the challenge of the future*, pp. 94–110.

9 Conclusion: from Community to Union

The history of post-1945 Europe reveals an emerging consensus for integration, even if the precise framework for its realization has been contentious. Not surprisingly, over this period Europe witnessed a number of fundamental transitions; the changes made to the institutional framework, first explored in the Schuman Declaration of 1950, reflect these developments. First the European Coal and Steel Community was launched, which was replaced by the European Economic Community, then by the European Community and, since 1 November 1993, by the European Union. These progressions are more than of semantic interest. This development – from the ESCU, to EEC, to EC, to EU – is emblematic of the expanding neo-functionalist process of spillover. The new European union, while still constrained in many ways, is consistent with a federalist and inclusive approach to integration. It represents the maturing of the 'idea of Europe', derived from Monnet, and signifies the continuing institutionalization of the integration process. The challenge of Monnet's conception of Europe remains fundamental to the European agenda of the 1990s. The previous chapters have, in their different ways, attempted to convey the link between the original aspirations of the founding Treaty framers and the developments, both supranational as well as intergovernmental, of the past four decades. Only through understanding the tension between these conflicting (and possibly mutually exclusive) forces and interpretations of integration – supranationalism and intergovernmentalism – can the European experience be adequately comprehended.

Six broad themes can be used to summarize the analysis of European integration presented here: the scope of involvement; the complexity of decision-making; the dynamism of the process; its experimental nature; the reliance of institutions; and, the implicit and explicit political context of integration.

First the Treaty on European Union has extended the Union's involvement into new policy spheres. However, as the analysis of the selected common policies discussed in Chapter 8 acknowledges, while competences are expanding neither the Community nor the Union as yet constitute a mayor invasive threat to national control of domestic policy areas. The introduction of the principle of subsidiarity may in fact limit any pervasive or surreptitious spread of European policy domains. The Commission's initial reaction confirmed that over 300 EC directives and regulations could be revoked under this principle. The emergence of a centralized, bureaucratic European Union dominating atrophied member states is a prospect based on myth not fact. The speed and depth of integration is still controlled intergovernmentally – as the Maastricht experience demonstrated. The potential for an expansion in Union authority is, however, contained within the Treaty on European Union's provisions for Economic and Monetary Union. If implemented, monetary union will signify a change in the balance of policy control favouring the Union over its composite member states. Whether this fundamental step will be possible remains in question for both political and economic reasons. Another area where Maastricht has already extended the Union's competences is in the execution of Common Foreign and Security policy as discussed in Chapter 5. The launching of the Union saw five 'joint actions' of the Union undertaken (Russia, the former Yugoslavia, the Middle-East, South Africa and security and stability in Europe) ; the decision prescribed bilateral national action in each case, a significant curtailment of traditional member state foreign policy autonomy and a more binding constraint than that exercised under the former EPC procedures. Similarly, immigration and issues of citizenship have shifted, if cautiously, out of exclusive national control under the TEU. Policy spillover remains in evidence and continues to be central to the future question of European integration.

Second the complexity of decision-making is almost labyrinthine and, in part, reflects the bureaucratic and elitist origins of the first Community. As outlined in Chapter 4, the functions of the various institutions can be simplified by distinguishing between the intergovernmental institutions (the European Council, Council of Ministers) and the supranational institutions (the Commission, European Parliament and the Court of Justice). The combination of national and Community-Union bodies within a single decision-making structure presents potential conflicts of interest; yet, as the Community experience has shown, the European system has been successful. Gradually, consensus decision-making has been moderated to allow for both explicit qualified majority voting, and implicit majoritarian style behaviour. However, as has become increasingly evident, the democratic deficit is a fundamental constitutional weakness within the system. as argued in Chapter 6, 'an ever closer Union' is jeopardized by the lack of popular involvement with or commitment to the European idea. Greater democratization and transparency in decision-making remain constitutional priorities despite, perhaps because of, the compromises and concessions made at Maastricht.

A third common theme that links the individual chapters is the dynamic nature of the European idea. Monnet's original conception did not envisage a static Community limited in shape, scope or size: on the contrary, the European idea has always been expansive and open to development. As demonstrated in Chapter 3, the reform of the community has been a typical procedure, of which Maastricht is simply the most recent example. The current Union is not the final structure as it too will be revised and reformed beginning with the 1996 intergovernmental conference already foreshadowed. The dynamism of the Community has also resulted in successive enlargements; again, there is no limitation on the future number of member states. The only criteria are those of democracy, economic development and geography. The 1994 negotiations on the fourth enlargement are therefore typical of the European experience: irrespective of whether Austria, Finland, Norway or Sweden accede, the Union will remain the dominant economic and political magnet within the European continent. By early in the next century enlargement will address the membership of Poland, Hungary, Slovakia, the Czech Republic, Malta, Cyprus, Slovenia, Estonia, Latvia, Lithuania and perhaps even Switzerland! Obviously, there are risks and costs involved in this dynamism. A Union of the Twenty-seven, for example, will be very different from that of the current Twelve let alone the original Six. To prosper and develop the Union's dynamism must be complemented by institutional and policy reform.

The fourth theme is the institutionalization of integration and is linked to both the dynamic nature of the Union and to the complexity in decision-making. As outlined in Chapter 1, Monnet advocated strong European institutions as the only feasible foundation for integration. Despite the democratic deficit already noted, the development of Europe's institutions has been both remarkable and indispensable to the process from Community to Union. Recent reforms, as well as *ad hoc* practice have seen additional institutions grafted onto the original triumvirate of Commission, Council and Assembly. The European Council is now formally incorporated within the Union, the Committee of the Regions and the European Monetary Institute established and, since 1979, the Parliament has evolved as a consequence of direct election. Institutions are not a sufficient condition for integration, but as Monnet argued they do constitute a necessary prerequisite.

The penultimate common theme is the experimental nature of the European idea. As discussed in Chapter 2, the original Community was designed, above all else, to stop Europeans slaughtering each other. To achieve this the destructive elements of nationalism were channelled into an untried structure where national sovereignty was pooled and collectively enhanced. But both the Community and the new Union remain experimental and historically unique. As such they facilitate the dynamism already noted, but also emphasize the fragility of the whole process. While it seems inconceivable for Europe to regress to its pre-1945 fragmented political structure, the events in the former Yugoslavia and in many of the former Soviet Republics and East European states serve as a cautionary reminder. The progression toward integration since 1950 is not, as yet, an irreversible process. As the experimental ambitions of Europeans increase (such as monetary union and a common foreign policy), the suppressed forces of intra-Union nationalisms have re-emerged. Arguably this has been a typical trend throughout Community history, each new *saut qualitif* producing a temporary national reaction (such as the French empty chair diplomacy of 1965, or the British objections to a Social Charter at Maastricht). The past success of the European idea over nationalism does not, necessarily, imply its continued supremacy. The continued construction of Europe remains subject to conflicting forces. As Monnet wisely cautioned, it is impossible to foretell the shape of future developments; all that is possible is 'to hold fast to the fixed principles that have guided us since the beginning'(Monnet,1978, p.524)

The final theme contained within this book, both explicitly and implicitly, is the importance of Europe as a political idea, and not just as an economic enterprise. Without trivializing the importance of economic integration and European policies such as the CAP or EMU, the European Union is about political integration *par exellence* . The Union is not simply a Single Market customs union; it involves joint political commitments in the fields of foreign affairs, democracy, citizenship and a commitment to supranationalism as an idea and a reality. While the political content of Europe is evident in every constitutional innovation since the Schuman Declaration, political elites have often been economic with the truth when advocating and explaining European integration domestically. For a large proportion of Europe's citizenship this political commitment has been either only vaguely appreciated or negatively interpreted. If for no other reason, the Maastricht process was valuable as it brought the political and federal implications of Union into the public centre-stage. The volatile and hesitant ratification given by some countries, both more recent as well as founding member states, signified that many concerns need to be addressed before the political idea of a united integrated European Union is able to capture the hearts and minds of Europe's citizens. Such a conversion is essential to the longevity of the Union.

To conclude, Monnet's ideas remain pertinent to the Europe of the 1990s. The distraction of contemporary policy disputes and the difficulties between competing political elites can disguise the underlying consistency that, since the 1950s, has characterized the development of the Community into the European Union. The guiding principle of supranationalism remains paramount despite the detours and revisions that have been made within the European experience. Enlargement, the changing international environment and the immanent next intergovernmental conference to reform the Union further, will all contribute to the evolution of the European construction. Despite pragmatic changes, to date the path towards European Union remains consistent with the idea of Europe articulated by Monnet and his colleagues. The objective of a supranational federal Union, that harnesses the power of nationalism through political and economic integration, is still on course to finally become a reality.

Appendix: Maastricht Treaty on European Union

As agreed by the European Council meeting of December 1991, amended and signed by the member states at Maastricht on 7 February 1992 (abridged version)

TITLE I – COMMON PROVISIONS

Article A

By this Treaty, the High Contracting Parties establish among themselves a European Union, hereinafter called the 'Union'.

This Treaty marks a new stage in the process creating an ever closer Union among the peoples of Europe, in which decisions are taken as closely as possible to the citizen.

The Union shall be founded on the European Communities supplemented by the policies and forms of co-operation established by this Treaty. Its task shall be to organize, in a manner demonstrating consistency and solidarity, relations between the Member States and between their peoples.

Article B

The Union shall set itself the following objectives:

– to promote economic and social progress which is balanced and sustainable in particular through the creation of an area without internal frontiers, through the strengthening of economic and social cohesion and the establishment of economic and monetary union, ultimately including a single currency in accordance with the provisions of this Treaty;
– to assert its identity on the international scene, in particular through the implementation of a common foreign and security policy including the eventual framing of a defence policy, which might in time lead to a common defence;
– to strengthen the protection of the rights and interests of the nationals of its Member States through the introduction of a citizenship of the Union;
– to develop close co-operation on justice and home affairs;
– to maintain in full the 'acquis communautaire' and build on it with a

view to considering through the procedure referred to in Article N(2), to what extent the policies and forms of co-operation introduced by this Treaty may need to be revised with the aim of ensuring the effectiveness of the mechanisms and the institutions of the Community.

The objectives of the Union shall be achieved as provided in this Treaty and in accordance with the conditions and the timetable set out therein while respecting the principle of subsidiarity as defined in Article 3b of the Treaty establishing the European Community.

Article C

The Union shall be served by a single institutional framework which shall ensure the consistency and the continuity of the activities carried out in order to attain its objectives while respecting and building upon the 'acquis communautaire'.

The Union shall in particular ensure the consistency of its external activities as a whole in the context of its external relations, security, economic and development policies. The Council and Commission shall be responsible for ensuring such consistency. They shall ensure the implementation of these policies, each in accordance with its respective powers.

Article D

The European Council shall provide the Union with the necessary impetus for its development and shall define the general political guidelines thereof.

The European Council shall bring together the Heads of State or of Government of the Member States and the President of the Commission. They shall be assisted by the Ministers for Foreign Affairs of the Member States and by a Member of the Commission. The European Council shall meet at least twice a year, under the chairmanship of the Head of State or of Government of the Member state which holds the Presidency of the Council.

The European Council shall submit to the European Parliament a report after each of its meetings and a yearly written report on the progress achieved by the Union.

Article E

The European Parliament, the Council, the Commission and the Court of Justice shall exercise their powers under the conditions and for the purposes provided for, on the one hand, by the provisions of the Treaties establishing the European Communities and of the subsequent Treaties and Acts modifying and supplementing them and, on the other hand, by the other provisions of this Treaty.

Article F

1. The Union shall respect the national identities of its Member States, whose systems of government are founded on the principles of democracy.

2. The Union shall respect fundamental rights, as guaranteed by the European Convention for the Protection of Human Rights and Fundamental Freedoms signed in Rome on 4 November 1950 and as they result from the constitutional traditions common to the Member States, as general principles of Community law.

3. The Union shall provide itself with the means necessary to attain its objectives and carry through its policies.

TITLE II – PROVISIONS AMENDING THE TREATY ESTABLISHING THE EUROPEAN ECONOMIC COMMUNITY WITH A VIEW TO ESTABLISHING THE EUROPEAN COMMUNITY

Article 2

The Community shall have as its task, by establishing a common market and an economic and monetary union and by implementing the common policies or activities referred to in Article 3 and 3a, to promote throughout the Community a harmonious and balanced development of economic activities, sustainable and non-inflationary growth respecting the environment, a high degree of convergence of economic performance, a high level of employment and of social protection, the raising of the standard of living and quality of life, and economic and social cohesion and solidarity among Member States.

Article 3

For the purposes set out in Article 2, the activities of the Community shall include, as provided in this Treaty and in accordance with the timetable set out therein:

(a) the elimination, as between Member States, of customs duties and quantitative restrictions on the import and export of goods, and of all other measures having equivalent effect;
(b) a common commercial policy;
(c) an internal market characterised by the abolition, as between Member States, of obstacles to the freedom of movement of goods, persons, services and capital;

(d) measures concerning the entry and movement of persons in the internal market as provided for in Article 100c;
(e) a common policy in the sphere of agriculture and fisheries;
(f) a common policy in the sphere of transport;
(g) a system ensuring that competition in the internal market is not distorted;
(h) the approximation of the laws of Member States to the extent required for the functioning of the common market;
(i) a policy in the social sphere comprising a European Social Fund;
(j) the strengthening of economic and social cohesion;
(k) a policy in the sphere of the environment;
(l) the strengthening of the competitiveness of Community industry;
(m) the promotion of research and technological development;
(n) encouragement for the establishment and development of trans-European networks;
(o) a contribution to the attainment of a high level of health protection;
(p) a contribution to education and training of high quality and to the flowering of the cultures of the Member States;
(q) a policy in the sphere of development co-operation;
(r) the association of the overseas countries and territories in order to increase trade and promote jointly economic and social development;
(s) a contribution to the strengthening of consumer protection;
(t) measures in the spheres of energy, civil protection and tourism.

Article 3b

The Community shall act within the limits of the powers conferred upon it by this Treaty and of the objectives assigned to it therein.

In the areas which do not fall within its exclusive competence, the Community shall take action, in accordance with the principle of subsidiarity, only if and in so far as the objectives of the proposed action cannot be sufficiently achieved by the Member States and can therefore, by reason of the scale or effects of proposed action, be better achieved by the Community.

Any action by the Community shall not go beyond what is necessary to achieve the objectives of this Treaty.

Article 4.2

The Council and the Commission shall be assisted by an Economic and Social Committee and a Committee of the Regions acting in an advisory capacity.

Article 4b

A European Investment Bank is hereby established, which shall act within the limits of the powers conferred upon it by this Treaty and the Statutes annexed thereto.

PART TWO – CITIZENSHIP OF THE UNION

Article 8

1. Citizenship of the Union is hereby established.
    Every person holding the nationality of a Member State shall be a citizen of the Union.

2. Citizens of the Union shall enjoy the rights conferred by this Treaty and shall be subject to the duties imposed thereby.

Article 8a

1. Every citizen of the Union shall have the right to move and reside freely within the territory of the Member States, subject to the limitations and conditions laid down in this Treaty and by the measures adopted to give it effect.

2. The Council may adopt provisions with a view to facilitating the exercise of the rights referred to in paragraph 1; save as otherwise provided in this Treaty, the Council shall act unanimously on a proposal from the Commission and after obtaining the assent of the European Parliament.

Article 8b

1. Every citizen of the Union residing in a Member State of which he is not a national shall have the right to vote and to stand as a candidate at municipal elections in the Member State in which he resides, under the same conditions as nationals of that State. This right shall be exercised subject to detailed arrangements to be adopted before 31 December 1994 by the Council, acting unanimously on a proposal from the Commission and after consulting the European Parliament; these arrangements may provide for derogations where warranted by problems specific to a Member State.

2. Without prejudice to the provisions of Article 138(3) and of the provisions adopted for its implementation, every citizen of the Union residing in a Member State of which he is not a national shall have the right to vote and to stand as a candidate in elections to the European

Parliament in the Member State in which he resides, under the same conditions as nationals of that State. This right shall be exercised subject to detailed arrangements to be adopted before 31 December 1993 by the Council, acting unanimously on a proposal from the Commission and after consulting the European Parliament; these arrangements may provide for derogations where warranted by problems specific to a Member State.

Article 8c

Every citizen of the Union shall, in the territory of a third country in which the Member State of which he is a national is not represented, be entitled to protection by the diplomatic or consular authorities of any Member State, on the same conditions as the nationals of that State. Before 31 December 1993, Member States shall establish the necessary rules among themselves and start the international negotiations required to secure this protection.

Article 8d

Every citizen of the Union shall have the right to petition the European Parliament in accordance with Article 138d.

Every citizen of the Union may apply to the Ombudsman established in accordance with Article 138e.

Article 8e

The Commission shall report to the European Parliament, to the Council and to the Economic and Social Committee before 31 December 1993 and then every three years on the application of the provisions of this Part. This report shall take account of the development of the Union. On this basis, and without prejudice to the other provisions of this Treaty, the Council, acting unanimously on a proposal from the Commission and after consulting the European Parliament, may adopt provisions to strengthen or to add to the rights laid down in this Part, which it shall recommend to the Member States for adoption in accordance with their respective constitutional requirements.

PART THREE - COMMUNITY POLICIES

TITLE V – COMMON RULES ON COMPETITION, TAXATION, APPROXIMATION OF LAWS.

Article 100

The Council shall, acting unanimously on a proposal from the Commission and after consulting the European Parliament and the Economic and Social Committee, issue directives for the approximation of such laws, regulations or administrative provisions of the Member States as directly affect the establishment or functioning of the common market.

Article 100c

1. The Council, acting unanimously on a proposal from the Commission and after consulting the European Parliament, shall determine the third countries whose nationals must be in possession of a visa when crossing the external borders of the Member States.

2. However, in the event of an emergency situation in a third country posing a threat of a sudden inflow of nationals from that country into the Community, the Council, acting by a qualified majority on a recommendation from the Commission, may introduce, for a period not exceeding six months, a visa requirement for nationals from the country in question. The visa requirement established under this paragraph may be extended in accordance with the procedure referred to in paragraph 1.

3. From 1 January 1996, the Council shall adopt the decisions referred to in paragraph 1 by a qualified majority. The Council shall, before that date, acting by a qualified majority on a proposal from the Commission and after consulting the European Parliament, adopt measures relating to a uniform format for visas.

4. In the areas referred to in this Article, the Commission shall examine any request made by a Member State that it submit a proposal to the Council.

5. This Article shall be without prejudice to the exercise of the responsibilities incumbent upon the Member States with regard to the maintenance of law and order and the safeguarding of internal security.

6. This Article shall apply to other areas if so decided pursuant to Article K.9 of the provisions of the Treaty on European Union which relate to co-operation in the fields of justice and home affairs, subject to the voting conditions determined at the same time.

7.   The provisions of the conventions in force between the Member States governing areas covered by this Article shall remain in force until their content has been replaced by directives or measures adopted pursuant thereto.

TITLE VII – COMMON COMMERCIAL POLICY

Article 113

1.   The common commercial policy shall be based on uniform principles, particularly in regard to changes in tariff rates, the conclusion of tariff and trade agreements, the achievement of uniformity in measures of liberalization, export policy and measures to protect trade such as those to be taken in the event of dumping or subsidies.

2.   The Commission shall submit proposals to the Council for implementing the common commercial policy.

3.   Where agreements with one or more States or international organizations need to be negotiated, the Commission shall make recommendations to the Council, which shall authorize the Commission to open the necessary negotiations.
     The Commission shall conduct these negotiations in consultation with a special committee appointed by the Council to assist the Commission in its task and within the framework of such directives as the Council may issue to it.
     The relevant provisions of Article 228 shall apply.

4.   In exercising the powers conferred upon it by this Article, the Council shall act by a qualified majority.

Article 115

In order to ensure that the execution of measures of commercial policy taken in accordance with this Treaty by any Member State is not obstructed by deflection of trade, or where differences between such measures lead to economic difficulties in one or more Member States, the Commission shall recommend the methods for the requisite co-operation between Member States. Failing this, the Commission may authorize Member States to take the necessary protective measures, the conditions and details of which it shall determine.

In the event of urgency, Member States may request authorization to take the necessary measures themselves from the Commission, which shall take a decision as soon as possible; the Member States concerned shall then notify the measures to the other Member States. The Commission may decide at any time that the Member States concerned shall amend or abolish the measures in question.

In the selection of such measures, priority shall be given to those which cause the least disturbance to the functioning of the common market.

TITLE XIV – ECONOMIC AND SOCIAL COHESION

Article 130a

In order to promote its overall harmonious development, the Community shall develop and pursue its actions leading to the strengthening of its economic and social cohesion.

In particular, the Community shall aim at reducing disparities between the levels of development of the various regions and the backwardness of the least-favoured regions, including rural areas.

Article 130b

Member States shall conduct their economic policies and shall co-ordinate them in such a way as, in addition, to attain the objectives set out in Article 130a. The formation and implementation of the Community's policies and actions and the implementation of the internal market shall take into account the objectives set out in Article 130a and shall contribute to their achievement. The Community shall also support the achievement of these objectives by the action it takes through the Structural Funds (European Agricultural Guidance and Guarantee Fund, Guidance Section; European Social Fund; European Regional Development Fund), the European Investment Bank and the other existing financial instruments.

The Commission shall submit a report to the European Parliament, the Council, the Economic and Social Committee and the Committee of the Regions every three years on the progress made towards achieving economic and social cohesion and on the manner in which the various means provided for in this Article have contributed to it. The report shall, if necessary be accompanied by appropriate proposals.

If specific actions prove necessary outside the Funds and without prejudice to the measures decided upon within the framework of the other Community policies, such actions may be adopted by the Council acting unanimously on a proposal from the Commission and after consulting the European Parliament, the Economic and Social Committee and the Committee of the Regions.

Article 130c

The European Regional Development Fund is intended to help to redress the main regional imbalances in the Community through participation in the development and structural adjustment of regions whose development is lagging behind and in the conversion of declining industrial regions.

Article 130d

Without prejudice to Article 130e, the Council, acting unanimously on a proposal from the Commission and after obtaining the assent of the European Parliament and consulting the Economic and Social Committee and the Committee of the Regions, shall define the tasks, priority objectives and the organization of the Structural Funds, which may involve grouping the Funds. The Council, acting by the same procedure, shall also define the general rules applicable to them and the provisions necessary to ensure their effectiveness and the co-ordination of the Funds with one another and with the other existing financial instruments.

The Council, acting in accordance with the same procedure, shall before the 31 December 1993 set up a Cohesion Fund to provide a financial contribution to projects in the fields of environment and trans-European networks in the area of transport infrastructure.

Article 130e

Implementing decisions relating to the European Regional Development Fund shall be taken by the Council, acting in accordance with the procedure referred to in Article 189c and after consulting the Economic and Social Committee and the Committee of the Regions.

With regard to the European Agricultural Guidance and Guarantee Fund, Guidance Section, and the European Social Fund, Articles 43 and 125 shall continue to apply respectively.

TITLE XVI – ENVIRONMENT

Article 130r

1. Community policy on the environment shall contribute to pursuit of the following objectives:
   - preserving, protecting and improving the quality of the environment;
   - protecting human health;
   - prudent and rational utilization of natural resources;
   - promoting measures at international level to deal with regional or worldwide environmental problems.

2. The Community policy on the environment shall aim at a high level of protection taking into account the diversity of situations in the various regions of the Community. It shall be based on the precautionary principle and on the principles that preventive action should be taken, that environmental damage should as a priority be rectified at source and that the polluter should pay. Environmental protection requirements must be integrated into the definition and implementation of other Community policies.

In this context, harmonization measures answering these requirements shall include, where appropriate, a safeguard clause allowing Member States to take provisional measures, for non-economic environmental reasons, subject to a Community inspection procedure.

3. In preparing its policy relating to the environment, the Community shall take account of:
   - available scientific and technical data;
   - environmental conditions in the various regions of the Community;
   - the potential benefits and costs of action or lack of action;
   - the economic and social development of the Community as a whole and the balanced development of its regions.

4. Within their respective spheres of competence, the Community and the Member States shall co-operate with third countries and with the competent international organizations. The arrangements for Community co-operation may be the subject of agreements between the Community and the third parties concerned, which shall be negotiated and concluded in accordance with Article 228.

The previous subparagraph shall be without prejudice to Member States' competence to negotiate in international bodies and to conclude international agreements.

Article 130s

1. The Council, acting in accordance with the procedure referred to in Article 189c and after consulting the Economic and Social Committee, shall decide what action is to be taken by the Community in order to achieve the objectives referred to in Article 130r.

2. By way of derogation from the decision-making procedure provided for in paragraph 1 and without prejudice to Article 100a, the Council, acting unanimously on a proposal from the Commission and after consulting the European Parliament and the Economic and Social Committee, shall adopt:
   - provisions primarily of a fiscal nature;

- measures concerning town and country planning, land use with the exception of waste management and measures of a general nature, and management of water resources;
- measures significantly affecting a Member State's choice between different energy sources and the general structure of energy supply.

The Council may, under the conditions laid down in the preceding subparagraph, define those matters referred to in this paragraph on which decisions are to be taken by a qualified majority.

3. In other areas, general action programmes setting out priority objectives to be attained shall be adopted by the Council, acting in accordance with the procedure referred to in Article 189b and after consulting the Economic and Social Committee.

    The Council, acting under the terms of paragraph 1 or paragraph 2 according to the case, shall adopt the measures necessary for the implementation of these programmes.

4. Without prejudice to certain measures of a Community nature, the Member States shall finance and implement the environment policy.

5. Without prejudice to the principle that the polluter should pay, if a measure based on the provisions of paragraph 1 involves costs deemed disproportionate for the public authorities of a Member State, the Council shall, in the act adopting that measure, lay down appropriate provisions in the form of:
    - temporary derogations and/or
    - financial support from the Cohesion Fund to be set up no later than 31 December 1993 pursuant to Article 130d.

Article 130t

The protective measures adopted pursuant to Article 130s shall not prevent any Member State from maintaining or introducing more stringent protective measures. Such measures must be compatible with this Treaty. They shall be notified to the Commission.

TITLE XVII – DEVELOPMENT CO-OPERATION

Article 130u

1. Community policy in the sphere of development co-operation, which shall be complementary to the policies pursued by the Member States, shall foster:
    - the sustainable economic and social development of the developing countries, and more particularly the most disadvantaged among them;

- the smooth and gradual integration of the developing countries into the world economy;
- the campaign against poverty in the developing countries.

2. Community policy in this area shall contribute to the general objective of developing and consolidating democracy and the rule of law, and to that of respecting human rights and fundamental freedoms.

3. The Community and the Member States shall comply with the commitments and take account of the objectives they have approved in the context of the United Nations and other competent international organizations.

Article 130v

The Community shall take account of the objectives referred to in Article 130u in the policies that it implements which are likely to affect developing countries.

Article 130w

1. Without prejudice to the other provisions of this Treaty the Council, acting in accordance with the procedure referred to in Article 189c, shall adopt the measures necessary to further the objectives referred to in Article 130u. Such action may take the form of multiannual programmes.

2. The European Investment Bank shall contribute, under the terms laid down in its Statute, to the implementation of the action referred to in paragraph 1.

3. The provisions of this Article shall not affect co-operation with the African, Caribbean and Pacific countries in the framework of the ACP-EEC Convention.

Article 130x

1. The Community and the Member States shall co-ordinate their policies on development co-operation and shall consult each other on their aid programmes, including in international organizations and during international conferences. They may undertake joint action. Member States shall contribute if necessary to the implementation of Community aid programmes.

2. The Commission may take any useful initiatives to promote the co-ordination referred to in paragraph 1.

Article 130y

Within their respective spheres of competence, the Community and the Member States shall co-operate with third countries and with the international organizations. The arrangements for Community co-operation may be the subject of agreements between the Community and the third parties concerned, which shall be negotiated and concluded in accordance with Article 228.

The previous paragraph shall be without prejudice to Member States' competence to negotiate in international bodies and to conclude international agreements.

PART FIVE – INSTITUTIONS OF THE COMMUNITY

Article 137

The European Parliament, which shall consist of representatives of the peoples of the States brought together in the Community, shall exercise the powers conferred upon it by this Treaty.

Article 138.3

The European Parliament shall draw up proposals for elections by direct universal suffrage in accordance with a uniform procedure in all Member States.

The Council shall, acting unanimously after obtaining the assent of the European Parliament, which shall act by a majority of its component members, lay down the appropriate provisions, which it shall recommend to Member States for adoption in accordance with their respective constitutional requirements.

Article 138b

In so far as provided in this Treaty, the European Parliament shall participate in the process leading up to the adoption of Community acts by exercising its powers under the procedures laid down in Articles 189b and 189c and by giving its assent or delivering advisory opinions.

The European Parliament may, acting by a majority of its members, request the Commission to submit any appropriate proposal on matters on which it considers that a Community act is required for the purpose of implementing this Treaty.

Article 138c

In the course of its duties, the European Parliament may, at the request of a quarter of its members, set up a temporary Committee of Inquiry to investigate, without prejudice to the powers conferred by this Treaty on other institutions or bodies, alleged contraventions or maladministration in the implementation of Community law, except where the alleged facts are being examined before a court and while the case is still subject to legal proceedings.

The temporary Committee of Inquiry shall cease to exist on the submission of its report.

The detailed provisions governing the exercise of the right of enquiry shall be determined by common agreement of the European Parliament, the Council and the Commission.

Article 138d

Any citizen of the Union, and any natural or legal person residing or having its registered office in a Member State of the Community, shall have the right to address, individually or in association with other citizens or persons, a petition to the European Parliament on a matter which comes within the Community's fields of activity and which affects him, her or it directly.

Article 138e

1. The European Parliament shall appoint an Ombudsman empowered to receive complaints from any citizen of the Union or any natural or legal person residing or having its registered office in a Member State concerning instances of maladministration in the activities of the Community institutions or bodies, with the exception of the Court of Justice and the Court of First Instance acting in their judicial role.

   In accordance with his duties, the Ombudsman shall conduct inquiries for which he finds grounds, either on his own initiative on the basis of complaints submitted to him direct or through a member of the European Parliament, except where the alleged facts are or have been the subject of legal proceedings. Where the Ombudsman establishes an instance of maladministration, he shall refer the matter to the institution concerned, which shall have a period of three months in which to inform him of its views. The Ombudsman shall then forward a report to the European Parliament and the institution concerned. The person lodging the complaint shall be informed of the outcome of such inquiries.

   The Ombudsman shall submit an annual report to the European Parliament on the outcome of his inquiries.

2. The Ombudsman shall be appointed after each election of the European Parliament for the duration of its term of office. The Ombudsman shall be eligible for reappointment.

    The Ombudsman may be dismissed by the Court of Justice at the request of the European Parliament if he no longer fulfils the conditions required for the performance of his duties or if he is guilty of serious misconduct.

3. The Ombudsman shall be completely independent in the performance of his duties. In the performance of those duties he shall neither seek nor take instructions from any body. The Ombudsman may not, during his term of office, engage in any other occupation, whether gainful or not.

4. The European Parliament shall, after seeking an opinion from the Commission and with the approval of the Council acting by a qualified majority, lay down the regulations and general conditions governing the performance of the Ombudsman's duties.

Article 151

1. A committee consisting of the Permanent Representatives of the Member States shall be responsible for preparing the work of the Council and for carrying out the tasks assigned to it by the Council.

2. The Council shall be assisted by a General Secretariat, under the direction of a Secretary-General. The Secretary-General shall be appointed by the Council acting unanimously.

    The Council shall decide on the organization of the General Secretariat.

3. The Council shall adopt its rules of procedure.

Article 157

1. The Commission shall consist of seventeen members who shall be chosen on the grounds of their general competence and whose independence is beyond doubt.

    The number of members of the Commission may be altered by the Council, acting unanimously.

    Only nationals of Member States may be members of the Commission.

    The Commission must include at least one national of each of the Member States, but may not include more than two members having the nationality of the same State.

Article 158

1. The Members of the Commission shall be appointed, in accordance with the procedure referred to in paragraph 2, for a period of five years, subject, if need be, to Article 144.

   Their term of office shall be renewable.

2. The governments of the Member States shall nominate by common accord, after consulting the European Parliament, the person they intend to appoint as President of the Commission.

   The governments of the Member States shall, in consultation with the nominee for President, nominate the other persons whom they intend to appoint as members of the Commission.

   The President and the other members of the Commission thus nominated shall be subject as a body to a vote of approval by the European Parliament. After approval by the European Parliament, the President and the other members of the Commission shall be appointed by common accord of the governments of the Member State.

Article 159

Apart from normal replacement, or death, the duties of a member of the Commission shall end when he resigns or is compulsorily retired.

The vacancy thus caused shall be filled for the remainder of the member's term of office by a new member appointed by common accord of the governments of the Member States. The Council may, acting unanimously, decide that such a vacancy need not be filled.

In the event of resignation, compulsory retirement or death, the President shall be replaced for the remainder of his term of office. The procedure laid down in Article 158(2) shall be applicable for the replacement of the President.

Save in the case of compulsory retirement under the provisions of Article 160, members of the Commission shall remain in office until they have been replaced.

Article 161

The Commission may appoint a Vice-President or two Vice-Presidents from among its members.

Article 168a

1. A Court of First Instance shall be attached to the Court of Justice with jurisdiction to hear and determine at first instance, subject to a right of appeal to the Court of Justice on points of law only and in accordance with the conditions laid down by the Statute, certain classes of action or proceeding defined in accordance with the conditions laid down in paragraph 2. The Court of First Instance shall not be competent to hear and determine questions referred for a preliminary ruling under Article 177.

2. At the request of the Court of Justice and after consulting the Commission and the European Parliament, the Council, acting unanimously, shall determine the classes of action or proceeding referred to in paragraph 1 and the composition of the Court of First Instance and shall adopt the necessary adjustments and additional provisions to the Statute of the Court of Justice. Unless the Council decides otherwise, the provisions of this Treaty relating to the Court of Justice, in particular the provisions of the Protocol on the Statute of the Court of Justice, shall apply to the Court of First Instance.

3. The members of the Court of First Instance shall be chosen from persons whose independence is beyond doubt and who possess the ability required for appointment to judicial office; they shall be appointed by common accord of the governments of the Member States for a term of six years. The membership shall be partially renewed every three years. Retiring members shall be eligible for re-appointment.

4. The Court of First Instance shall establish its rules of procedure in agreement with the Court of Justice. Those rules shall require the unanimous approval of the Council.

Article 171

2. If the Commission considers that the Member State concerned has not taken such measures it shall, after giving that State the opportunity to submit its comments, issue a reasoned opinion specifying the points on which the Member State concerned has not complied with the judgment of the Court of Justice.

    If the member State concerned fails to take the necessary measures to comply with the Court's judgment within the time-limit laid down by the Commission, the latter may bring the case before the Court of Justice. In so doing it shall specify the amount of the lump sum or penalty payment to be paid by the Member State concerned which it considers appropriate in the circumstances. If the Court of Justice finds that the

Member State concerned has not complied with its judgment it may impose a lump sum or penalty payment on it.

This procedure shall be without prejudice to Article 170.

Article 173

The Court of Justice shall review the legality of acts of the European Parliament and the Council, of acts of the Council, of the Commission and of the ECB (European Central Bank), other than recommendations and opinions, and of acts of the European Parliament intended to produce legal effects vis-à-vis third parties.

It shall for this purpose have jurisdiction in actions brought by a Member State, the Council or the Commission on grounds of lack of competence, infringement of an essential procedural requirement, infringement of this Treaty or of any rule of law relating to its application, or misuse of powers.

The Court shall have jurisdiction under the same conditions in actions brought by the European Parliament and by the ECB for the purpose of protecting their prerogatives.

Article 189

1. In order to carry out their task and in accordance with the provisions of this Treaty, the European Parliament acting jointly with the Council, the Council and the Commission shall make regulations and issue directives, take decisions, make recommendations or deliver opinions.

Article 189a

1. Where, in pursuance of this Treaty, the Council acts on a proposal from the Commission, unanimity shall be required for an act constituting an amendment to that proposal, subject to Article 189b(4) and (5).

2. As long as the Council has not acted, the Commission may alter its proposal at any time during the procedures leading to the adoption of a Community act.

Article 189b

1. Where reference is made in this Treaty to this Article for the adoption of an act, the following procedure shall apply.

2. The Commission shall submit a proposal to the European Parliament and the Council.

The Council, acting by a qualified majority after obtaining the opinion of the European Parliament, shall adopt a common position. The common position shall be communicated to the European Parliament. The Council shall inform the European Parliament fully of the reasons which led it to adopt its common position. The Commission shall inform the European Parliament fully of its position.

If, within three months of such communication, the European Parliament:

(a) approves the common position, the Council shall definitively adopt the act in question in accordance with that common position;

(b) has not taken a decision, the Council shall adopt the act in question in accordance with its common position;

(c) indicates, by an absolute majority of its component members, that it intends to reject the common position, it shall immediately inform the Council. The Council may convene a meeting of the Conciliation Committee referred to in paragraph 3 to explain further its position. The European Parliament shall thereafter either confirm, by an absolute majority of its component members, its rejection of the common position, in which event the proposed act shall be deemed not to have been adopted, or propose amendments in accordance with subparagraph (d) of this paragraph;

(d) proposes amendments to the common position by an absolute majority of its component members, the amended text shall be forwarded to the Council and to the Commission, which shall deliver an opinion on those amendments.

3. If, within three months of the matter being referred to it, the Council, acting by a qualified majority, approves all the amendments of the European Parliament, it shall amend its common position accordingly and adopt the act in question; however, the Council shall act unanimously on the amendments on which the Commission has delivered a negative opinion. If the Council does not approve the act in question, the President of the Council, in agreement with the President of the European Parliament, shall forthwith convene a meeting of the Conciliation Committee.

4. The Conciliation Committee, which shall be composed of the members of the Council or their representatives and an equal number of representatives of the European Parliament, shall have the task of reaching agreement on a joint text, by a qualified majority of the members of the Council or their representatives and by a majority of the representatives of the European Parliament. The Commission shall take part in the Conciliation Committee's proceedings and shall take all the necessary

initiatives with a view to reconciling the positions of the European Parliament and the Council.

5. If, within six weeks of its being convened, the Conciliation Committee approves a joint text, the European Parliament, acting by an absolute majority of the votes cast, and the Council, acting by a qualified majority, shall have a period of six weeks from that approval in which to adopt the act in question in accordance with the joint text. If one of the two institutions fails to adopt the proposed act, it shall be deemed not to have been adopted.

6. Where the Conciliation Committee does not approve a joint text, the proposed act shall not be deemed not to have been adopted unless the Council, acting by a qualified majority within six weeks of expiry of the period granted to the Conciliation Committee, confirms the common position to which it agreed before the conciliation procedure was initiated, possibly with amendments proposed by the European Parliament. In this case, the act in question shall be finally adopted unless the European Parliament, within six weeks of the date of confirmation by the Council, rejects the text by an absolute majority of its component members, in which case the proposed act shall be deemed not to have been adopted.

7. The periods of three months and six weeks referred to in this Article may be extended by a maximum of one month and two weeks respectively by common accord of the European Parliament and the Council. The period of three months referred to in paragraph 2 shall be automatically extended by two months where paragraph 2(c) applies.

8. The scope of the procedure under this Article may be widened, in accordance with the procedure provided for in Article N(2) of the Treaty on European Union, on the basis of a report to be submitted to the Council by the Commission by 1996 at the latest.

Article 198a

A Committee consisting of representatives of regional and local bodies, hereinafter referred to as the 'Committee of the Regions', is hereby established with advisory status.

The number of members of the Committee of the Regions shall be as follows: Belgium 12; Denmark 9; Germany 24; Greece 12; Spain 21; France 24; Ireland 9; Italy 24; Luxembourg 6; Netherlands 12; Portugal 12; United Kingdom 24.

The members of the Committee and an equal number of alternate members shall be appointed for four years by the Council acting unanimously on proposals from the respective Member States. Their term of office shall be renewable.

The members of the Committee may not be bound by any mandatory instructions. They shall be completely independent in the performance of their duties, in the general interest of the Community.

Article 198b

The Committee of the Regions shall elect its chairman and officers from among its members for a term of two years.

It shall adopt its rules of procedure and shall submit them for approval to the Council, acting unanimously.

The Committee shall be convened by its chairman at the request of the Council or of the Commission. It may also meet on its own initiative.

Article 198c

The Committee of the Regions shall be consulted by the Council or by the Commission where this Treaty so provides and in all other cases in which one of these two institutions considers it appropriate.

The Council or the Commission shall, if it considers it necessary, set the Committee, for the submission of its opinion, a time-limit which may not be less than one month from the date on which the chairman receives notification to this effect. Upon expiry of the time-limit, the absence of an opinion shall not prevent further action.

Where the Economic and Social Committee is consulted pursuant to Article 198, the Committee of the Regions shall be informed by the Council or the Commission of the request for an opinion. Where it considers that specific regional interests are involved, the Committee of the Regions may submit an opinion on the matter.

It may issue an opinion on its own initiative in cases in which it considers such action appropriate.

The opinion of the Committee, together with a record of the proceedings, shall be forwarded to the Council and to the Commission.

Article 201

Without prejudice to other revenue, the budget shall be financed wholly from own resources.

The Council, acting unanimously on a proposal from the Commission and after consulting the European Parliament, shall lay down provisions relating to the system of own resources of the Community, which it shall recommend to the Member States for adoption in accordance with their respective constitutional requirements.

Article 201a

With a view to maintaining budgetary discipline, the Commission shall not make any proposal for a Community act, nor alter its proposals, or adopt any implementing measure which is likely to have appreciable implications for the budget without providing the assurance that that proposal or that measure is capable of being financed within the limit of the Community's own resources arising under provisions laid down by the Council pursuant to Article 201.

Article 206

1. The European Parliament, acting on a recommendation from the Council which shall act by a qualified majority, shall give a discharge to the Commission in respect of the implementation of the budget. To this end, the Council and the European Parliament in turn shall examine the accounts and the financial statement referred to in Article 205a, the annual report by the Court of Auditors together with the replies of the institutions under audit to the observations of the Court of Auditors and any relevant special reports by the Court of Auditors.

2. Before giving a discharge to the Commission, or for any other purpose in connection with the exercise of its powers over the implementation of the budget, the European Parliament may ask to hear the Commission give evidence with regard to the execution of expenditure or the operation of financial control systems. The Commission shall submit any necessary information to the European Parliament at the latter's request.

3. The Commission shall take all appropriate steps to act on the observations in the decisions giving discharge and on other observations by the European Parliament relating to the execution of expenditure, as well as on comments accompanying the recommendations on discharge adopted by the Council.

    At the request of the European Parliament or the Council, the Commission shall report on the measures taken in the light of these observations and comments and in particular on the instructions given to the departments which are responsible for the implementation of the budget. These reports shall also be forwarded to the Court of Auditors.

Article 228

1. Where this Treaty provides for the conclusion of agreements between the Community and one or more States or international organizations, the Commission shall make recommendations to the Council, which shall authorize the Commission to open the necessary negotiations. The Commission shall conduct these negotiations in consultation with special committees appointed by the Council to assist it in this task, and within the framework of such directives as the Council may issue to it.

   In exercising the powers bestowed upon it by this paragraph, the Council shall act by a qualified majority, except in the cases provided for in the second sentence of paragraph 2, for which it shall act unanimously.

2. Subject to the powers vested in the Commission in this field, the agreements shall be concluded by the Council, acting by a qualified majority on a proposal from the Commission. The Council shall act unanimously when the agreement covers a field for which unanimity is required for the adoption of internal rules, and for the agreements referred to in Article 238.

3. The Council shall conclude agreements after consulting the European Parliament, except for the agreements referred to in Article 113(3), including cases when the agreement covers a field for which the procedure referred to in Article 189b or that referred to in Article 189c is required for the adoption of internal rules. The European Parliament shall deliver its opinion within a time limit which the Council may lay down according to the urgency of the matter. In the absence of an opinion within that time limit, the Council may act.

   By way of derogation from the provisions of the previous subparagraph, agreements referred to in Article 238, other agreements establishing a specific institutional framework by organizing co-operation procedures, agreements having important budgetary implications for the Community and agreements entailing amendment of an act adopted under the procedure referred to in Article 189b shall be concluded after the assent of the European Parliament has been obtained.

   The Council and the European Parliament may, in an urgent situation, agree upon a time limit for the assent.

4. When concluding an agreement, the Council may, by way of derogation from the provisions of paragraph 2, empower the Commission to approve modifications on behalf of the Community where the agreement provides for them to be adopted by a simplified procedure or by

a body set up by the agreement; it may attach specific conditions to such empowerment.

5. When the Council envisages concluding an agreement which calls for amendments to this Treaty, the amendments must first be adopted in accordance with the procedure laid down in Article N of the Treaty on European Union.

6. The Council, the Commission or a Member State may obtain the opinion of the Court of Justice as to whether the agreement envisaged is compatible with the provisions of this Treaty. Where the opinion of the Court of Justice is adverse, the agreement may enter into force only in accordance with Article N of the Treaty on European Union.

7. Agreements concluded under the conditions set out in this Article shall be binding on the institutions of the Community and on Member States.

Article 228a

Where it is provided, in a common position or a joint action adopted according to the provisions of the Treaty on the Union relating to the common foreign and security policy, for an action by the Community to interrupt or to reduce, in part or completely, economic relations with one or more third countries, the Council shall take the necessary urgent measures. The Council shall act by a qualified majority on a proposal from the Commission.

Article 238

The Community may conclude with one or more States or international organizations agreements establishing an association involving reciprocol rights and obligations, common action and special procedures.

TITLE V – PROVISIONS ON A COMMON FOREIGN AND SECURITY POLICY

Article J

A common foreign and security policy is hereby established which shall be governed by the following provisions.

Article J.1

1. The Union and its Member States shall define and implement a common foreign and security policy, governed by the provisions of this Title and covering all areas of foreign and security policy.

2. The objectives of the common foreign and security policy shall be:
   – to safeguard the common values, fundamental interests and independence of the Union;
   – to strengthen the security of the Union and its Member States in all ways;
   – to preserve peace and strengthen international security , in accordance with the principles of the United Nations Charter as well as the principles of the Helsinki Final Act and the objectives of the Paris Charter;
   – to promote international co-operation;
   – to develop and consolidate democracy and the rule of law, and respect for human rights and fundamental freedoms.

3. The Union shall pursue these objectives:
   – by establishing systematic co-operation between Member States in the conduct of policy, in accordance with Article J.2;
   – by gradually implementing, in accordance with Article J.3, joint action in the areas in which the Member States have important interests in common.

4. The Member States shall support the Union's external and security policy actively and unreservedly in a spirit of loyalty and mutual solidarity. They shall refrain from any action which is contrary to the interests of the Union or likely to impair its effectiveness as a cohesive force in international relations. The Council shall ensure that these principles are complied with.

Article J.2

1. Member States shall inform and consult one another within the Council on any matter of foreign and security policy of general interest in order to ensure that their combined influence is exerted as effectively as possible by means of concerted and convergent action.

2. Whenever it deems it necessary, the Council shall define a common position.

   Member States shall ensure that their national policies conform to the common positions.

3. Member States shall co-ordinate their action in international organizations and at international conferences. They shall uphold the common positions in such fora.

   In international organizations and at international conferences where not all Member States participate, those which do take part shall uphold the common positions.

Article J.3

The procedure for adopting joint action in matters covered by the foreign and security policy shall be the following:

1. The Council shall decide, on the basis of general guidelines from the European Council, that a matter should be the subject of joint action.

    Whenever the Council decides on the principle of joint action, it shall lay down the specific scope, the Union's general and specific objectives in carrying out such action, if necessary its duration, and the means procedures and conditions for its implementation.

2. The Council shall, when adopting the joint action and at any stage during its development, define those matters on which decisions are to be taken by a qualified majority.

    Where the Council is required to act by a qualified majority pursuant to the preceding subparagraph, the votes of its members shall be weighted in accordance with Article 148(2) of the Treaty establishing the European Community, and for their adoption, acts of the Council shall require at least fifty-four votes in favour, cast by at least eight members.

3. If there is a change in circumstances having a substantial effect on a question subject to joint action, the Council shall review the principles and objectives of that action and take the necessary decisions. As long as the Council has not acted, the joint action shall stand.

4. Joint actions shall commit the Member States in the positions they adopt and in the conduct of their activity.

5. Whenever there is any plan to adopt a national position or take national action pursuant to a joint action, information shall be provided in time to allow, if necessary, for prior consultations within the Council. The obligation to provide prior information shall not apply to measures which are merely a national transposition of Council decisions.

6. In cases of imperative need arising from changes in the situation, and failing a Council decision, Member States may take the necessary measures as a matter of urgency having regard to the general objectives of joint action. The Member State concerned shall inform the Council immediately of any such measures.

7. Should there be any major difficulties in implementing a joint action, a Member State shall refer them to the Council which shall discuss them and seek appropriate solutions. Such solutions shall not run counter to the objectives of the joint action or impair its effectiveness.

Article J.4

1. The common foreign and security policy shall include all questions related to the security of the Union, including the eventual framing of a common defence policy, which might in time lead to a common defence.

2. The Union requests the Western European Union (WEU), which is an integral part of the development of the European Union, to elaborate and implement decisions and actions of the Union which have defence implications. The Council shall, in agreement with the institutions of the WEU, adopt the necessary practical arrangements.

3. Issues having defence implications dealt with under this Article shall not be subject to the procedures set out in Article J.3.

4. The policy of the Union in accordance with this Article shall not prejudice the specific character of the security and defence policy of certain Member States and shall respect the obligations of certain Member States under the North Atlantic Treaty and be compatible with the common security and defence policy established within that framework.

5. The provisions of this Article shall not prevent development of closer co-operation between two or more Member States on a bilateral level, in the framework of the WEU and the Atlantic Alliance provided such co-operation does not run counter to or impede that provided for in this Title.

6. With a view to furthering the objective of this Treaty, and having in view the date of 1998 in the context of Article XII of the Brussels Treaty, the provisions of this Article may be revised as provided for in Article N(2) on the basis of a report to be presented in 1996 by the Council to the European Council, which shall include an evaluation of the progress made and the experience gained until then.

Article J.5

1. The Presidency shall represent the Union in matters coming within the common foreign and security policy.

2. The Presidency shall be responsible for the implementation of common measures; in that capacity it shall in principle express the position of the Union in international organizations and international conferences.

3. In the tasks referred to in paragraphs 1 and 2, the Presidency shall be assisted if need be by the previous and next Member States to hold the Presidency. The Commission shall be fully associated in these tasks.

4. Without prejudice to the provisions of Article J.2(3) and Article J.3(4), Member States represented in international organizations or international conferences where not all the Member States participate shall keep the latter informed of any matter of common interest.

Member States which are also members of the United Nations Security Council will concert and keep the other Member States fully informed. Member States which are permanent members of the Security Council will, in the execution of their functions, ensure the defence of the positions and the interests of the Union, without prejudice to their responsibilities under the provisions of the United Nations Charter.

Article J.6

The diplomatic and consular missions of the Member States and the Commission Delegations in third countries and international conferences, and their representations to international organizations, shall co-operate in ensuring that the common positions and common measures adopted by the Council are complied with and implemented.

They shall set up co-operation by exchanging information, carrying out joint assessments and contributing to the implementation of the provisions referred to in Article 8c of the Treaty establishing the European Community.

Article J.7

The Presidency shall consult the European Parliament on the main aspects and the basic choices of the common foreign and security policy and shall ensure that the views of the European Parliament are duly taken into consideration. The European Parliament shall be kept regularly informed by the Presidency and the Commission of the development of the Union's foreign and security policy.

The European Parliament may ask questions of the Council or make recommendations to it. It shall hold an annual debate on progress in implementing the common foreign and security policy.

Article J.8

1. The European Council shall define the principles of and general guidelines for the common foreign and security policy.

2. The Council shall take the decisions necessary for defining and implementing common foreign and security policy on the basis of the general guidelines adopted by the European Council. It shall ensure the unity, consistency and effectiveness of action by the Union.

The Council shall act unanimously, except for procedural questions and in the case referred to in Article J.3(2).

3. Any Member State or the Commission may refer to the Council any question relating to the common foreign and security policy and may submit proposals to the Council.

4. In cases requiring a rapid decision, the Presidency, of its own motion, or at the request of the Commission or a Member State, shall convene an extraordinary Council meeting within forty-eight hours or, in an emergency, within a shorter period.

5. Without prejudice to Article 151 of the Treaty establishing the European Community, a Political Committee consisting of Political Directors shall monitor the international situation in the areas covered by Common foreign and security policy and contribute to the definition of policies by delivering opinions to the Council at the request of the Council or on its own initiative. It shall also monitor the implementation of agreed policies, without prejudice to the responsibility of the Presidency and the Commission.

Article J.9

The Commission shall be fully associated with the work carried out in the common foreign and security policy field.

Article J.10

On the occasion of any review of the security provisions under Article J.4, the Conference which is convened to that effect shall also examine whether any other amendments need to be made to provisions relating to the common foreign and security policy.

Article J.11

1. The provisions referred to in Articles 137, 138 to 142, 146, 147, 150 to 153, 157 to 163 and 217 of the Treaty establishing the European Community shall apply to the provisions relating to the areas referred to in this Title.

2. Administrative expenditure which the provisions relating to the areas referred to in this Title entail for the institutions shall be charged to the budget of the European Communities.

The Council may also:
– either decide unanimously that operational expenditure to which the implementation of those provisions gives rise is to be charged to

the budget of the European Communities; in that event, the budgetary procedure laid down in the Treaty establishing the European Community shall be applicable;
– or determine that such expenditure should be charged to the Member States, where appropriate in accordance with a scale to be decided.

TITLE VII – FINAL PROVISIONS

Article L

The provisions of the Treaty establishing the European Community, the Treaty establishing the European Coal and Steel Community and the Treaty establishing the European Atomic Energy Community concerning the powers of the Court of Justice of the European Communities and the exercise of those powers shall apply only to the following provisions of this Treaty:
(a) provisions amending the Treaty establishing the European Economic Community with a view to establishing the European Community, the Treaty establishing the European Coal and Steel Community and the Treaty establishing the European Atomic Energy Community;
(b) the third subparagraph of Article K.3(2) (c);
(c) Articles L to S.

Article M

Subject to provisions amending the Treaty establishing the European Economic Community with a view to establishing the European Community, the Treaty establishing the European Coal and Steel Community and the Treaty establishing the European Atomic Energy Community, and to these final provisions, nothing in this Treaty shall affect the Treaties establishing the European Communities or any subsequent Treaties and Acts modifying or supplementing them.

Article N

1. The government of any Member State or the Commission may submit to the Council proposals for the amendment of the Treaties on which the Union is founded.

   If the Council, after consulting the European Parliament and, where appropriate, the Commission, delivers an opinion in favour of calling a conference of representatives of the governments of the Member States, the conference shall be convened by the President of the Council for the purpose of determining by common accord the amendments to be made to those Treaties. The European Central Bank shall also be consulted in the case of institutional changes in the monetary area.

The amendments shall enter into force after being ratified by all the Member States in accordance with their respective constitutional requirements.

2.   A conference of representatives of the governments of the Member States shall be convened in 1996 to examine those provisions of this Treaty for which revision is provided, in accordance with the objectives set out in Articles A and B.

Article O

Any European State may apply to become a Member of the Union. It shall address its application to the Council, which shall act unanimously after consulting the Commission and after receiving the assent of the European Parliament, which shall act by an absolute majority of its component members.

The conditions of admission and the adjustments to the Treaties on which the Union is founded which such admission entails shall be the subject of an agreement between the Member States and the applicant State. This agreement shall be submitted for ratification by all the Contracting States in accordance with their respective constitutional requirements.

Article P

1.   Articles 2 to 7 and 10 to 19 of the Treaty establishing a single Council and a single Commission of the European Communities, signed in Brussels on 8 April 1965, are hereby repealed.

2.   Article 2, Article 3(2) and Title III of the Single European Act signed in Luxembourg on 17 February 1986 and in The Hague on 28 February 1986 are hereby repealed.

Article Q

This Treaty is concluded for an unlimited period.

Article R

1.   This Treaty shall be ratified by the High Contracting Parties in accordance with their respective constitutional requirements. The instruments of ratification shall be deposited with the government of the Italian Republic.

2.   This Treaty will enter into force on 1 January 1993, provided that all the instruments of ratification have been deposited, or, failing that, on

the first day of the month following the deposit of the instrument of ratification by the last signatory State to take this step.

Article S

This Treaty, drawn up in a single original in the Danish, Dutch, English, French, German, Greek, Irish, Italian, Portuguese and Spanish languages, the texts in each of these languages being equally authentic, shall be deposited in the archives of the government of the Italian Republic, which will transmit a certified copy to each of the governments of the other signatory States.

IN WITNESS WHEREOF, the undersigned Plenipotentiaries have signed this Treaty.

Done at Maastricht on 7 February 1992.

PROTOCOL ON ECONOMIC AND SOCIAL COHESION

The High Contracting Parties,

RECALLING that the Union has set itself the objective of promoting economic and social progress, inter alia, through the strengthening of economic and social cohesion;

RECALLING that Article 2 of the Treaty establishing the European Community includes the task of promoting economic and social cohesion and solidarity between Member States and that the strengthening of economic and social cohesion figures among the activities of the Community listed in Article 3;

RECALLING that the provisions of Part Three, Title XIV, on economic and social cohesion as a whole provide the legal basis for consolidating and further developing the Community's action in the field of economic and social cohesion, including the creation of a new fund;

RECALLING that the provisions of Part Three, Title XII on trans-European networks and Title XVI on environment envisage a Cohesion Fund to be set up before 31 December 1993;

STATING their belief that progress towards Economic and Monetary Union will contribute to the economic growth of all Member States;

NOTING that the Community's Structural Funds are being doubled in real terms between 1987 and 1993, implying large transfers especially as a proportion of GDP of the less prosperous Member States;

NOTING that the European Investment Bank is lending large and increasing amounts for the benefit of the poorer regions;

NOTING the desire for greater flexibility in the arrangements for allocations from the Structural Funds;

NOTING the desire for modulation of the levels of Community participation in programmes and projects in certain countries;

NOTING the proposal to take greater account of the relative prosperity of Member States in the system of own resources,

REAFFIRM that the promotion of economic and social cohesion is vital to the full development and enduring success of the Community, and underline the importance of the inclusion of economic and social cohesion in the Articles 2 and 3 of this Treaty;

REAFFIRM their conviction that the Structural Funds should continue to play a considerable part in achievement of Community objectives in the field of cohesion;

REAFFIRM their conviction that the European Investment Bank should continue to devote the majority of its resources to promotion of economic and social cohesion, and declare their willingness to review the capital needs of the European Investment Bank as soon as this is necessary for that purpose;

REAFFIRM the need for a thorough evaluation of operation and effectiveness of the Structural Funds in 1992, and the need to review, on that occasion, the appropriate size of these Funds in the light of the tasks of the Community in the area of economic and social cohesion;

AGREE that the Cohesion Fund to be set up before 31 December 1993 will provide Community financial contributions to projects in the fields of environment and trans-European networks in Member States with a per capita GNP of less than 90% of Community average which have a programme relating to the fulfilment of the conditions of economic convergence as set out in Article 104c;

DECLARE their intention of allowing a greater margin of flexibility in allocating financing from the Structural Funds to specific needs not covered under present Structural Funds regulations;

DECLARE their willingness to modulate the levels of Community participation in the context of programmes and projects of the Structural Funds, with a view to avoiding excessive increases in budgetary expenditure in the less prosperous Member States;

RECOGNIZE the need to monitor regularly the progress made towards achieving economic and social cohesion and state their willingness to study all necessary measures in this respect;

DECLARE their intention of taking greater account of the contributive capacity of individual Member States in the system of own resources, and of examining means of correcting, for the less prosperous Member States regressive elements existing in the present own resources system;

AGREE to annex this Protocol to the Treaty establishing the European Community.

PROTOCOL ON SOCIAL POLICY

The High Contracting Parties,

NOTING that eleven Member States . . . wish to continue along the path laid down in the 1989 Social Charter; that they have adopted among themselves an Agreement to this end; that this Agreement is annexed to this Protocol; that this Protocol and the said Agreement are without prejudice to the provisions of this Treaty, particularly those relating to social policy which constitute an integral part of the "acquis communautaire":

1. Agree to authorize those eleven Member States to have recourse to the institutions, procedures and mechanisms of the Treaty for the purposes of taking among themselves and applying as far as they are concerned the acts and decisions required for giving effect to the abovementioned Agreement.

2. The United Kingdom of Great Britain and Northern Ireland shall not take part in the deliberations and the adoption by the Council of Commission proposals made on the basis of this Protocol and the abovementioned Agreement.

By way of derogation from Article 148(2) of the Treaty, acts of the Council which are made pursuant to this Protocol and which must be adopted by a qualified majority shall be deemed to be so adopted if they have received at least forty-four votes in favour. The unanimity of all members of the Council, with the exception of the United Kingdom of Great Britain and Northern Ireland, shall be necessary for acts of the Council which must be adopted unanimously and for those amending the Commission proposal.

Acts adopted by the Council and any financial consequences other than administrative costs entailed for the institutions shall not be applicable to the United Kingdom of Great Britain and Northern Ireland.

3.   This Protocol shall be annexed to the Treaty establishing the European Community.

AGREEMENT ON SOCIAL POLICY CONCLUDED BETWEEN THE MEMBER STATES OF THE EUROPEAN COMMUNITY WITH THE EXCEPTION OF THE UNITED KINGDOM OF GREAT BRITAIN AND NORTHERN IRELAND

The undersigned eleven HIGH CONTRACTING PARTIES, . . .
WISHING to implement the 1989 Social Charter on the basis of the "acquis communautaires",
CONSIDERING the protocol on Social policy:
Have AGREED as follows:

Article 1

The Community and the Member States shall have as their objectives the promotion of employment, improved living and working conditions, proper social protection, dialogue between management and labour, the development of human resources with a view to lasting high employment and the combatting of exclusion. To this end the Community and the Member States shall implement measures which take account of the diverse forms of national practices, in particular in the field of contractual relations, and the need to maintain the competitiveness of the Community economy.

Article 2

1.   With a view to achieving the objectives of Article 1, the Community shall support and complement the activities of the Member States in the following fields:
     – improvement in particular of the working environment to protect workers' health and safety;
     – working conditions;
     – the information and consultation of workers;

– equality between men and women with regard to labour market opportunities and treatment at work;
– the integration of persons excluded from the labour market, without prejudice to Article 127 of the Treaty establishing the European Community (hereinafter referred to as "the Treaty").

2. To this end, the Council may adopt, by means of directives, minimum requirements for gradual implementation, having regard to the conditions and technical rules obtaining in each of the Member States. Such directives shall avoid imposing administrative, financial and legal constraints in a way which would hold back the creation and development of small and medium-sized undertakings.

   The Council shall act in accordance with the procedure referred to in Article 189c of the Treaty after consulting the Economic and Social Committee.

3. However, the Council shall act unanimously on a proposal from the Commission, after consulting the European Parliament and the Economic and Social Committee, in the following areas:
   – social security and social protection of workers;
   – protection of workers where their employment contract is terminated;
   – representation and collective defence of the interests of workers and employers, including co-determination, subject to paragraph 6;
   – conditions of employment for third-country nationals legally residing in Community territory;
   – financial contributions for promotion of employment and job-creation, without prejudice to the provisions relating to the Social Fund.

4. A Member State may entrust management and labour, at their joint request, with the implementation of directives adopted pursuant to paragraphs 2 and 3.

   In this case, it shall ensure that, no later than the date on which a directive must be transposed in accordance with Article 189, management and labour have introduced the necessary measures by agreement, the Member State concerned being required to take any necessary measure enabling it any time to be in a position to guarantee the results imposed by that directive.

5. The provisions adopted pursuant to this Article shall not prevent any Member State from maintaining or introducing more stringent measures compatible with this Treaty.

6. The provisions of this Article shall not apply to pay, the right of association, the right to strike or the right to impose lock-outs.

Article 3

1. The Commission shall have the task of promoting the consultation of management and labour at Community level and shall take any relevant measure to facilitate their dialogue by ensuring balanced support for the parties.

2. To this end, before submitting proposals in the social policy field, the Commission shall consult management and labour on the possible direction of Community action.

3. If, after such consultation, the Commission considers Community action advisable, it shall consult management and labour on the content of the envisaged proposal. Management and labour shall forward to the Commission an opinion or, where appropriate, a recommendation.

4. On the occasion of such consultation, management and labour may inform the Commission of their wish to initiate the process provided for in Article 4. The duration of the procedure shall not exceed nine months, unless the management and labour concerned and the Commission decide jointly to extend it.

Article 4

1. Should management and labour so desire, the dialogue between them at Community level may lead to contractual relations, including agreements.

2. Agreements concluded at Community level shall be implemented either in accordance with the procedures and practices specific to management and labour and the Member States or, in matters covered by Article 2, at the joint request of the signatory parties, by a Council decision on a proposal from the Commission.

    The Council shall act by qualified majority, except when the agreement in question contains one or more provisions relating to one of the areas referred to in Article 2(3), in which case it shall act unanimously.

Article 5

With a view to achieving the objectives of Article 1 and without prejudice to the other provisions of the Treaty, the Commission shall encourage co-operation between the Member States and facilitate the co-ordination of their action in all social fields under this Agreement.

Article 6

1. Each Member State shall ensure that the principle of equal pay for male and female workers for equal work is applied.

2. For the purpose of this Article, 'pay' means the ordinary basic or minimum wage or salary and any other consideration, whether in cash or in kind, which the worker receives directly or indirectly, in respect of his employment, from his employer.

    Equal pay without discrimination based on sex means:
    (a) that pay for the same work at piece rates shall be calculated on the basis of the same unit of measurement;
    (b) that pay for work at time rates shall be the same for the same job.

3. This Article shall not prevent any Member State from maintaining or adopting measures providing for specific advantages in order to make it easier for women to pursue a vocational activity or to prevent or compensate for disadvantages in their professional careers.

Articles 7

The Commission shall draw up a report each year on progress in achieving the objectives of Article 1, including the demographic situation in the Community. It shall forward the report to the European Parliament, the Council and the Economic and Social Committee.

The European Parliament may invite the Commission to draw up reports on particular problems concerning the social situation.

DECLARATION ON WESTERN EUROPEAN UNION

I. DECLARATION

by Belgium, Germany, Spain, France, Italy, Luxembourg, the Netherlands, Portugal and the United Kingdom of Great Britain and Northern Ireland which are members of the Western European Union and also members of the European Union

THE ROLE OF WEU AND ITS RELATIONS WITH THE EUROPEAN UNION AND WITH THE ATLANTIC ALLIANCE

INTRODUCTION

1. WEU Member States agree on the need to develop a genuine European security and defence identity and a greater European responsibility on

defence matters. This identity will be pursued though a gradual process involving successive phases. WEU will form an integral part of the process of the development of the European Union and will enhance its contribution to solidarity within the Atlantic Alliance. WEU Member States agree to strengthen the role of WEU, in the longer term perspective of a common defence policy within the European Union which might in time lead to a common defence, compatible with that of the Atlantic Alliance.

2. WEU will be developed as the defence component of the European Union and as a means to strengthen the European pillar of the Atlantic Alliance. To this end, it will formulate common European defence policy and carry forward its concrete implementation through the further development of its own operational role.

WEU Member States take note of Article J.4 relating to the common foreign and security policy of the Treaty on European Union which reads as follows:

"1. The common foreign and security policy shall include all questions related to the security of the Union, including the eventual framing of a common defence policy, which might in time lead to a common defence.

2. The Union requests the Western European Union (WEU), which is an integral part of the development of the Union, to elaborate and implement decisions and actions of the Union which have defence implications. The Council shall, in agreement with the institutions of the WEU, adopt the necessary practical arrangements.

3. Issues having defence implications dealt with under this Article shall not be subject to the procedures set out in Article J.3.

4. The policy of the Union in accordance with this Article shall not prejudice the specific character of the security and defence policy of certain Member States and shall respect the obligations of certain Member States under the North Atlantic Treaty and be compatible with the common security and defence policy established within that framework.

5. The provisions of this Article shall not prevent development of closer co-operation between two or more Member States on a bilateral level, in the framework of the WEU and the Atlantic Alliance, provided such co-operation does not run counter to or impede that provided for in this Title.

6. With a view to furthering the objective of this Treaty, and having in view the date of 1998 in the context of Article XII of the Brussels

Treaty, the provisions of this Article may be revised as provided for in Article N(2) on the basis of a report to be presented in 1996 by the Council to the European Council which shall include an evaluation of the progress made and the experience gained until then."

A. WEU's relations with European Union

3. The objective is to build up WEU in stages as the defence component of the European Union. To this end, WEU is prepared, at the request of the European Union, to elaborate and implement decisions and actions of the Union which have defence implications.

To this end, WEU will take the following measures to develop a close working relationship with the Union:

– as appropriate, synchronization of the dates and venues of meetings and harmonization of working methods;
– establishment of close co-operation between the Council and Secretariat-General of WEU on the one hand, and the Council of the Union and Secretariat-General of the Council on the other;
– consideration of the harmonization of the sequence and duration of the respective Presidencies;
– arranging for appropriate modalities so as to ensure that the Commission of the European Communities is regularly informed and, as appropriate, consulted on WEU activities in accordance with the role of the Commission in the common foreign and security policy as defined in the Treaty on European Union;
– encouragement of closer co-operation between the Parliamentary Assembly of WEU and the European Parliament.

The WEU Council shall, in agreement with the competent bodies of the European Union, adopt the necessary practical arrangements.

B. WEU's relations with the Atlantic Alliance

4. The objective is to develop WEU as a means to strengthen the European pillar of the Atlantic Alliance. Accordingly WEU is prepared to develop further the close working links between WEU and the Alliance and to strengthen the role, responsibilities and contributions of WEU Member States in the Alliance. This will be undertaken on the basis of the necessary transparency and complementarity between the emerging European security and defence identity and the Alliance. WEU will act in conformity with the positions adopted in the Atlantic Alliance.

– WEU Member States will intensify their co-ordination on Alliance

issues which represent an important common interest with the aim of introducing joint positions agreed in WEU into the process of consultation in the Alliance which will remain the essential forum for consultation among its members and the venue for agreement on policies bearing on the security and defence commitments of Allies under the North Atlantic Treaty.
– Where necessary, dates and venues of meetings will be synchronized and working methods harmonized.
– Close co-operation will be established between the Secretariats-General of WEU and NATO.

C. Operational role of WEU

5.   WEU's operational role will be strengthened by examining and defining appropriate missions, structures and means, covering in particular:

– WEU planning cell;
– closer military co-operation complementary to the Alliance in particular in the fields of logistics, transport, training and strategic surveillance;
– meetings of WEU Chiefs of Defence Staff;
– military units answerable to WEU.

Other proposals will be examined further, including:

– enhanced co-operation in the field of armaments with the aim of creating a European armaments agency;
– development of the WEU Institute into a European Security and Defence Academy.

Arrangements aimed at giving WEU a stronger operational role will be fully compatible with the military dispositions necessary to ensure the collective defence of all Allies.

D. Other measures

6.   As a consequence of the measures set out above, and in order to facilitate the strengthening of WEU's role, the seat of the WEU Council and Secretariat will be transferred to Brussels.

7.   Representation on the WEU Council must be such that the Council is able to exercise its functions continuously in accordance with Article VIII of the modified Brussels Treaty. Member States may draw on a double-hatting formula, to be worked out, consisting of their representatives to the Alliance and to the European Union.

8.   WEU notes that, in accordance with the provisions of Article J.4(6)

concerning 'the common foreign and security policy of the Treaty on European Union, the Union will decide to review the provisions of this Article with a view to furthering the objective to be set by it in accordance with the procedure defined. The WEU will re-examine the present provisions in 1996. This re-examination will take account of the progress and experience acquired and will extend to relations between WEU and the Atlantic Alliance.

II. DECLARATION

by Belgium, Germany, Spain, France, Italy, Luxembourg, the Netherlands, Portugal and the United Kingdom of Great Britain and Northern Ireland which are members of the Western European Union and also members of the European Union

"The Member States of WEU welcome the development of the European security and defence identity. They are determined, taking into account the role of WEU as the defence component of the European Union and as the means to strengthen the European pillar of the Atlantic Alliance, to put the relationship between WEU and the other European States on a new basis for the sake of stability and security in Europe. In this spirit, they propose the following:

States which are members of the European Union are invited to accede to WEU on conditions to be agreed in accordance with Article XI of the modified Brussels Treaty, or to become observers if they so wish. Simultaneously, other European Member States of NATO are invited to become associate members of WEU in a way which will give them the possibility of participating fully in the activities of WEU.

The Member States of WEU assume that treaties and agreements corresponding with the above proposals will be concluded before 31 December 1992."

Index